Mastering Zabbix
Second Edition

Learn how to monitor your large IT environments using
Zabbix with this one-stop, comprehensive guide to the
Zabbix world

Andrea Dalle Vacche

[PACKT] open source*
PUBLISHING
community experience distilled

BIRMINGHAM - MUMBAI

Mastering Zabbix
Second Edition

First published: December 2013

Second edition: September 2015

Production reference: 1080915

Published by Packt Publishing Ltd.
Livery Place
35 Livery Street
Birmingham B3 2PB, UK.

ISBN 978-1-78528-926-2

www.packtpub.com

Credits

Author
Andrea Dalle Vacche

Reviewers
Grigory Chernyshev

Nitish Kumar

Nicholas Pier

Timothy Scoppetta

Commissioning Editor
Dipika Gaonkar

Acquisition Editor
Kevin Colaco

Content Development Editor
Adrian Raposo

Technical Editor
Parag Topre

Copy Editor
Sarang Chari

Project Coordinator
Sanchita Mandal

Proofreader
Safis Editing

Indexer
Monica Ajmera Mehta

Graphics
Sheetal Aute

Disha Haria

Jason Monteiro

Abhinash Sahu

Production Coordinator
Nilesh R. Mohite

Cover Work
Nilesh R. Mohite

About the Author

Andrea Dalle Vacche is a highly skilled IT professional with over 15 years of industry experience.

He graduated from Univerità degli Studi di Ferrara with an information technology certification. This laid the technology foundation that Andrea has built on ever since. He has acquired various other industry-respected accreditations from big players in the IT industry, which include Cisco, Oracle, ITIL, and of course, Zabbix. He also has a Red Hat Certified Engineer certification. Throughout his career, he has worked on many large-scale environments, often in roles that have been very complex, on a consultant basis. This has further enhanced his growing skillset, adding to his practical knowledge base and concreting his appetite for theoretical technical studying.

Andrea's love for Zabbix came from the time he spent in the Oracle world as a database administrator/developer. His time was mainly spent on reducing "ownership costs" with specialization in monitoring and automation. This is where he came across Zabbix and the technical and administrative flexibility that it offered. With this as a launch pad, Andrea was inspired to develop Orabbix, the first piece of open source software to monitor Oracle that is completely integrated with Zabbix. He has published a number of articles on Zabbix-related software, such as DBforBIX. His projects are publicly available on his website at http://www.smartmarmot.com.

Currently, Andrea is working as a senior architect for a leading global investment bank in a very diverse and challenging environment. His involvement is very wide ranging, and he deals with many critical aspects of the Unix/Linux platforms and pays due diligence to the many different types of third-party software that are strategically aligned to the bank's technical roadmap.

Andrea also plays a critical role within the extended management team for the security awareness of the bank, dealing with disciplines such as security, secrecy, standardization, auditing, regulator requirements, and security-oriented solutions.

In addition to this book, he has also authored the following books:

- *Mastering Zabbix, Packt Publishing*
- *Zabbix Network Monitoring Essentials, Packt Publishing*

Acknowledgments

First, I would like to thank my wife, Anna, for her support and encouragement during the writing of this book. I highly appreciate her help and advice. Many thanks to Fifi for her relaxing company and fluffy stress relief.

I would like to give a special thanks to the whole team at Packt Publishing and a particular thanks to Adrian. Their advice, effort, and suggestions have been really valuable. The whole team has been very professional and helpful.

About the Reviewers

Grigory Chernyshev is senior release manager / DevOps engineer in the Online Games department at Mail.Ru Group. He specializes in managing configurations, automating the build pipeline, monitoring, releasing versions, and writing scripts in Python. He has experience in projects such as Allods Online and Skyforge — AAA MMORPG games that are known around the globe. In his regular work, he uses Zabbix to monitor internal game servers, heterogeneous build agents, and a lot of infrastructure servers.

Besides that, he writes plugins for Atlassian Jira and JetBrains Teamcity — for the latter, he even won the 2015 WordPress Plugins contest!

I would like to thank my wife for her patience, my parents for my happy childhood, and the project coordinator, Sanchita, for her never-ending enthusiasm and support.

Nitish Kumar is a Wintel lead at HT Media Ltd. and an independent tech blogger on various technologies. He has been working on several Microsoft technologies and open source solutions (including, but not limited to, Spiceworks, ManageEngine products, Zabbix, MS Active Directory, MS Exchange Servers, and so on) for 8 years now, of which the last couple of years have been spent on bringing cost-effective solutions to corporates to simplify their complex requirements and improve the time management of their staff. Nitish is a technology enthusiast and has been a participant at various corporate events and public webinars. Mobile technologies are of special interest to him and he often writes about various gadgets and technologies. Nitish holds an MS degree in software from J.K Institute of Applied Physics and Technology, and his areas of interest include Microsoft technologies, open source software, and mobile gadgets. He occasionally blogs at http://nitishkumar.net and can be reached at nitish@nitishkumar.net.

Nitish coauthored *Getting Started with Spiceworks, Packt Publishing*. Also, he has been a technical reviewer for other books on topics such as Zabbix and Spiceworks.

Nicholas Pier is a network engineer in the managed services and professional services fields. His experience includes web development, designing data center network infrastructures with virtualization and SAN solutions, and writing middleware for business applications. As of this date, Nicholas holds a number of industry certifications, including Cisco CCNP, VMware VCP-DCV, and various other Cisco and CompTIA certifications. He has a passion for craft beer, long-distance running, and reading, in which he indulges in his free time.

Timothy Scoppetta is a systems engineer who specializes in automation, continuous integration, and creating fault-tolerant infrastructures. Having held positions at Google and a number of start-ups, he now focuses on bringing cutting-edge tools and industry best practices to higher education.

www.PacktPub.com

Support files, eBooks, discount offers, and more

For support files and downloads related to your book, please visit.

Did you know that Packt offers eBook versions of every book published, with PDF and ePub files available? You can upgrade to the eBook version at www.PacktPub.com and as a print book customer, you are entitled to a discount on the eBook copy. Get in touch with us at service@packtpub.com for more details.

At www.PacktPub.com, you can also read a collection of free technical articles, sign up for a range of free newsletters and receive exclusive discounts and offers on Packt books and eBooks.

https://www2.packtpub.com/books/subscription/packtlib

Do you need instant solutions to your IT questions? PacktLib is Packt's online digital book library. Here, you can search, access, and read Packt's entire library of books.

Why subscribe?

- Fully searchable across every book published by Packt
- Copy and paste, print, and bookmark content
- On demand and accessible via a web browser

Free access for Packt account holders

If you have an account with Packt at www.PacktPub.com, you can use this to access PacktLib today and view 9 entirely free books. Simply use your login credentials for immediate access.

Table of Contents

Preface

Ever since its first public release in 2001, Zabbix has distinguished itself as a very powerful and effective monitoring solution. As an open source product, it's easy to obtain and deploy, and its unique approach to metrics and alarms has helped to set it apart from its competitors, both open and commercial. It's a powerful, compact package with very low requirements in terms of hardware and supporting software for a basic yet effective installation. If you add a relative ease of use, it's clear that it can be a very good contender for small environments with a tight budget. But it's when it comes to managing a huge number of monitored objects, with a complex configuration and dependencies, that Zabbix's scalability and inherently distributed architecture really shines. More than anything, Zabbix can be an ideal solution in large and complex distributed environments, where being able to manage efficiently and extract meaningful information from monitored objects and events is just as important if not more important than the usual considerations about costs, accessibility, and the ease of use.

This is a second edition book, the first having been coauthored by Andrea Dalle Vacche and Stefano Kewan Lee.The purpose of this book is to help you make the most of your Zabbix installation to leverage all of its power to monitor any large and complex environment effectively.

The purpose of this book is to help you make the most of your Zabbix installation to leverage all of its power to monitor any large and complex environment effectively.

What this book covers

Chapter 1, Deploying Zabbix, focuses on choosing the optimal hardware and software configuration for the Zabbix server and database in relation to the current IT infrastructure, monitoring goals, and possible evolution. This chapter also includes a section that covers an interesting database-sizing digression, which is useful in calculating the final database size using a standard environment as the baseline. Correct environment sizing and a brief discussion about metrics and measurements that can also be used for capacity planning will be covered here. The chapter contains practical examples and calculations framed in a theoretical approach to give the reader the skills required to adapt the information to real-world deployments.

Chapter 2, Distributed Monitoring, explores various Zabbix components both on the server side and the agent side. Different distributed solutions will be given to the same example networks to highlight the advantages and possible drawbacks of each. In addition to the deployment and configuration of agents, the chapter takes proxies, maintenance, and change management into account too. This section will cover all the possible architectural implementations of Zabbix and add the pros and cons considerations.

Chapter 3, High Availability and Failover, covers the subjects of high availability and failover. For each of the three main Zabbix tiers, you will learn to choose among different HA options. The discussion will build on the information provided in the previous two chapters in order to end the first part of the book with a few complete deployment scenarios that will include high-availability servers and databases hierarchically organized in tiered, distributed architectures geared toward monitoring thousands of objects scattered in different geographical locations. This chapter will include a real-world, practical example and certain possible scenarios that have been implemented.

Chapter 4, Collecting Data, moves beyond simple agent items and SNMP queries to tackle a few complex data sources. The chapter will explore powerful Zabbix built-in functionalities, how to use them, and how to choose the best metrics to ensure thorough monitoring without overloading the system. There will also be special considerations about aggregated values and their use in monitoring complex environments with clusters or the more complex grid architectures.

Chapter 5, Visualizing Data, focuses on getting the most out of the data visualization features of Zabbix. This is quite a useful chapter, especially if you need to explain or chase a hardware expansion/improvement to the business unit. You will learn how to leverage live monitoring data to make dynamic maps and how to organize a collection of graphs for big-screen visualization in control centers and implement a general qualitative view. This chapter will cover the data center quality view slide show completely, which is really useful in highlighting problems and warning the first-level support in a proactive approach. The chapter will also explore some best practices concerning the IT services and SLA-reporting features of Zabbix.

Chapter 6, Managing Alerts, gives examples of complex triggers and trigger conditions as well as advice on choosing the right amount of trigger and alerting actions. The purpose is to help you walk the fine line between being blind to possible problems and being overwhelmed by false positives. You will also learn how to use actions to automatically fix simple problems, raise actions without the need for human intervention to correlate different triggers and events, and tie escalations to your operations management workflow. This section will make you aware of what can be automated, reducing your administrative workload and optimizing the administration process in a proactive way.

Chapter 7, Managing Templates, offers guidelines for effective template management: building complex template schemes out of simple components, understanding and managing the effects of template modification, maintaining existing monitored objects, and assigning templates to discovered hosts. This will conclude the second part of the book that is dedicated to the different Zabbix monitoring and data management options. The third and final part will discuss Zabbix's interaction with external products and all its powerful extensibility features.

Chapter 8, Handling External Scripts, helps you learn how to write scripts to monitor objects that are not covered by the core Zabbix features. The relative advantages and disadvantages of keeping the scripts on the server side or agent side, how to launch or schedule them, and a detailed analysis of the Zabbix agent protocol will also be covered. This chapter will make you aware of all the possible side effects, delays, and load caused by scripts; you will be able to implement all the needed external checks, as you will be well aware of all that is connected with them and the relative observer effect. The chapter will include different implementations of working with Bash, Java, and Python so that you can easily write your own scripts to extend and enhance Zabbix's monitoring possibilities.

Chapter 9, Extending Zabbix, delves into the Zabbix API and how to use it to build specialized frontends and complex extensions. It also covers how to harvest monitoring data for further elaboration and reporting. It will include simple example implementations written in Python that will illustrate how to export and further manipulate data, how to perform massive and complex operations on monitored objects, and finally, how to automate different management aspects such as user creation and configuration, trigger activation, and the like.

Chapter 10, Integrating Zabbix, wraps things up by discussing how to make other systems know about Zabbix and the other way around. This is key to the successful management of any large and complex environment. You will learn how to use built-in Zabbix features, API calls, or direct database queries to communicate with different upstream and downstream systems and applications. There will be concrete examples of possible interaction with inventory applications, trouble ticket systems, and data warehouse systems.

Who this book is for

As the book's title is *Mastering Zabbix, Second Edition*, you won't find any detailed, step-by-step tutorials (well, except the installation that will be covered from scratch, but with some useful tips) on the basic usage of Zabbix. Although you may find a lot of detailed information about installing the server or configuring items, triggers, and screens, you are expected to have at least a basic, working knowledge of how it all works so that you can focus on a more advanced approach for the same subjects. That said, it is possible to profit from the contents of this book even if you have no previous experience with Zabbix, but in that case, you are strongly encouraged to refer to the official Zabbix documentation that you can find at `https://www.zabbix.com/documentation/2.4/manual` to fill in any possible gaps in your knowledge.

What you need for this book

Before going deep into the Zabbix setup, it is important to know that the proposed setup covered here has been tested on a large-production environment (more than 1,800 hosts monitored, more than 89,500 monitored items, and more than 30,000 triggers) and that they can be considered valid for most large and very large environments. The high-availability solution proposed in this book has been widely tested, not purely as a disaster recovery exercise but during a real disaster (network cables were accidentally sheared by an excavating machine).

In this book, it is important to understand that most of the choices made have been on a practical basis and not driven by passion. One of the main choices made is using PostgreSQL as the official Zabbix RDBMS. We came across PostgreSQL as an RDBMS mostly for the mature and production ready features offered:

- Hot backup is available by design
- Atomicity, consistency, isolation, and durability — in short, it is fully ACID compliant
- Many different, native standby configurations (hot standby, synchronous replication, and so on)
- Efficient partitioning

Zabbix's database is a critical component, especially if you need to keep historical data available and guarantee constant performances day by day while the database is growing.

We have made some assumptions in this book: the packaging system used in our examples is yum, and then the distribution is obviously Red Hat Enterprise Linux. Anyway, excluding details such as package names and packet manager, the whole book is valid for all the Linux distributions. Furthermore, the proposed architectures and their implementations are not directly tied to a particular distribution. We did not use any Red Hat-specific clustering system or make any choice that you cannot reproduce on your favorite Linux distribution.

On reading this book, you will find different pieces of open source software, but out of all of them, it would be better if you are familiar with the following:

- **Apache**: http://www.apache.org/
- **Pacemaker**: http://clusterlabs.org/
- **PostgreSQL**: http://www.postgresql.org/
- **DRBD**: http://www.drbd.org

This book also focuses on system administrators who have some programming skills. We propose different workings for the implemented code snippet. With the proposed example, all well documented, you should be able to implement your own plugin or external software that is fully integrated with Zabbix. The code snippets proposed are in two different and widely diffused languages: Java and Python. These cover most of the current programmers' preferences and show, once you know how to implement the Zabbix protocol, how simple it is to switch between them.

Zabbix is more than a piece of monitoring software; it is an open source monitoring solution that can be explained as you want, and this book will make you aware of all the pros and cons of the possible solutions.

So, now it is time to go deep into Zabbix land!

Conventions

In this book, you will find a number of styles of text that distinguish between different kinds of information. Here are some examples of these styles, and an explanation of their meaning.

Code words in text, database table names, folder names, filenames, file extensions, pathnames, dummy URLs, user input, and Twitter handles are shown as follows: "Most of these parameters are contained inside the php.ini file."

A block of code is set as follows:

```
zabbixsrv=zabbixsvr
[ -e /etc/sysconfig/$syscf ] && . /etc/sysconfig/$syscf

start()
{
    echo -n $"Starting Zabbix server: "
```

When we wish to draw your attention to a particular part of a code block, the relevant lines or items are set in bold:

```
; Maximum size of POST data that PHP will accept.
; http://www.php.net/manual/en/ini.core.php#ini.post-max-size
post_max_size = 16M
```

Any command-line input or output is written as follows:

```
# yum list postgres*
```

New terms and **important** words are shown in bold. Words that you see on the screen, in menus or dialog boxes for example, appear in the text like this: "Once we fill this form, we can click on **Next**."

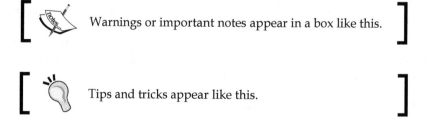

Warnings or important notes appear in a box like this.

Tips and tricks appear like this.

Reader feedback

Feedback from our readers is always welcome. Let us know what you think about this book—what you liked or may have disliked. Reader feedback is important for us to develop titles that you really get the most out of.

To send us general feedback, simply send an e-mail to feedback@packtpub.com, and mention the book title via the subject of your message.

If there is a topic that you have expertise in and you are interested in either writing or contributing to a book, see our author guide on www.packtpub.com/authors.

Customer support

Now that you are the proud owner of a Packt book, we have a number of things to help you to get the most from your purchase.

Downloading the example code

You can download the example code files for all Packt books you have purchased from your account at http://www.packtpub.com. If you purchased this book elsewhere, you can visit http://www.packtpub.com/support and register to have the files e-mailed directly to you.

Errata

Although we have taken every care to ensure the accuracy of our content, mistakes do happen. If you find a mistake in one of our books—maybe a mistake in the text or the code—we would be grateful if you would report this to us. By doing so, you can save other readers from frustration and help us improve subsequent versions of this book. If you find any errata, please report them by visiting http://www.packtpub.com/submit-errata, selecting your book, clicking on the **errata submission form** link, and entering the details of your errata. Once your errata are verified, your submission will be accepted and the errata will be uploaded on our website, or added to any list of existing errata, under the Errata section of that title. Any existing errata can be viewed by selecting your title from http://www.packtpub.com/support.

Piracy

Piracy of copyright material on the Internet is an ongoing problem across all media. At Packt, we take the protection of our copyright and licenses very seriously. If you come across any illegal copies of our works, in any form, on the Internet, please provide us with the location address or website name immediately so that we can pursue a remedy.

Please contact us at copyright@packtpub.com with a link to the suspected pirated material.

We appreciate your help in protecting our authors, and our ability to bring you valuable content.

Questions

You can contact us at questions@packtpub.com if you are having a problem with any aspect of the book, and we will do our best to address it.

1
Deploying Zabbix

If you are reading this book, you have, most probably, already used and installed Zabbix. Most likely, you did so on a small/medium environment, but now things have changed, and your environment today is a large one with new challenges coming in regularly. Nowadays, environments are rapidly growing or changing, and it is a difficult task to be ready to support and provide a reliable monitoring solution.

Normally, an initial deployment of a system, a monitoring system, is done by following a tutorial or how-to, and this is a common error. This kind of approach is valid for smaller environments, where the downtime is not critical, where there are no disaster recovery sites to handle, or, in short, where things are easy.

Most likely, these setups are not done by looking forward to the possible new quantity of new items, triggers, and events that the server should elaborate. If you have already installed Zabbix and you need to plan and expand your monitoring solution, or, instead, you need to plan and design the new monitoring infrastructure, this chapter will help you.

This chapter will also help you to perform the difficult task of setting up/upgrading Zabbix in large and very large environments. This chapter will cover every aspect of this task, starting with the definition of a large environment until using Zabbix as a capacity planning resource. The chapter will introduce all the possible Zabbix solutions, including a practical example with an installation ready to handle a large environment, and go ahead with possible improvements.

At the end of this chapter, you will understand how Zabbix works, which tables should be kept under special surveillance, and how to improve the housekeeping on a large environment, which, with a few years of trends to handle, is a really heavy task.

This chapter will cover the following topics:

- Knowing when you are in front of a large environment and defining when an environment can be considered a large environment
- Setting up/upgrading Zabbix on a large environment and a very large environment
- Installing Zabbix on a three-tier system and having a readymade solution to handle a large environment
- Database sizing and finally knowing the total amount of space consumed by the data acquired by us
- Knowing the database's heavy tables and tasks
- Improving the housekeeping to reduce the RDBMS load and improving the efficiency of the whole system
- Learning fundamental concepts about capacity planning bearing in mind that Zabbix is a capacity-planning tool

Defining the environment size

Since this book is focused on a large environment, we need to define or at least provide basic fixed points to identify a large environment. There are various things to consider in this definition; basically, we can identify an environment as large when:

- There are more than one different physical locations
- The number of monitored devices is high (hundreds or thousands)
- The number of checks and items retrieved per second is high (more than 500)
- There are lots of items, triggers, and data to handle (the database is larger than 100 GB)
- The availability and performance are both critical

All of the preceding points define a large environment; in this kind of environment, the installation and maintenance of Zabbix infrastructure play a critical role.

The installation, of course, is a task that is defined well on a timely basis and, probably, is one of the most critical tasks; it is really important to go live with a strong and reliable monitoring infrastructure. Also, once we go live with the monitoring in place, it will not be so easy to move/migrate pieces without any loss of data. There are certain other things to consider: we will have a lot of tasks related to our monitoring system, most of which are daily tasks, but in a large environment, they require particular attention.

In a small environment with a small database, a backup will keep you busy for a few minutes, but if the database is large, this task will consume a considerable amount of time to be completed.

The restore and relative-restore plans should be considered and tested periodically to be aware of the time needed to complete this task in the event of a disaster or critical hardware failure.

Between maintenance tasks, we need to consider testing and putting into production upgrades with minimal impact, along with the daily tasks and daily checks.

Zabbix architectures

Zabbix can be defined as a distributed monitoring system with a centralized web interface (on which we can manage almost everything). Among its main features, we will highlight the following ones:

- Zabbix has a centralized web interface
- The server can be run on most Unix-like operating systems
- This monitoring system has native agents for most Unix, Unix-like, and Microsoft Windows operation systems
- The system is easy to integrate with other systems, thanks to the API available in many different programming languages and the option that Zabbix itself provides
- Zabbix can monitor via SNMP (v1, v2, and v3), IPMI, JMX, ODBC, SSH, HTTP(s), TCP/UDP, and Telnet
- This monitoring system gives us the possibility of creating custom items and graphs and interpolating data
- The system is easy to customize

The following diagram shows the three-tier system of a Zabbix architecture:

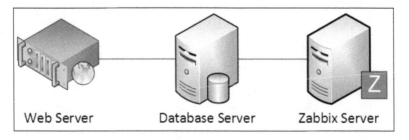

The Zabbix architecture for a large environment is composed of three different servers/components (that should be configured on HA as well). These three components are as follows:

- A web server
- A database server
- A Zabbix server

The whole Zabbix infrastructure in large environments allows us to have two other actors that play a fundamental role. These actors are the Zabbix agents and the Zabbix proxies. An example is represented in the following figure:

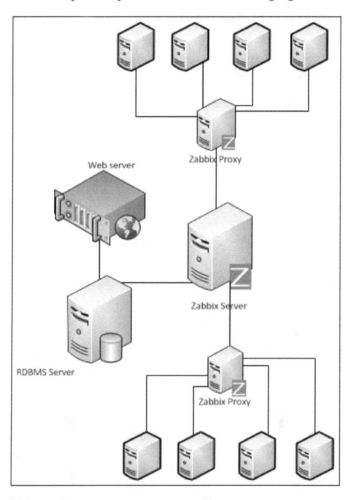

On this infrastructure, we have a centralized Zabbix server that is connected to different proxies, usually one for each server farm or a subnetwork.

The **Zabbix server** will acquire data from **Zabbix proxies**, the proxies will acquire data from all the **Zabbix agents** connected to it, all the data will be stored on a dedicated RDBMS, and the frontend will be exposed with a web interface to the users. Looking at the technologies used, we see that the web interface is written in PHP and that the server, proxies, and agents are written in C.

 The server, proxies, and agents are written in C to give the best performance and least resource usage possible. All the components are deeply optimized to achieve the best performance.

We can implement different kinds of architecture using proxies. There are several types of architectures and, in the order of complexity, we find the following ones:

- The single-server installation
- One server and many proxies
- Distributed installation (available only until 2.3.0)

The single-server installation is not suggested in a large environment. It is the basic installation, where single servers do the monitoring, and it can be considered a good starting point.

Most likely, in our infrastructure, we might already have a Zabbix installation. Zabbix is quite flexible, and this permits us to upgrade this installation to the next step: proxy-based monitoring.

Proxy-based monitoring is implemented with one Zabbix server and several proxies, that is, one proxy per branch or data center. This configuration is easy to maintain and offers the advantage to have a centralized monitoring solution. This kind of configuration is the right balance between large environment monitoring and complexity. From this point, we can (with a lot of effort) expand our installation to a complete and distributed monitoring architecture. The installation consisting of one server and many proxies is the one shown in the previous diagram.

Starting from the 2.4.0 version of Zabbix, the distributed scenarios that include nodes are no longer a possible setup. Indeed, if you download the source code of the Zabbix distribution discussed in this book, and then Zabbix 2.4.3, you'll see that the branch of code that was managing the nodes has been removed.

All the possible Zabbix architectures will be discussed in detail in *Chapter 2, Distributed Monitoring*.

Installing Zabbix

The installation that will be covered in this chapter is the one consisting of a server for each of the following base components:

- A web frontend
- A Zabbix server
- A Zabbix database

We will start describing this installation because:

- It is a basic installation that is ready to be expanded with proxies and nodes
- Each component is on a dedicated server
- This kind of configuration is the starting point to monitor large environments
- It is widely used
- Most probably, it will be the starting point of your upgrade and expansion of the monitoring infrastructure.

Actually, this first setup for a large environment, as explained here, can be useful if you are looking to improve an existing monitoring infrastructure. If your current monitoring solution is not implemented in this way, the first thing to do is plan the migration on three different dedicated servers.

Once the environment is set up on three tiers but is still giving poor performance, you can plan and think which kind of large environment setup will be a perfect fit for your infrastructure.

When you monitor your large environment, there are some points to consider:

- Use a dedicated server to keep things easy to extend
- Keep things easy to extend and implement a high-availability setup
- Keep things easy to extend and implement a fault-tolerant architecture

On this three-layer installation, the CPU usage of the server component will not be really critical at least for the Zabbix server. The CPU consumption is directly related to the number of items to store and the refresh rate (number of samples per minute) rather than the memory.

Indeed, the Zabbix server will not consume excessive CPU but is a bit greedier for memory. We can consider that four CPU cores with 8 GB of RAM can be used for more than 1,000 quad hosts without any issues.

Basically, there are two ways to install Zabbix:

- Downloading the latest source code and compiling it
- Installing it from packages

There is also another way to have a Zabbix server up and running, that is, by downloading the virtual appliance, but we don't consider this case as it is better to have full control of our installation and be aware of all the steps. Also, the major concern about the virtual appliance is that Zabbix itself defines the virtual appliance that is not production ready directly on the download page `http://www.zabbix.com/download.php`.

The installation from packages gives us the following benefits:

- It makes the process of upgrading and updating easier
- Dependencies are automatically sorted

The source code compilation also gives us benefits:

- We can compile only the required features
- We can statically build the agent and deploy it on different Linux flavors
- We can have complete control over the update

It is quite usual to have different versions of Linux, Unix, and Microsoft Windows in a large environment. These kinds of scenarios are quite diffused on a heterogeneous infrastructure, and if we use the agent distribution package of Zabbix on each Linux server, we will, for sure, have different versions of the agent and different locations for the configuration files.

The more standardized we are across the server, the easier it will be to maintain and upgrade the infrastructure. `--enable-static` gives us a way to standardize the agent across different Linux versions and releases, and this is a strong benefit. The agent, if statically compiled, can be easily deployed everywhere, and, for sure, we will have the same location (and we can use the same configuration file apart from the node name) for the agent and their configuration file. The deployment will be standardized; however, the only thing that may vary is the start/stop script and how to register it on the right `init` runlevel.

The same kind of concept can be applied to commercial Unix bearing in mind its compilation by vendors, so the same agent can be deployed on different versions of Unix released by the same vendor.

Prerequisites

Before compiling Zabbix, we need to take a look at the prerequisites. The web frontend will need at least the following versions:

- Apache (1.3.12 or later)
- PHP (5.3.0 or later)

Instead, the Zabbix server will need:

- An RDBMS: The open source alternatives are PostgreSQL and MySQL
- `zlib-devel`
- `mysql-devel`: This is used to support MySQL (not needed on our setup)
- `postgresql-devel`: This is used to support PostgreSQL
- `glibc-devel`
- `curl-devel`: This is used in web monitoring
- `libidn-devel`: The `curl-devel` depends on it
- `openssl-devel`: The `curl-devel` depends on it
- `net-snmp-devel`: This is used on SNMP support
- `popt-devel`: `net-snmp-devel` might depend on it
- `rpm-devel`: `net-snmp-devel` might depend on it
- `OpenIPMI-devel`: This is used to support IPMI
- `iksemel-devel`: This is used for the Jabber protocol
- `Libssh2-devel`
- `sqlite3`: This is required if SQLite is used as the Zabbix backend database (usually on proxies)

To install all the dependencies on a Red Hat Enterprise Linux distribution, we can use `yum` (from `root`), but first of all, we need to include the EPEL repository with the following command:

```
# yum install epel-release
```

Using `yum install`, install the following package:

```
# yum install zlib-devel postgresql-devel glibc-devel curl-devel gcc
automake postgresql libidn-devel openssl-devel net-snmp-devel rpm-devel
OpenIPMI-devel iksemel-devel libssh2-devel openldap-devel
```

The `iksemel-devel` package is used to send a Jabber message. This is a really useful feature as it enables Zabbix to send chat messages, Furthermore, Jabber is managed as a media type on Zabbix, and you can also set your working time, which is a really useful feature to avoid the sending of messages when you are not in the office.

Setting up the server

Zabbix needs a user and an unprivileged account to run. Anyway, if the daemon is started from root, it will automatically switch to the Zabbix account if this one is present:

```
# groupadd zabbix
# useradd -m -s /bin/bash -g zabbix zabbix
# useradd -m -s /bin/bash -g zabbix zabbixsvr
```

 The server should never run as root because this will expose the server to a security risk.

The preceding lines permit you to enforce the security of your installation. The server and agent should run with two different accounts; otherwise, the agent can access the Zabbix server's configuration. Now, using the Zabbix user account, we can download and extract the sources from the `tar.gz` file:

```
# wget  http://sourceforge.net/projects/zabbix/files/ZABBIX%20Latest%20
Stable/2.4.4/zabbix-2.4.4.tar.gz/download -O zabbix-2.4.4.tar.gz
# tar -zxvf zabbix-2.4.4.tar.gz
```

Now, we will configure the sources where `help` is available:

```
# cd zabbix-2.4.3
# ./configure --help
```

To configure the source for our server, we can use the following options:

```
# ./configure --enable-server --enable-agent --with-postgresql --with-
libcurl --with-jabber --with-net-snmp --enable-ipv6 --with-openipmi
--with-ssh2 --with-ldap
```

 The `zabbix_get` and `zabbix_send` commands are generated only if `--enable-agent` is specified during server compilation.

If the configuration is complete without errors, we should see something similar to this:

```
config.status: executing depfiles commands



Configuration:


  Detected OS:              linux-gnu
  Install path:             /usr/local
  Compilation arch:         linux


  Compiler:                 gcc
  Compiler flags:           -g -O2    -I/usr/include       -I/usr/include/rpm
-I/usr/local/include -I/usr/lib64/perl5/CORE -I. -I/usr/include -I/usr/
include -I/usr/include -I/usr/include


  Enable server:            yes
  Server details:
    With database:          PostgreSQL
    WEB Monitoring:         cURL
    Native Jabber:          yes
    SNMP:                   yes
    IPMI:                   yes
    SSH:                    yes
    ODBC:                   no
    Linker flags:           -rdynamic      -L/usr/lib64       -L/usr/lib64
-L/usr/lib -L/usr/lib -L/usr/lib
    Libraries:              -lm -ldl -lrt  -lresolv     -lpq  -liksemel
-lnetsnmp -lssh2 -lOpenIPMI -lOpenIPMIposix -lldap -llber   -lcurl


  Enable proxy:             no


  Enable agent:             yes
  Agent details:
    Linker flags:           -rdynamic    -L/usr/lib
    Libraries:              -lm -ldl -lrt  -lresolv    -lldap -llber
-lcurl


  Enable Java gateway:      no
```

```
LDAP support:            yes
IPv6 support:            yes


***************************************************************
*                                                             *
*              Now run 'make install'                         *
*                                                             *
*              Thank you for using Zabbix!                    *
*              <http://www.zabbix.com>                        *
*                                                             *
***************************************************************
```

We will not run make install but only the compilation with # make. To specify a different location for the Zabbix server, we need to use a -- prefix on the configure options, for example, --prefix=/opt/zabbix. Now, follow the instructions as explained in the *Installing and creating the package* section.

Setting up the agent

To configure the sources to create the agent, we need to run the following command:

./configure --enable-agent

make

> With the make command followed by the --enable-static option, you can statically link the libraries, and the compiled binary will not require any external library; this is very useful to distribute the agent across different dialects of Linux.

Installing and creating the package

In both the previous sections, the command line ends right before the installation; indeed, we didn't run the following command:

make install

I advise you not to run the make install command but use the checkinstall software instead. This software will create the package and install the Zabbix software.

You can download the software from ftp://ftp.pbone.net/mirror/ftp5.gwdg.de/pub/opensuse/repositories/home:/ikoinoba/CentOS_CentOS-6/x86_64/checkinstall-1.6.2-3.el6.1.x86_64.rpm.

Note that checkinstall is only one of the possible alternatives that you have to create a distributable system package.

> We can also use a prebuild checkinstall. The current release is checkinstall-1.6.2-20.4.i686.rpm (on Red Hat/CentOS); the package will also need rpm-build; then, from root, we need to execute the following command:
>
> ```
> # yum install rpm-build rpmdevtools
> ```
>
> We also need to create the necessary directories:
>
> ```
> # mkdir -p ~/rpmbuild/{BUILD,RPMS,SOURCES,SPECS,SRPMS}
> ```

The package made things easy; it is easy to distribute and upgrade the software, plus we can create a package for different versions of a package manager: RPM, deb, and tgz.

> checkinstall can produce a package for Debian (option -D), Slackware (option -S), and Red Hat (option -R). This is particularly useful to produce the Zabbix's agent package (statically linked) and to distribute it around our server.

Now, we need to convert to root or use the sudo checkinstall command followed by its options:

```
# checkinstall --nodoc -R --install=no -y
```

If you don't face any issue, you should get the following message:

```
******************************************************************
 Done. The new package has been saved to
 /root/rpmbuild/RPMS/x86_64/zabbix-2.4.4-1.x86_64.rpm
 You can install it in your system anytime using:
      rpm -i zabbix-2.4.4-1.x86_64.rpm
******************************************************************
```

Now, to install the package from root, you need to run the following command:

```
# rpm -i zabbix-2.4.4-1.x86_64.rpm
```

Finally, Zabbix is installed. The server binaries will be installed in <prefix>/sbin, utilities will be in <prefix>/bin, and the man pages will be under the <prefix>/share location.

Installing from packages

To provide a complete picture of all the possible install methods, you need to be aware of the steps required to install Zabbix using the prebuilt `rpm` packages.

The first thing to do is install the repository:

```
# rpm -ivh http://repo.zabbix.com/zabbix/2.4/rhel/6/x86_64/
zabbix-2.4.4-1.el6.x86_64.rpm
```

This will create the yum repo file, `/etc/yum.repos.d/zabbix.repo`, and will enable the repository.

> If you take a look at the Zabbix repository, you can see that inside the "non-supported" tree: `http://repo.zabbix.com/non-supported/rhel/6/x86_64/`, you have available these packages: `iksemel`, `fping`, `libssh2`, and `snmptt`.

Now, it is easy to install our Zabbix server and web interface; you can simply run this command on the server:

```
# yum install zabbix-server-pgsql
```

And in the web server, bear in mind to first add the `yum` repository:

```
# yum install zabbix-web-pgsql
```

To install the agent, you only need to run the following command:

```
# yum install zabbix-agent
```

> If you have decided to use the RPM packages, please bear in mind that the configuration files are located under `/etc/zabbix/`. The book anyway will continue to refer to the standard configuration: `/usr/local/etc/`.

Also, if you have a local firewall active where you're deploying your Zabbix agent, you need to properly configure `iptables` to allow the traffic against Zabbix's agent port with the following command that you need to run as root:

```
# iptables -I INPUT 1 -p tcp --dport 10050 -j ACCEPT
# iptables-save
```

Configuring the server

For the server configuration, we only have one file to check and edit:

`/usr/local/etc/zabbix_server.conf`

The configuration files are located inside the following directory:

`/usr/local/etc`

We need to change the `/usr/local/etc/zabbix_server.conf` file and write the username, relative password, and the database name there; note that the database configuration will be done later on in this chapter and that, by now, you can write the planned username/password/database name. Then, in the `zabbix` account, you need to edit:

`# vi /usr/local/etc/zabbix_server.conf`

Change the following parameters:

`DBHost=localhost`

`DBName=zabbix`

`DBUser=zabbix`

`DBPassword=<write-here-your-password>`

> Now, our Zabbix server is configured and almost ready to go. `zabbix_server.conf location` depends on the `sysconfdir` compile-time installation variable. Don't forget to take appropriate measures to protect access to the configuration file with the following command:
>
> `chmod 600/usr/local/etc/zabbix_server.conf`

The location of the default external scripts will be as follows:

`/usr/local/share/zabbix/externalscripts`

This depends on the `datadir` compile-time installation variable. The `alertscripts` directory will be in the following location:

`/usr/local/share/zabbix/alertscripts`

> This can be changed during compilation, and it depends on the `datadir` installation variable.

Now, we need to configure the agent. The configuration file is where we need to write the IP address of our Zabbix server. Once done, it is important to add two new services to the right runlevel to be sure that they will start when the server enters on the right runlevel.

To complete this task, we need to install the start/stop scripts on the following:

- `/etc/init.d/zabbix-agent`
- `/etc/init.d/zabbix-proxy`
- `etc/init.d/zabbix-server`

There are several scripts prebuilt inside the `misc` folder located at the following location:

`zabbix-2.4.4/misc/init.d`

This folder contains different startup scripts for different Linux variants, but this tree is not actively maintained and tested, and may not be up to date with the most recent versions of Linux distributions, so it is better to take care and test it before going live.

Once the start/stop script is added inside the `/etc/init.d` folder, we need to add them to the service list:

```
# chkconfig --add zabbix-server
# chkconfig --add zabbix-agentd
```

Now, all that is left is to tell the system which runlevel it should start them on; we are going to use runlevels 3 and 5:

```
# chkconfig --level 35 zabbix-server on
# chkconfig --level 35 zabbix-agentd on
```

Also, in case you have a local firewall active in your Zabbix server, you need to properly configure `iptables` to allow traffic against Zabbix's server port with the following command that you need to run as root:

```
# iptables -I INPUT 1 -p tcp --dport 10051 -j ACCEPT
# iptables-save
```

Currently, we can't start the server; before starting up our server, we need to configure the database.

Installing the database

Once we complete the previous step, we can walk through the database server installation. All those steps will be done on the dedicated database server. The first thing to do is install the PostgreSQL server. This can be easily done with the package offered from the distribution, but it is recommended that you use the latest 9.x stable version.

Red Hat is still distributing the 8.x on RHEL6.4. Also, its clones, such as CentOS and ScientificLinux, are doing the same. PosgreSQL 9.x has many useful features; at the moment, the latest stable, ready-for-production environment is Version 9.2.

To install PostgreSQL 9.4, there are some easy steps to follow:

1. Locate the `.repo` files:

    ○   **Red Hat**: This is present at `/etc/yum/pluginconf.d/rhnplugin.conf` `[main]`

    ○   **CentOS**: This is present at `/etc/yum.repos.d/CentOS-Base.repo`, `[base]` and `[updates]`

2. Append the following line on the section(s) identified in the preceding step:
    `exclude=postgresql*`

3. Browse to `http://yum.postgresql.org` and find your correct RPM. For example, to install PostgreSQL 9.4 on RHEL 6, go to `http://yum.postgresql.org/9.4/redhat/rhel-6-x86_64/pgdg-redhat94-9.4-1.noarch.rpm`.

4. Install the repo with `yum localinstall http://yum.postgresql.org/9.4/redhat/rhel-6-x86_64/pgdg-centos94-9.4-1.noarch.rpm`.

5. Now, to list the entire `postgresql` package, use the following command:
    `# yum list postgres*`

6. Once you find our package in the list, install it using the following command:
    `# yum install postgresql94 postgresql94-server postgresql94-contrib`

7. Once the packages are installed, we need to initialize the database:
    `# service postgresql-9.4 initdb`

    Alternatively, we can also initialize this database:
    `# /etc/init.d/postgresql-9.4 initdb`

8. Now, we need to change a few things in the configuration file /var/lib/pgsql/9.4/data/postgresql.conf. We need to change the listen address and the relative port:

```
listen_addresses = '*'
port = 5432
```

We also need to add a couple of entries for zabbix_db right after the following lines:

```
# TYPE   DATABASE         USER              ADDRESS
METHOD

# "local" is for Unix domain socket connections only

local    all              all
trust

in /var/lib/pgsql/9.4/data/pg_hba.conf

# configuration for Zabbix

local    zabbix_db    zabbix                         md5

host     zabbix_db    zabbix      <CIDR-address>     md5
```

The local keyword matches all the connections made in the Unix-domain sockets. This line is followed by the database name (zabbix_db), the username (zabbix), and the authentication method (in our case, md5).

The host keyword matches all the connections that are coming from TCP/IP (this includes SSL and non-SSL connections) followed by the database name (zabbix_db), username (zabbix), network, and mask of all the hosts that are allowed and the authentication method (in our case md5).

9. The network mask of the allowed hosts in our case should be a network mask because we need to allow the web interface (hosted on our web server) and the Zabbix server that is on a different dedicated server, for example, 10.6.0.0/24 (a small subnet) or even a large network. Most likely, the web interface as well as the Zabbix server will be in a different network, so make sure that you express all the network and relative masks here.

10. Finally, we can start our PosgreSQL server using the following command:

```
# service postgresql-9.4  start
```

Alternatively, we can use this command:

```
# /etc/init.d/postgresql-9.4  start
```

To create a database, we need to be a postgres user (or the user that in your distribution is running PostgreSQL). Create a user for the database (our Zabbix user) and log in as that user to import the schema with the relative data.

The code to import the schema is as follows:

```
# su - postgres
```

Once we become `postgres` users, we can create the database (in our example, it is `zabbix_db`):

```
-bash-4.1$ psql
postgres=#  CREATE USER zabbix WITH PASSWORD '<YOUR-ZABBIX-PASSWORD-HERE>';
CREATE ROLE
postgres=# CREATE DATABASE zabbix_db WITH OWNER zabbix ENCODING='UTF8';
CREATE DATABASE
postgres=# \q
```

The database creation scripts are located in the `/database/postgresql` folder of the extracted source files. They need to be installed exactly in this order:

```
# cat schema.sql |  psql –h <DB-HOST-IP-ADDRESS> -W -U zabbix zabbix_db
# cat images.sql |  psql –h <DB-HOST-IP-ADDRESS> -W -U zabbix zabbix_db
# cat data.sql |  psql –h <DB-HOST-IP-ADDRESS> -W -U zabbix zabbix_db
```

The `-h <DB-HOST-IP-ADDRESS>` option used on the `psql` command will avoid the use of the local entry contained in the standard configuration file `/var/lib/pgsql/9.4/data/pg_hba.conf`.

Now, finally, it is the time to start our Zabbix server and test the whole setup for our Zabbix server/database:

```
# /etc/init.d/zabbix-server start
Starting Zabbix server:                                  [  OK  ]
```

A quick check of the log file can give us more information about what is currently happening in our server. We should be able to get the following lines from the log file (the default location is `/tmp/zabbix_server.log`):

```
  26284:20150114:034537.722 Starting Zabbix Server. Zabbix 2.4.4
(revision 51175).
  26284:20150114:034537.722 ****** Enabled features ******
  26284:20150114:034537.722 SNMP monitoring:          YES
  26284:20150114:034537.722 IPMI monitoring:          YES
  26284:20150114:034537.722 WEB monitoring:           YES
```

```
26284:20150114:034537.722 VMware monitoring:          YES
26284:20150114:034537.722 Jabber notifications:        YES
26284:20150114:034537.722 Ez Texting notifications:    YES
26284:20150114:034537.722 ODBC:                        YES
26284:20150114:034537.722 SSH2 support:                YES
26284:20150114:034537.722 IPv6 support:                YES
26284:20150114:034537.725 ******************************
26284:20150114:034537.725 using configuration file: /usr/local/etc/
zabbix/zabbix_server.conf
26284:20150114:034537.745 current database version (mandatory/optional):
02040000/02040000
26284:20150114:034537.745 required mandatory version: 02040000
26284:20150114:034537.763 server #0 started [main process]
26289:20150114:034537.763 server #1 started [configuration syncer #1]
26290:20150114:034537.764 server #2 started [db watchdog #1]
26291:20150114:034537.764 server #3 started [poller #1]
26293:20150114:034537.765 server #4 started [poller #2]
26294:20150114:034537.766 server #5 started [poller #3]
26296:20150114:034537.770 server #7 started [poller #5]
26295:20150114:034537.773 server #6 started [poller #4]
26297:20150114:034537.773 server #8 started [unreachable poller #1]
26298:20150114:034537.779 server #9 started [trapper #1]
26300:20150114:034537.782 server #11 started [trapper #3]
26302:20150114:034537.784 server #13 started [trapper #5]
26301:20150114:034537.786 server #12 started [trapper #4]
26299:20150114:034537.786 server #10 started [trapper #2]
26303:20150114:034537.794 server #14 started [icmp pinger #1]
26305:20150114:034537.790 server #15 started [alerter #1]
26312:20150114:034537.822 server #18 started [http poller #1]
26311:20150114:034537.811 server #17 started [timer #1]
26310:20150114:034537.812 server #16 started [housekeeper #1]
26315:20150114:034537.829 server #20 started [history syncer #1]
26316:20150114:034537.844 server #21 started [history syncer #2]
26319:20150114:034537.847 server #22 started [history syncer #3]
26321:20150114:034537.852 server #24 started [escalator #1]
26320:20150114:034537.849 server #23 started [history syncer #4]
```

```
26326:20150114:034537.868 server #26 started [self-monitoring #1]
26325:20150114:034537.866 server #25 started [proxy poller #1]
26314:20150114:034537.997 server #19 started [discoverer #1]
```

Actually, the default log location is not the best ever as /tmp will be cleaned up in the event of reboot and, for sure, the logs are not rotated and managed properly.

We can change the default location by simply changing an entry in /etc/zabbix_server.conf. You can change the file as follows:

```
### Option: LogFile
LogFile=/var/log/zabbix/zabbix_server.log
```

Create the directory structure with the following command from root:

```
# mkdir -p /var/log/zabbix
# chown zabbixsvr:zabbixsvr /var/log/zabbix
```

Another important thing to change is logrotate as it is better to have an automated rotation of our log file. This can be quickly implemented by adding the relative configuration in the logrotate directory /etc/logrotate.d/.

To do that, create the following file by running the command from the root account:

```
# vim  /etc/logrotate.d/zabbix-server
```

Use the following content:

```
/var/log/zabbix/zabbix_server.log {
        missingok
        monthly
        notifempty
        compress
        create 0664 zabbix zabbix
}
```

Once those changes have been done, you need to restart your Zabbix server with the following command (run it using root):

```
# /etc/init.d/zabbix-server restart
Shutting down Zabbix server:                        [  OK  ]
Starting Zabbix server:                             [  OK  ]
```

Another thing to check is whether our server is running with our user:

```
# ps aux | grep "[z]abbix_server"
502 28742 1  0 13:39 ?    00:00:00 /usr/local/sbin/zabbix_server
```

```
502 28744 28742 0 13:39 ? 00:00:00 /usr/local/sbin/zabbix_server
502 28745 28742 0 13:39 ? 00:00:00 /usr/local/sbin/zabbix_server
...
```

The preceding lines show that `zabbix_server` is running with the user `502`. We will go ahead and verify that `502` is the user we previously created:

```
# getent passwd 502
zabbixsvr:x:502:501::/home/zabbixsvr:/bin/bash
```

The preceding lines show that all is fine. The most common issue normally is the following error:

```
28487:20130609:133341.529 Database is down. Reconnecting in 10 seconds.
```

There are different actors that cause this issue:

- Firewall (local on our servers or an infrastructure firewall)
- The `postgres` configuration
- Wrong data in `zabbix_server.conf`

> We can try to isolate the problem by running the following command on the database server:
>
> ```
> serverpsql -h <DB-HOST-IP> -U zabbix zabbix_dbPassword
> for user zabbix:psql (9.4)Type "help" for help
> ```
>
> If we have a connection, we can try the same command from the Zabbix server; if it fails, it is better to check the firewall configuration. If we get the fatal identification-authentication failed error, it is better to check the `pg_hba.conf` file.

Now, the second thing to check is the local firewall and then `iptables`. You need to verify that the PostgreSQL port is open on the database server. If the port is not open, you need to add a firewall rule using the root account:

```
# iptables -I INPUT 1 -p tcp --dport 5432 -j ACCEPT
# iptables-save
```

Now, it is time to check how to start and stop your Zabbix installation. The scripts that follow are a bit customized to manage the different users for the server and the agent.

The following startup script works fine with the standard compilation without using a -- prefix or the zabbixsvr user. If you are running on a different setup, make sure that you customize the executable location and the user:

```
exec=/usr/local/sbin/zabbix_server
zabbixsrv=zabbixsvr
```

For `zabbix-server`, create the `zabbix-server` file at `/etc/init.d` with the following content:

```
#!/bin/sh
#
# chkconfig: - 85 15
# description: Zabbix server daemon
# config: /usr/local/etc/zabbix_server.conf
#

### BEGIN INIT INFO
# Provides: zabbix
# Required-Start: $local_fs $network
# Required-Stop: $local_fs $network
# Default-Start:
# Default-Stop: 0 1 2 3 4 5 6
# Short-Description: Start and stop Zabbix server
# Description: Zabbix server
### END INIT INFO

# Source function library.
. /etc/rc.d/init.d/functions

exec=/usr/local/sbin/zabbix_server
prog=${exec##*/}
lockfile=/var/lock/subsys/zabbix
syscf=zabbix-server
```

The next parameter, `zabbixsvr`, is specified inside the `start()` function, and it determines which user will be used to run our Zabbix server:

```
zabbixsrv=zabbixsvr
[ -e /etc/sysconfig/$syscf ] && . /etc/sysconfig/$syscf

start()
{
    echo -n $"Starting Zabbix server: "
```

In the preceding code, the user (who will own our Zabbix's server process) is specified inside the `start` function:

```
daemon --user $zabbixsrv $exec
```

Remember to change the ownership of the server log file and configuration file of Zabbix. This is to prevent a normal user from accessing sensitive data that can be acquired with Zabbix. `Logfile` is specified as follows:

```
/usr/local/etc/zabbix_server.conf
On 'LogFile''LogFile' properties      rv=$?
    echo
    [ $rv -eq 0 ] && touch $lockfile
    return $rv
}

stop()
{
    echo -n $"Shutting down Zabbix server: "
```

Here, inside the `stop` function, we don't need to specify the user as the start/stop script runs from root, so we can simply use `killproc $prog` as follows:

```
        killproc $prog
        rv=$?
        echo
        [ $rv -eq 0 ] && rm -f $lockfile
        return $rv
}

restart()
{
    stop
    start
}

case "$1" in
    start|stop|restart)
        $1
        ;;
    force-reload)
        restart
        ;;
    status)
        status $prog
        ;;
```

```
    try-restart|condrestart)
        if status $prog >/dev/null ; then
            restart
        fi
        ;;
    reload)
        action $"Service ${0##*/} does not support the reload
         action: " /bin/false
        exit 3
        ;;
    *)
        echo $"Usage: $0 {start|stop|status|restart|try-restart|force-
reload}"
        exit 2
        ;;
esac
```

> The following startup script works fine with the standard
> compilation without using a -- prefix or the zabbix_usr
> user. If you are running on a different setup, make sure that
> you customize the executable location and the user:
>   exec=/usr/local/sbin/zabbix_agentd
>   zabbix_usr=zabbix

For zabbix_agent, create the following zabbix-agent file at /etc/init.d/zabbix-agent:

```
#!/bin/sh
#
# chkconfig: - 86 14
# description: Zabbix agent daemon
# processname: zabbix_agentd
# config: /usr/local/etc/zabbix_agentd.conf
#

### BEGIN INIT INFO
# Provides: zabbix-agent
# Required-Start: $local_fs $network
# Required-Stop: $local_fs $network
# Should-Start: zabbix zabbix-proxy
# Should-Stop: zabbix zabbix-proxy
# Default-Start:
# Default-Stop: 0 1 2 3 4 5 6
# Short-Description: Start and stop Zabbix agent
```

```
# Description: Zabbix agent
### END INIT INFO

# Source function library.
. /etc/rc.d/init.d/functions

exec=/usr/local/sbin/zabbix_agentd
prog=${exec##*/}
syscf=zabbix-agent
lockfile=/var/lock/subsys/zabbix-agent
```

The following `zabbix_usr` parameter specifies the account that will be used to run Zabbix's agent:

```
zabbix_usr=zabbix
[ -e /etc/sysconfig/$syscf ] && . /etc/sysconfig/$syscf

start()
{
    echo -n $"Starting Zabbix agent: "
```

The next command uses the value of the `zabbix_usr` variable and permits us to have two different users, one for the server and one for the agent, preventing the Zabbix agent from accessing the `zabbix_server.conf` file that contains our database password:

```
        daemon --user $zabbix_usr $exec
        rv=$?
        echo
        [ $rv -eq 0 ] && touch $lockfile
        return $rv
}

stop()
{
    echo -n $"Shutting down Zabbix agent: "
    killproc $prog
    rv=$?
    echo
    [ $rv -eq 0 ] && rm -f $lockfile
    return $rv
}

restart()
{
```

```
        stop
        start
    }

    case "$1" in
        start|stop|restart)
            $1
            ;;
        force-reload)
            restart
            ;;
        status)
            status $prog
            ;;
        try-restart|condrestart)
            if status $prog >/dev/null ; then
                restart
            fi
            ;;
        reload)
            action $"Service ${0##*/} does not support the reload action:
" /bin/false
            exit 3
            ;;
        *)
            echo $"Usage: $0 {start|stop|status|restart|try-restart|force-
reload}"
            exit 2
            ;;
    esac
```

With that setup, we have the agent that is running with zabbix_usr and the server
with Unix accounts of zabbixsvr:

```
zabbix_usr_  4653 1 0 15:42 ?              00:00:00 /usr/local/sbin/zabbix_
agentd

zabbix_usr 4655 4653   0 15:42 ?    00:00:00 /usr/local/sbin/zabbix_agentd

zabbixsvr 4443 1   0 15:32 ?    00:00:00 /usr/local/sbin/zabbix_server

zabbixsvr 4445 4443   0 15:32 ? 00:00:00 /usr/local/sbin/zabbix_server
```

Some considerations about the database

Zabbix uses an interesting way to keep the database the same size at all times. The database size indeed depends upon:

- The number of processed values per second
- The housekeeper settings

Zabbix uses two ways to store the collected data:

- History
- Trends

While on history, we will find all the collected data (it doesn't matter what type of data will be stored in history); trends will collect only numerical data. Its minimum, maximum, and average calculations are consolidated by hour (to keep the trend a lightweight process).

 All the *strings* items, such as character, log, and text, do not correspond to trends since trends store only values.

There is a process called the housekeeper that is responsible for handling the retention against our database. It is strongly advised that you keep the data in history as small as possible so that you do not overload the database with a huge amount of data, and store the trends for as long as you want.

Now, since Zabbix will also be used for capacity planning purposes, we need to consider using a baseline and keeping at least a whole business period. Normally, the minimum period is one year, but it is strongly advised that you keep the trend history on for at least 2 years. These historical trends will be used during the business opening and closure to have a baseline and quantify the overhead for a specified period.

 If we indicate 0 as the value for trends, the server will not calculate or store trends at all. If history is set to 0, Zabbix will be able to calculate only triggers based on the last value of the item itself as it does not store historical values at all.

The most common issue that we face when aggregating data is the presence of values influenced by positive spikes or fast drops in our hourly trends, which means that huge spikes can produce a mean value per hour that is not right.

Trends in Zabbix are implemented in a smart way. The script creation for the trend table is as follows:

```
CREATE TABLE trends(
itemid bigin NOT NULL, clock integer DEFAULT '0'
NOT NULL, num integer DEFAULT '0'
NOT NULL, value_min numeric(16, 4) DEFAULT '0.0000'
NOT NULL, value_avg numeric(16, 4) DEFAULT '0.0000'
NOT NULL, value_max numeric(16, 4) DEFAULT '0.0000'
NOT NULL, PRIMARY KEY(itemid, clock));

CREATE TABLE trends_uint(
Itemid bigint NOT NULL, Clock integer DEFAULT '0'
NOT NULL, Num integer DEFAULT '0'
NOT NULL, value_min numeric(20) DEFAULT '0'
NOT NULL, value_avg numeric(20) DEFAULT '0'
NOT NULL, value_max numeric(20) DEFAULT '0'
NOT NULL, PRIMARY KEY(itemid, clock));
```

As you can see, there are two tables showing trends inside the Zabbix database:

- Trends
- Trends_uint

The first table, Trends, is used to store the float value. The second table, trends_uint, is used to store the unsigned integer. Both tables own the concept of keeping the following for each hour:

- Minimum value (value_min)
- Maximum value (value_max)
- Average value (value_avg)

This feature permits us to find out and display the trends graphically by using the influence of spikes and fast drops against the average value and understanding how and how much this value has been influenced. The other tables used for historical purposes are as follows:

- history: This is used to store numeric data (float)
- history_log: This is used to store logs (for example, the text field on the PostgreSQL variable has unlimited length)
- history_str: This is used to store strings (up to 255 characters)
- history_text: This is used to store the text value (again, this is a text field, so it has unlimited length)
- history_uint: This is used to store numeric values (unsigned integers)

Sizing the database

Calculating the definitive database size is not an easy task because it is hard to predict how many items and the relative rate per second we will have on our infrastructure and how many events will be generated. To simplify this, we will consider the worst-case scenario, where we have an event generated every second.

In summary, the database size is influenced by:

- **Items**: The number of items in particular
- **Refresh rate**: The average refresh rate of our items
- **Space to store values**: This value depends on RDBMS

The space used to store the data may vary from database to database, but we can simplify our work by considering mean values that quantify the maximum space consumed by the database. We can also consider the space used to store values on history to be around 50 bytes per value, the space used by a value on the trend table to be around 128 bytes, and the space used for a single event to be normally around 130 bytes.

The total amount of used space can be calculated with the following formula:

Configuration + History + Trends + Events

Now, let's look into each of the components:

- **Configuration**: This refers to Zabbix's configuration for the server, the web interface, and all the configuration parameters that are stored in the database; this is normally around 10 MB
- **History**: The history component is calculated using the following formula:
  ```
  History retention days* (items/refresh rate)*24*3600* 50 bytes
  (History bytes usage average)
  ```
- **Trends**: The trends component is calculated using the following formula:
  ```
  days*(items/3600)*24*3600*128 bytes (Trend bytes usage average)
  ```
- **Events**: The event component is calculated using the following formula:
  ```
  days*events*24*3600*130 bytes (Event bytes usage average)
  ```

Now, coming back to our practical example, we can consider 5,000 items to be refreshed every minute, and we want to have 7 days of retention; the used space will be calculated as follows:

```
History: retention (in days) * (items/refresh rate)*24*3600* 50 bytes
```

50 bytes is the mean value of the space consumed by a value stored on history.

Considering a history of 30 days, the result is the following:

- History will be calculated as:

```
30 * 5000/60 * 24*3600 *50 = 10.8GB
```

- As we said earlier, to simplify, we will consider the worst-case scenario (one event per second) and will also consider keeping 5 years of events

- Events will be calculated using the following formula:

```
retention days*events*24*3600* Event bytes usage (average)
```

When we calculate an event, we have:

```
5*365*24*3600* 130 = 15.7GB
```

 130 bytes is the mean value for the space consumed by a value stored on events.

- Trends will be calculated using the following formula:

```
retention in days*(items/3600)*24*3600*Trend bytes usage (average)
```

When we calculate trends, we have:

```
5000*24*365* 128 = 5.3GB per year or 26.7GB for 5 years.
```

 128 bytes is the mean value of the space consumed by a value stored on trends.

The following table shows the retention in days and the space required for the measure:

Type of measure	Retention in days	Space required
History	30	10.8 GB
Events	1825 (5 years)	15.7 GB
Trends	1825 (5 years)	26.7 GB
Total	N.A.	53.2 GB

The calculated size is not the initial size of our database, but we need to keep in mind that this one will be our target size after 5 years. We are also considering a history of 30 days, so keep in mind that this retention can be reduced if there are issues since the trends will keep and store our baseline and hourly trends.

The history and trend retention policy can be changed easily for every item. This means that we can create a template with items that have a different history retention by default. Normally, the history is set to 7 days, but for some kind of measure, such as in a web scenario or an other measures, we may need to keep all the values for more than a week. This permits us to change the value for each item.

In our example, we considered a worst-case scenario with 30 days of retention, but it is a piece of good advice to keep the history only for 7 days or even less in large environments. If we perform a basic calculation of an item that is updated every 60 seconds and has its history preserved for 7 days, it will generate *(update interval)* * *(hours in a day)* * *(number of days in history)* $=60*24*7=10,080$.

This mean that, for each item, we will have 10,080 lines in a week, and that gives us an idea of the number of lines that we will produce on our database.

The following screenshot represents the details of a single item:

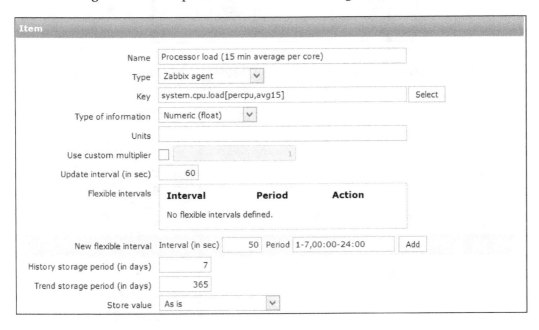

Some considerations about housekeeping

Housekeeping can be quite a heavy process. As the database grows, housekeeping will require more and more time to complete his/her work. This issue can be sorted using the `delete_history()` database function.

There is a way to deeply improve the housekeeping performance and fix this performance drop. The heaviest tables are: `history`, `history_uint`, `trends`, and `trends_uint`.

A solution is PostgreSQL table partitioning and the partitioning of the entire table on a monthly basis. The following figure displays the standard and nonpartitioned history table on the database:

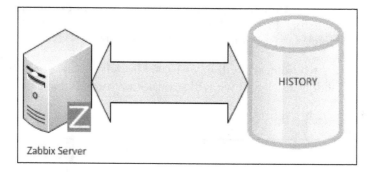

The following figure shows how a partitioned history table will be stored in the database:

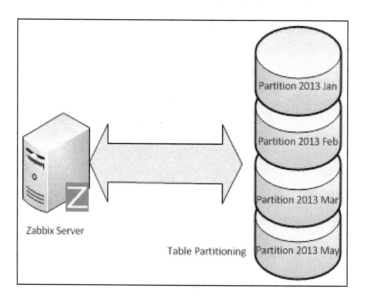

Partitioning is basically the splitting of a large logical table into smaller physical pieces. This feature can provide several benefits:

- The performance of queries can be improved dramatically in situations where there is heavy access of the table's rows in a single partition.

- The partitioning will reduce the index size, making it more likely to fit in the memory of the parts that are being used heavily.

- Massive deletes can be accomplished by removing partitions, instantly reducing the space allocated for the database without introducing fragmentation and a heavy load on index rebuilding. The `delete partition` command also entirely avoids the *vacuum* overhead caused by a bulk *delete*.

- When a query updates or requires access to a large percentage of the partition, using a sequential scan is often more efficient than using the index with random access or scattered reads against that index.

All these benefits are only worthwhile when a table is very large. The strongpoint of this kind of architecture is that the RDBMS will directly access the needed partition, and the delete will simply be a delete of a partition. Partition deletion is a fast process and requires few resources.

Unfortunately, Zabbix is not able to manage the partitions, so we need to disable the housekeeping and use an external process to accomplish the housekeeping.

The partitioning approach described here has certain benefits compared to the other partitioning solutions:

- This does not require you to prepare the database to partition it with Zabbix

- This does not require you to create/schedule a cron job to create the tables in advance

- This is simpler to implement than other solutions

This method will prepare partitions under the desired partitioning schema with the following convention:

- Daily partitions are in the form of `partitions.tablename_pYYYYMMDD`

- Monthly partitions are in the form of `partitions.tablename_pYYYYMM`

All the scripts here described are available at `https://github.com/smartmarmot/Mastering_Zabbix`.

To set up this feature, we need to create a schema where we can place all the partitioned tables; then, within a `psql` section, we need to run the following command:

```
CREATE SCHEMA partitions AUTHORIZATION zabbix;
```

Now, we need a function that will create the partition. So, to connect to Zabbix, you need to run the following code:

```
CREATE OR REPLACE FUNCTION trg_partition()
RETURNS TRIGGER AS
$BODY$
DECLARE
    prefix text:= 'partitions.';
    timeformat text;
    selector text;
    _interval INTERVAL;
    tablename text;
    startdate text;
    enddate text;
    create_table_part text;
    create_index_part text;
BEGIN
selector = TG_ARGV[0];
IF selector = 'day'
    THEN
    timeformat:= 'YYYY_MM_DD';
ELSIF selector = 'month'
    THEN
    timeformat:= 'YYYY_MM';
END IF;

_interval:= '1 ' || selector;
tablename:= TG_TABLE_NAME || '_p' || TO_CHAR(TO_TIMESTAMP(NEW.clock),
timeformat);

EXECUTE 'INSERT INTO ' || prefix || quote_ident(tablename) || ' SELECT
($1).*'
USING NEW;
RETURN NULL;

EXCEPTION
    WHEN undefined_table THEN
```

```
startdate:= EXTRACT(epoch FROM date_trunc(selector, TO_TIMESTAMP(NEW.
clock)));
enddate:= EXTRACT(epoch FROM date_trunc(selector, TO_TIMESTAMP(NEW.
clock) + _interval));

create_table_part:= 'CREATE TABLE IF NOT EXISTS ' || prefix || quote_
ident(tablename) || ' (CHECK ((clock >= ' || quote_literal(startdate)
|| ' AND clock < ' || quote_literal(enddate) || '))) INHERITS (' ||
TG_TABLE_NAME || ')';
create_index_part:= 'CREATE INDEX ' || quote_ident(tablename) || '_1
on ' || prefix || quote_ident(tablename) || '(itemid,clock)';

EXECUTE create_table_part;
EXECUTE create_index_part;

--insert it again
EXECUTE 'INSERT INTO ' || prefix || quote_ident(tablename) || ' SELECT
($1).*'
USING NEW;
RETURN NULL;

END;
$BODY$
LANGUAGE plpgsql VOLATILE
COST 100;
ALTER FUNCTION trg_partition()
OWNER TO zabbix;
```

> Please ensure that your database has been set up with the user
> Zabbix. If you're using a different role/account, please change
> the last line of the script accordingly:
>
> **ALTER FUNCTION trg_partition()**
>
> **OWNER TO <replace with your database owner here>;**

Now, we need a trigger connected to each table that we want to separate. This trigger
will run an INSERT statement, and if the partition is not ready or created yet, the
function will create the partition right before the INSERT statement:

```
CREATE TRIGGER partition_trg BEFORE INSERT ON history
FOR EACH ROW EXECUTE PROCEDURE trg_partition('day');
CREATE TRIGGER partition_trg BEFORE INSERT ON history_sync
FOR EACH ROW EXECUTE PROCEDURE trg_partition('day');
CREATE TRIGGER partition_trg BEFORE INSERT ON history_uint
FOR EACH ROW EXECUTE PROCEDURE trg_partition('day');
```

```
CREATE TRIGGER partition_trg BEFORE INSERT ON history_str_sync
FOR EACH ROW EXECUTE PROCEDURE trg_partition('day');
CREATE TRIGGER partition_trg BEFORE INSERT ON history_log
FOR EACH ROW EXECUTE PROCEDURE trg_partition('day');
CREATE TRIGGER partition_trg BEFORE INSERT ON trends
FOR EACH ROW EXECUTE PROCEDURE trg_partition('month');
CREATE TRIGGER partition_trg BEFORE INSERT ON trends_uint
FOR EACH ROW EXECUTE PROCEDURE trg_partition('month');
```

At this point, we miss only the housekeeping function that will replace the one built in Zabbix and disable Zabbix's native one. The function that will handle housekeeping for us is as follows:

```
CREATE OR REPLACE FUNCTION delete_partitions(intervaltodelete
INTERVAL, tabletype text)
  RETURNS text AS
$BODY$
DECLARE
result RECORD ;
prefix text := 'partitions.';
table_timestamp TIMESTAMP;
delete_before_date DATE;
tablename text;
BEGIN
    FOR result IN SELECT * FROM pg_tables WHERE schemaname =
'partitions' LOOP
        table_timestamp := TO_TIMESTAMP(substring(result.tablename
FROM '[0-9_]*$'), 'YYYY_MM_DD');
        delete_before_date := date_trunc('day', NOW() -
intervalToDelete);
        tablename := result.tablename;
        IF tabletype != 'month' AND tabletype != 'day' THEN
      RAISE EXCEPTION 'Please specify "month" or "day" instead of %',
tabletype;
        END IF;
    --Check whether the table name has a day (YYYY_MM_DD) or month
(YYYY_MM) format
        IF LENGTH(substring(result.tablename FROM '[0-9_]*$')) = 10
AND tabletype = 'month' THEN
            --This is a daily partition YYYY_MM_DD
            -- RAISE NOTICE 'Skipping table % when trying
to delete "%" partitions (%)', result.tablename, tabletype,
length(substring(result.tablename from '[0-9_]*$'));
            CONTINUE;
```

```
            ELSIF LENGTH(substring(result.tablename FROM '[0-9_]*$')) = 7
AND tabletype = 'day' THEN
                --this is a monthly partition
                --RAISE NOTICE 'Skipping table % when trying to delete "%"
partitions (%)', result.tablename, tabletype, length(substring(result.
tablename from '[0-9_]*$'));
                CONTINUE;
            ELSE
                --This is the correct table type. Go ahead and check if it
needs to be deleted
        --RAISE NOTICE 'Checking table %', result.tablename;
            END IF;
    IF table_timestamp <= delete_before_date THEN
            RAISE NOTICE 'Deleting table %', quote_ident(tablename);
            EXECUTE 'DROP TABLE ' || prefix || quote_ident(tablename) ||
';';
    END IF;
        END LOOP;
RETURN 'OK';
    END;
    $BODY$
    LANGUAGE plpgsql VOLATILE
    COST 100;
ALTER FUNCTION delete_partitions(INTERVAL, text)
    OWNER TO zabbix;
```

Now you have the housekeeping ready to run. To enable housekeeping, we can use crontab by adding the following entries:

```
@daily psql -h<your database host here> -d zabbix_db -q -U zabbix -c
"SELECT delete_partitions('7 days', 'day')"
@daily psql  -h<your database host here> -d zabbix_db -q -U zabbix -c
"SELECT delete_partitions('24 months', 'month')"
```

Those two tasks should be scheduled on the database server's crontab. In this example, we will keep the history of 7 days and trends of 24 months.

Now, we can finally disable the Zabbix housekeeping. To disable the housekeeping on Zabbix 2.4, the best way is use the web interface by selecting **Administration | General | Housekeeper**, and there, you can disable the housekeeping for the **Trends** and **History** tables, as shown in the following screenshot:

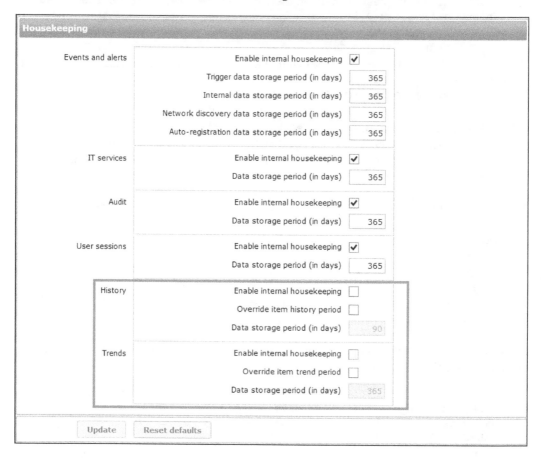

Now the built-in housekeeping is disabled, and you should see a lot of improvement in the performance. To keep your database as lightweight as possible, you can clean up the following tables:

- `acknowledges`
- `alerts`
- `auditlog`
- `events`
- `service_alarms`

Once you have chosen your own retention, you need to add a retention policy; for example, in our case, it will be 2 years of retention. With the following crontab entries, you can delete all the records older than 63072000 (2 years expressed in seconds):

```
@daily psql -q -U zabbix -c "delete from acknowledges where clock <
(SELECT (EXTRACT( epoch FROM now() ) - 63072000))"
@daily psql -q -U zabbix -c "delete from alerts where clock < (SELECT
(EXTRACT( epoch FROM now() ) - 63072000))"
@daily psql -q -U zabbix -c "delete from auditlog where clock <
(SELECT (EXTRACT( epoch FROM now() ) - 62208000))"
@daily psql -q -U zabbix -c "delete from events where clock < (SELECT
(EXTRACT( epoch FROM now() ) - 62208000))"
@daily psql -q -U zabbix -c "delete from service_alarms where clock <
(SELECT (EXTRACT( epoch FROM now() ) - 62208000))"
```

To disable housekeeping, we need to drop the triggers created:

```
DROP TRIGGER partition_trg ON history;
DROP TRIGGER partition_trg ON history_sync;
DROP TRIGGER partition_trg ON history_uint;
DROP TRIGGER partition_trg ON history_str_sync;
DROP TRIGGER partition_trg ON history_log;
DROP TRIGGER partition_trg ON trends;
DROP TRIGGER partition_trg ON trends_uint;
```

All those changes need to be tested and changed/modified as they fit your setup. Also, be careful and back up your database.

The web interface

The web interface installation is quite easy; there are certain basic steps to execute. The web interface is completely written in PHP, so we need a web server that supports PHP; in our case, we will use Apache with the PHP support enabled.

The entire web interface is contained inside the php folder at frontends/php/ that we need to copy on our htdocs folder:

```
/var/www/html
```

Use the following commands to copy the folders:

```
# mkdir <htdocs>/zabbix
# cd frontends/php
# cp -a . <htdocs>/zabbix
```

 Be careful—you might need proper rights and permissions as all those files are owned by Apache and they also depend on your httpd configuration.

The web wizard – frontend configuration

Now, from your web browser, you need to open the following URL:

```
http://<server_ip_or_name>/zabbix
```

The first screen that you will meet is a welcome page; there is nothing to do there other than to click on **Next**. When on the first page, you may get a warning on your browser that informs you that the date / time zone is not set. This is a parameter inside the php.ini file. All the possible time zones are described on the official PHP website at http://www.php.net/manual/en/timezones.php.

The parameter to change is the date/time zone inside the php.ini file. If you don't know the current PHP configuration or where it is located in your php.ini file, and you need detailed information about which modules are running or the current settings, then you can write a file, for example, php-info.php, inside the Zabbix directory with the following content:

```
<?phpphpinfo();phpinfo(INFO_MODULES);
?>
```

Now point your browser to http://your-zabbix-web-frontend/zabbix/php-info.php.

You will have your full configuration printed out on a web page. The following screenshot is more important; it displays a prerequisite check, and, as you can see, there is at least one prerequisite that is not met:

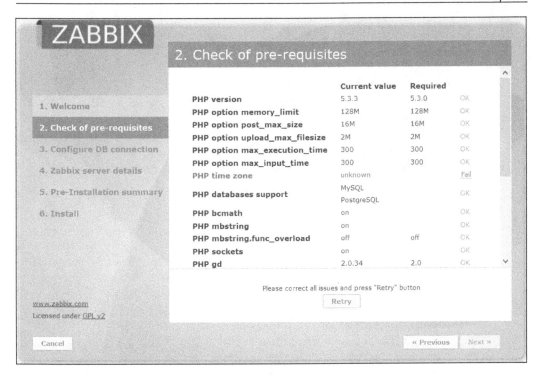

On standard Red-Hat/CentOS 6.6, you only need to set the time zone; otherwise, if you're using an older version, you might have to change the following prerequisites that most likely are not fulfilled:

```
PHP option post_max_size          8M    16M    Fail
PHP option max_execution_time     30    300    Fail
PHP option max_input_time         60    300    Fail
PHP bcmath                        no           Fail
PHP mbstring                      no           Fail
PHP gd  unknown                         2.0    Fail
PHP gd PNG support                no           Fail
PHP gd JPEG support               no           Fail
PHP gd FreeType support           no           Fail
PHP xmlwriter                     no           Fail
PHP xmlreader                     no           Fail
```

Most of these parameters are contained inside the php.ini file. To fix them, simply change the following options inside the /etc/php.ini file:

```
[Date]
; Defines the default timezone used by the date functions
```

```
; http://www.php.net/manual/en/datetime.configuration.php#ini.date.
timezone
date.timezone = Europe/Rome


; Maximum size of POST data that PHP will accept.
; http://www.php.net/manual/en/ini.core.php#ini.post-max-size
post_max_size = 16M


; Maximum execution time of each script, in seconds
; http://www.php.net/manual/en/info.configuration.php#ini.max-
execution-time
max_execution_time = 300


; Maximum amount of time each script may spend parsing request data.
It's a good
; idea to limit this time on productions servers in order to eliminate
unexpectedly
; long running scripts.
; Default Value: -1 (Unlimited)
; Development Value: 60 (60 seconds)
; Production Value: 60 (60 seconds)
; http://www.php.net/manual/en/info.configuration.php#ini.max-input-
time
max_input_time = 300


; Maximum amount of time each script may spend parsing request data.
It's a good
; idea to limit this time on productions servers in order to eliminate
unexpectedly
; long running scripts.
; Default Value: -1 (Unlimited)
; Development Value: 60 (60 seconds)
; Production Value: 60 (60 seconds)
; http://www.php.net/manual/en/info.configuration.php#ini.max-input-
time
max_input_time = 300
```

To solve the issue of the missing library, we need to install the following packages:

- php-xml
- php-bcmath
- php-mbstring
- php-gd

We will use the following command to install these packages:

```
# yum install php-xml php-bcmath php-mbstring php-gd
```

The whole list or the prerequisite list is given in the following table:

Prerequisite	Min value	Solution
PHP Version	5.3.0	
PHP `memory_limit`	128M	In `php.ini`, change `memory_limit=128M`.
PHP `post_max_size`	16M	In `php.ini`, change `post_max_size=16M`.
PHP `upload_max_filesize`	2M	In `php.ini`, change `upload_max_filesize=2M`.
PHP `max_execution_time` option	300 Seconds	In `php.ini`, change `max_execution_time=300`.
PHP `max_input_time` option	300 seconds	In `php.ini`, change `max_input_time=300`.
PHP `session.auto_start`	Disabled	In `php.ini`, change `session.auto_start=0`.
`bcmath`		Use `php-bcmath` extension
`mbstring`		Use `php-mbstring` extension
PHP `mbstring.func_overload`	Must be disabled	In `php.ini` change `mbstring.func_overload = 0`.
PHP `always_populate_raw_post_data`	Must be set to -1	In `php.ini` change `always_populate_raw_post_data = -1`.
`sockets`		This extension is required for user script support: `php-net-socket module`
`gd`		The PHP GD extension must support PNG images (`--with-png-dir`), JPEG (`--with-jpeg-dir`) images, and FreeType 2 (`--with-freetype-dir`)
`libxml`	2.6.15	Use `php-xml` or `php5-dom`

Prerequisite	Min value	Solution
`xmlwriter`		Use `php-xmlwriter`
`xmlreader`		Use `php-xmlreader`
`ctype`		Use `php-ctype`
`session`		Use `php-session`
`gettext`		Use `php-gettext`. Since 2.2.1 is not a mandatory requirement, anyway, you can have issues with the GUI translations

Every time you change a `php.ini` file or install a PHP extension, the `httpd` service needs a restart to get the change. Once all the prerequisites are met, we can click on **Next** and go ahead. On the next screen, we need to configure the database connection. We simply need to fill out the form with the username, password, IP address, or hostname and specify the kind of database server we are using, as shown in the following screenshot:

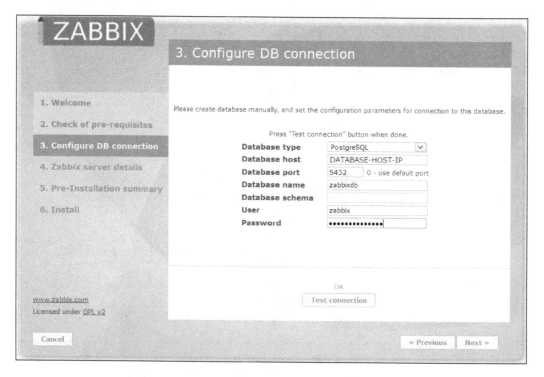

If the connection is fine (this can be checked with a test connection), we can proceed to the next step. Here, you only need to set the proper database parameters to enable the web GUI to create a valid connection, as shown in the following screenshot:

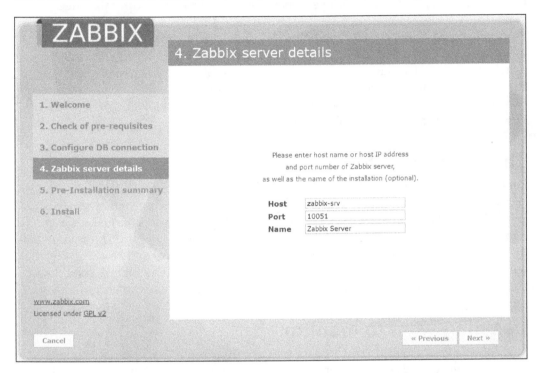

There is no check for the connection available on this page, so it is better to verify that it is possible to reach the Zabbix server from the network. In this form, it is necessary to fill **Host** (or IP address) of our Zabbix server. Since we are installing the infrastructure on three different servers, we need to specify all the parameters and verify that the Zabbix server port is available on the outside of the server.

Once we fill this form, we can click on **Next**. After this, the installation wizard prompts us to view **Pre-Installation summary**, which is a complete summary of all the configuration parameters. If all is fine, just click on **Next**; otherwise, we can go back and change our parameters. When we go ahead, we see that the configuration file has been generated (for example, in this installation the file has been generated in /usr/share/zabbix/conf/zabbix.conf.php).

It can happen that you may get an error instead of a success notification, and most probably, it is about the directory permission on our conf directory at /usr/share/zabbix/conf. Remember to make the directory writable to the httpd user (normally, Apache is writable) at least for the time needed to create this file. Once this step is completed, the frontend is ready and we can perform our first login.

Capacity planning with Zabbix

Quite often, people mix up the difference between capacity planning and performance tuning. Well, the scope of performance tuning is to optimize the system you already have in place for better performance. Using your current performance acquired as a baseline, capacity planning determines what your system needs and when it is needed. Here, we will see how to organize our monitoring infrastructure to achieve this goal and provide us a with useful baseline. Unfortunately, this chapter cannot cover all the aspects of this argument; we should have one whole book about capacity planning, but after this section, we will look at Zabbix with a different vision and will be aware of what to do with it.

The observer effect

Zabbix is a good monitoring system because it is really lightweight. Unfortunately, every observed system will spend a bit of its resources to run the agent that acquires and measures data and metrics against the operating system, so it is normal if the agent introduces a small (normally very small) overhead on the guest system. This is known as the **observer effect**. We can only accept this burden on our server and be aware that this will introduce a slight distortion in data collection, bearing in mind that we should keep it lightweight to a feasible extent while monitoring the process and our custom checks.

Deciding what to monitor

The Zabbix agent's job is to collect data periodically from the monitored machine and send metrics to the Zabbix server (that will be our aggregation and elaboration server). Now, in this scenario, there are certain important things to consider:

- What are we going to acquire?
- How are we going to acquire these metrics (the way or method used)?
- What is the frequency with which this measurement is performed?

Considering the first point, it is important to think what should be monitored on our host and the kind of work that our host will do; or, in other words, what function it will serve.

There are some basic metrics of operating systems that are, nowadays, more or less standardized, and those are: the CPU workload, percentage of free memory, memory usage details, usage of swap, the CPU time for a process, and all this family of measure, all of them are built-in on the Zabbix agent.

Having a set of items with built-in measurement means that they are optimized to produce as little workload as possible on the monitored host; the whole of Zabbix's agent code is written in this way.

All the other metrics can be divided by the service that our server should provide.

 Here, templates are really useful! (Also, it is an efficient way to aggregate our metrics by type.)

Doing a practical example and considering monitoring the RDBMS, it will be fundamental to acquire:

- All the operating system metrics
- Different custom RDBMS metrics

Our different custom RDBMS metrics can be: the number of users connected, the use of cache systems, the number of full table scans, and so on.

All those kinds of metrics will be really useful and can be easily interpolated and compared against the same time period in a graph. Graphs have some strongpoints:

- They are useful to understand (also from the business side)
- It is often nice to present and integrate on slides to enforce our speech

Coming back to our practical example, well, currently we are acquiring data from our RDBMS and our operating system. We can compare the workload of our RDBMS and see how this reflects the workload against our OS. Now?

Most probably, our core business is the revenue of a website, merchant site, or a web application. We assume that we need to keep a website in a three-tier environment under control because it is quite a common case. Our infrastructure will be composed of the following actors:

- A web server
- An application server
- The RDBMS

In real life, most probably, this is the kind of environment that Zabbix will be configured in. We need to be aware that every piece and every component that can influence our service should be measured and stored inside our Zabbix monitoring system. Generally, we can consider it to be quite normal to see people with a strong system administration background to be more focused on operating system-related items as well. We also saw people writing Java code that needs to be concentrated on some other obscure measure, such as the number of threads. The same kind of reasoning can be done if the capacity planner talks with a database administrator or a specific guy from every sector.

This is a quite important point because the Zabbix implementer should have a global vision and should remember that, when buying new hardware, the interface will most likely be a business unit.

This business unit very often doesn't know anything about the number of threads that our system can support but will only understand customer satisfaction, customer-related issues, and how many concurrent users we can successfully serve.

Having said that, it is really important to be ready to talk in their language, and we can do that only if we have certain efficient items to graph.

Defining a baseline

Now, if we look at the whole infrastructure from a client's point of view, we can think that if all our pages are served in a reasonable time, the browsing experience will be pleasant.

Our goal in this case is to make our clients happy and the whole infrastructure reliable. Now, we need to have two kinds of measures:

- The one felt from the user's side (the response time of our web pages)
- Infrastructure items related to it

We need to quantify the response time related to the user's navigation, and we need to know how much a user can wait in front of a web page to get a response, keeping in mind that the whole browsing experience needs to be pleasant. We can measure and categorize our metrics with these three levels of response time:

- **0.2 seconds**: It gives the feel of an instantaneous response. The user feels the browser reaction was caused by him/her and not from a server with a business logic.

- **1-2 seconds**: The user feels that the browsing is continuous, without any interruption. The user can move freely rather than waiting for the pages to load.

- **10 seconds**: The likes for our website will drop. The user will want better performance and can definitely be distracted by other things.

Now, we have our thresholds and we can measure the response of a web page during normal browsing, and in the meantime, we can set a trigger level to warn us when the response time is more than two seconds for a page.

Now we need to relate that to all our other measures: the number of users connected, the number of sessions in our application server, and the number of connections to our database. We also need to relate all our measures to the response time and the number of users connected. Now, we need to measure how our system is serving pages to users during normal browsing.

This can be defined as a baseline. It is where we currently are and is a measure of how our system is performing under a normal load.

Load testing

Now that we know how we are, and we have defined the threshold for our goal, along with the pleasant browsing experience, let's move forward.

We need to know which one is our limit and, more importantly, how the system should reply to our requests. Since we can't hire a room full of people that can click on our website like crazy, we need to use software to simulate this kind of behavior. There is interesting open source software that does exactly this. There are different alternatives to choose from — one of them is Siege (`https://www.joedog.org/2013/07/siege-3-0-3-url-encoding/`).

Seige permits us to simulate a stored browser history and load it on our server. We need to keep in mind that users, real users, will never be synchronized between them. So, it is important to introduce a delay between all the requests. Remember that if we have a login, then we need to use a database of users because application servers cache their object, and we don't want to measure how good the process is in caching them. The basic rule is to create a real browsing scenario against our website, so users who login can log out with just a click and without any random delay.

The stored scenarios should be repeated x times with a growing number of users, meaning Zabbix will store our metrics, and, at a certain point, we will pass our first threshold (1-2 seconds per web page). We can go ahead until the response time reaches the value of our second threshold. There is no way to see how much load our server can take, but it is well known that appetite comes with eating, so I will not be surprised if you go ahead and load your server until it crashes one of the components of your infrastructure.

Drawing graphs that relate the response time to the number of users on a server will help us to see whether our three-tier web architecture is linear or not. Most probably, it will grow in a linear pattern until a certain point. This segment is the one on which our system is performing fine. We can also see the components inside Zabbix, and from this point, we can introduce a kind of delay and draw some conclusions.

Now, we know exactly what to expect from our system and how the system can serve our users. We can see which component is the first that suffers the load and where we need to plan a tuning.

Capacity planning can be done without digging and going deep into what to optimize. As we said earlier, there are two different tasks — performance tuning and capacity planning — that are related, of course, but different. We can simply review our performance and plan our infrastructure expansion.

 A planned hardware expansion is always cheaper than an unexpected, emergency hardware improvement.

We can also perform performance tuning, but be aware that there is a relation between the time spent and the performance obtained, so we need to understand when it is time to stop our performance tuning, as shown in the following graph:

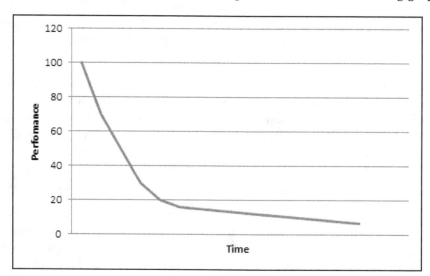

Forecasting the trends

One of the most important features of Zabbix is the capacity to store historical data. This feature is of vital importance during the task of predicting trends. Predicting our trends is not an easy task and is important considering the business that we are serving, and when looking at historical data, we should see whether there are repetitive periods or whether there is a sort of formula that can express our trend.

For instance, it is possible that the online web store we are monitoring needs more and more resources during a particular period of the year, for example, close to public holidays if we sell travels. While doing a practical example, you can consider the used space on a specific server disk. Zabbix gives us the export functionality to get our historical data, so it is quite easy to import them in a spreadsheet. Excel has a curve fitting option that will help us a lot. It is quite easy to find a trend line using Excel that will tell us when we are going to exhaust all our disk space. To add a trend line into Excel, we need to create, at first, a "scatter graph" with our data; here, it is also important to graph the disk size. After this, we can try to find a mathematical equation that is more close to our trend. There are different kinds of formulae that we can choose; in this example, I used a linear equation because the graphs are growing with a linear relation.

 The trend line process is also known as the **curve fitting process**.

The graph that comes out from this process permits us to know, with a considerable degree of precision, when we will run out of space.

Now, it is clear how important it is to have a considerable amount of historical data, bearing in mind the business period and how it influences data.

 It is important to keep track of the trend/regression line used and the relative formula with the R-squared value so that it is possible to calculate it with precision and, if there aren't any changes in trends, when the space will be exhausted.

The graph obtained is shown in the following screenshot, and from this graph, it is simple to see that if the trends don't change, we are going to run out of space on June 25, 2015:

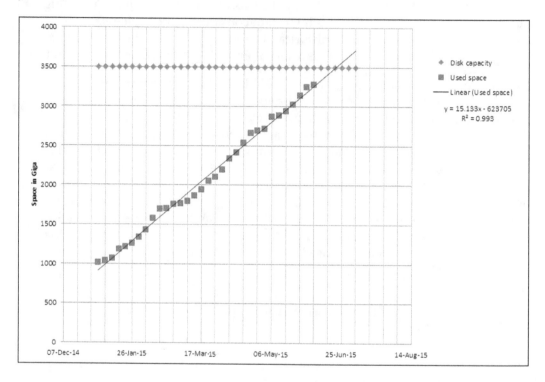

Summary

In this chapter, we completed a Zabbix setup in a three-tier environment. This environment is a good starting point to handle all the events generated from a large or very large environment.

In the next chapter, you will go deep into nodes, proxies, and all possible infrastructure evolution, and, as you will see, all of them are an improvement on the initial setup. This does not mean that the extensions described in the next chapter are easy to implement, but all the infrastructural improvements use this three-tier setup as a starting point. Basically, in the next chapter, you will learn how to expand and evolve this setup and also see how the distributed scenarios can be integrated into our installation. The next chapter will also include an important discussion about security in a distributed environment, making you aware of the possible security risks that may arise in distributed environments.

Distributed Monitoring

Zabbix is a fairly lightweight monitoring application that is able to manage thousands of items with a single-server installation. However, the presence of thousands of monitored hosts, a complex network topology, or the necessity to manage different geographical locations with intermittent, slow, or faulty communications can all show the limits of a single-server configuration. Likewise, the necessity to move beyond a monolithic scenario towards a distributed one is not necessarily a matter of raw performance, and, therefore, it's not just a simple matter of deciding between buying many smaller machines or just one big, powerful one. Many DMZs and network segments with a strict security policy don't allow two-way communication between any hosts on either side, so it is impossible for a Zabbix server to communicate with all the agents on the other side of a firewall. Different branches in the same company or different companies in the same group may need some sort of independence in managing their respective networks, while also needing some coordination and higher-level aggregation of monitored data. Different labs of a research facility may find themselves without a reliable network connection, so they may need to retain monitored data for a while and then send it asynchronously for further processing.

Thanks to its distributed monitoring features, Zabbix can thrive in all these scenarios and provide adequate solutions, whether the problem is about performance, network segregation, administrative independence, or data retention in the presence of faulty links.

While the judicious use of Zabbix agents could be considered from a point of view to be a simple form of distributed monitoring, in this chapter, we will concentrate on Zabbix's supported distributed monitoring mode with proxies. In this chapter, you will learn how to set up, size, and properly configure a Zabbix proxy.

There will also be considerations about security between proxies and the Zabbix server communication so that, by the end of this chapter, you will have all the information you need to apply Zabbix's distributed features to your environment.

Zabbix proxies

A Zabbix proxy is another member of the Zabbix suite of programs that sits between a full-blown Zabbix server and a host-oriented Zabbix agent. Just as with a server, it's used to collect data from any number of items on any number of hosts, and it can retain that data for an arbitrary period of time, relying on a dedicated database to do so. Just as with an agent, it doesn't have a frontend and is managed directly from the central server. It also limits itself to data collection without triggering evaluations or actions.

All these characteristics make the Zabbix proxy a simple, lightweight tool to deploy if you need to offload some checks from the central server or if your objective is to control and streamline the flow of monitored data across networks (possibly segregated by one or more firewalls) or both.

A basic distributed architecture involving Zabbix proxies would look as follows:

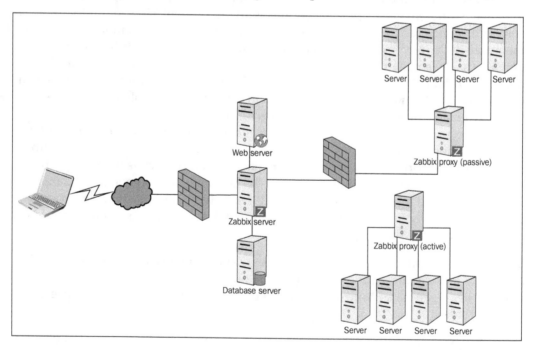

By its very nature, a Zabbix proxy should run on a dedicated machine, which is different than the main server. A proxy is all about gathering data; it doesn't feature a frontend, and it doesn't perform any complex queries or calculations; therefore, it's not necessary to assign a powerful machine with a lot of CPU power or disk throughput. In fact, a small, lean hardware configuration is often a better choice; proxy machines should be lightweight enough—not only to mirror the simplicity of the software component, but also because they should be an easy and affordable way to expand and distribute your monitoring architecture without creating too much impact on deployment and management costs.

A possible exception to the *small, lean, and simple* guideline for proxies can arise if you end up assigning hundreds of hosts with thousands of monitored items to a single proxy. In that case, instead of upgrading the hardware to a more powerful machine, it's often cheaper to just split up the hosts into different groups and assign them to different smaller proxies. In most cases, this would be the preferred option as you are not just distributing and evening out the load, but you are also considering the possibility of huge data loss if a single machine charged with the monitoring of a large portion of your network were to go down for any reason. Consider using small, lightweight embedded machines as Zabbix proxies. They tend to be cheap, easy to deploy, reliable, and quite frugal when it comes to power requirements. These are ideal characteristics for any monitoring solution that aims to leave as little a footprint as possible on the monitored system. There is one other consideration: if you have a very segregated network, that is perhaps even distributed in many different geographical locations, it is better to consider a very good persistent database on the back of it. This reason is driven by the fact that a network outage, which can endure for a considerable period of time, will force the proxy to preserve a considerable amount of data for an important period of time, and here, if the proxy goes down, it can be a serious problem.

That said, quantifying the period of time that the proxy needs to survive without any connectivity with the server can be quite complex as it depends on two particular factors: the number of the hosts that are monitored by a particular proxy, and, moreover, the number of items or acquired metrics that the proxy needs to store in its local database. Here, it is easy to understand that this kind of thinking will drive the database choice. Whether the proxy is on your local network or not, the decision will go in favor of a lightweight and performing database, such as SQLite3; otherwise, we will be obliged to choose a different kind of database that can maintain data for a long period of time and can be more crash tolerant than MySQL or PostgreSQL.

Deploying a Zabbix proxy

A Zabbix proxy is compiled together with the main server if you add `--enable-proxy` to the compilation options. The proxy can use any kind of database backend, just as the server does, but if you don't specify an existing DB, it will automatically create a local SQLite database to store its data. If you intend to rely on SQLite, just remember to add `--with-sqlite3` to the options as well.

When it comes to proxies, it's usually advisable to keep things light and simple as much as we can; of course, this is valid only if the network design permits us to take this decision. A proxy DB will just contain configuration and measurement data that, under normal circumstances, is almost immediately synchronized with the main server. Dedicating a full-blown database to it is usually overkill, so unless you have very specific requirements, the SQLite option will provide the best balance between performance and ease of management.

If you didn't compile the proxy executable the first time you deployed Zabbix, just run `configure` again with the options you need for the proxies:

```
$ ./configure --enable-proxy --enable-static --with-sqlite3 --with-net-
snmp --with-libcurl --with-ssh2 --with-openipmi
```

> In order to build the proxy statically, you must have a static version of every external library needed. The configure script doesn't do this kind of check.

Compile everything again using the following command:

```
$ make
```

> Be aware that this will compile the main server as well; just remember not to run `make install`, nor copy the new Zabbix server executable over the old one in the destination directory.

The only files you need to take and copy over to the proxy machine are the proxy executable and its configuration file. The `$PREFIX` variable should resolve to the same path you used in the configuration command (`/usr/local` by default):

```
# cp src/zabbix_proxy/zabbix_proxy $PREFIX/sbin/zabbix_proxy
# cp conf/zabbix_proxy.conf $PREFIX/etc/zabbix_proxy.conf
```

Next, you need to fill out relevant information in the proxy's configuration file. The default values should be fine in most cases, but you definitely need to make sure that the following options reflect your requirements and network status:

```
ProxyMode=0
```

This means that the proxy machine is in an active mode. Remember that you need at least as many Zabbix trappers on the main server as the number of proxies you deploy. Set the value to 1 if you need or prefer a proxy in the passive mode. See the *Understanding the Zabbix monitoring data flow* section for a more detailed discussion on proxy modes. The following code captures this discussion:

```
Server=n.n.n.n
```

This should be the IP number of the main Zabbix server or of the Zabbix node that this proxy should report to:

```
Hostname=Zabbix proxy
```

This must be a unique, case-sensitive name that will be used in the main Zabbix server's configuration to refer to the proxy:

```
LogFile=/tmp/zabbix_proxy.log
LogFileSize=1
DebugLevel=2
```

If you are using a small, embedded machine, you may not have much disk space to spare. In that case, you may want to comment all the options regarding the log file and let syslog send the proxy's log to another server on the Internet:

```
# DBHost=
# DBSchema=
# DBUser=
# DBPassword=
# DBSocket=
# DBPort=
```

We need now create the SQLite database; this can be done with the following commands:

```
$ mkdir -p /var/lib/sqlite/
```

```
$ sqlite3 /var/lib/sqlite/zabbix.db < /usr/share/doc/zabbix-proxy-
sqlite3-2.4.4/create/schema.sql
```

Now, in the `DBName` parameter, we need to specify the full path to our SQLite database:

```
DBName=/var/lib/sqlite/zabbix.db
```

The proxy will automatically populate and use a local SQLite database. Fill out the relevant information if you are using a dedicated, external database:

```
ProxyOfflineBuffer=1
```

This is the number of hours that a proxy will keep monitored measurements if communications with the Zabbix server go down. Once the limit has been reached, the proxy will housekeep away the old data. You may want to double or triple it if you know that you have a faulty, unreliable link between the proxy and server.

```
CacheSize=8M
```

This is the size of the configuration cache. Make it bigger if you have a large number of hosts and items to monitor.

Zabbix's runtime proxy commands

There is a set of commands that you can run against the proxy to change runtime parameters. This set of commands is really useful if your proxy is struggling with items, in the sense that it is taking longer to deliver the items and maintain our Zabbix proxy up and running.

You can force the configuration cache to get refreshed from the Zabbix server with the following:

```
$ zabbix_proxy -c /usr/local/etc/zabbix_proxy.conf -R config_cache_reload
```

This command will invalidate the configuration cache on the proxy side and will force the proxy to ask for the current configuration to our Zabbix server.

We can also increase or decrease the log level quite easily at runtime with `log_level_increase` and `log_level_decrease`:

```
$ zabbix_proxy -c /usr/local/etc/zabbix_proxy.conf -R log_level_increase
```

This command will increase the log level for the proxy process; the same command also supports a target that can be PID, process type or process type, number here. What follow are a few examples.

Increase the log level of the three poller process:

```
$ zabbix_proxy -c /usr/local/etc/zabbix_proxy.conf -R log_level_
increase=poller,3
```

Increase the log level of the PID to 27425:

```
 $ zabbix_proxy -c /usr/local/etc/zabbix_proxy.conf -R log_level_
increase=27425
```

Increase or decrease the log level of icmp pinger or any other proxy processes with:

```
$ zabbix_proxy -c /usr/local/etc/zabbix_proxy.conf -R log_level_
increase="icmp pinger"
```

```
zabbix_proxy [28064]: command sent successfully
```

```
$ zabbix_proxy -c /usr/local/etc/zabbix_proxy.conf -R log_level_
decrease="icmp pinger"
```

```
zabbix_proxy [28070]: command sent successfully
```

We can quickly see the changes reflected in the log file here:

```
28049:20150412:021435.841 log level has been increased to 4 (debug)
```

```
28049:20150412:021443.129 Got signal [signal:10(SIGUSR1),sender_
pid:28034,sender_uid:501,value_int:770(0x00000302)].
```

```
 28049:20150412:021443.129 log level has been decreased to 3 (warning)
```

Deploying a Zabbix proxy using RPMs

Deploying a Zabbix proxy using the RPM is a very simple task. Here, there are fewer steps required as Zabbix itself distributes a prepackaged Zabbix proxy that is ready to use.

What you need to do is simply add the official Zabbix repository with the following command that must be run from root:

```
$ rpm -ivh http://repo.zabbix.com/zabbix/2.4/rhel/6/x86_64/
zabbix-2.4.4-1.el6.x86_64.rpm
```

Now, you can quickly list all the available `zabbix-proxy` packages with the following command, again from root:

```
$ yum search zabbix-proxy
=============== N/S Matched: zabbix-proxy =================
zabbix-proxy.x86_64 : Zabbix Proxy common files
zabbix-proxy-mysql.x86_64 : Zabbix proxy compiled to use MySQL
zabbix-proxy-pgsql.x86_64 : Zabbix proxy compiled to use PostgreSQL
zabbix-proxy-sqlite3.x86_64 : Zabbix proxy compiled to use SQLite3
```

In this example, the command is followed by the relative output that lists all the available `zabbix-proxy` packages; here, all you have to do is choose between them and install your desired package:

```
$ yum install zabbix-proxy-sqlite3
```

Now, you've already installed the Zabbix proxy, which can be started up with the following command:

```
$ service zabbix-proxy start
Starting Zabbix proxy:                              [  OK  ]
```

 Please also ensure that you enable your Zabbix proxy when the server boots with the `$ chkconfig zabbix-proxy on` command.

That done, if you're using iptables, it is important to add a rule to enable incoming traffic on the `10051` port (that is the standard Zabbix proxy port) or, in any case, against the port that is specified in the configuration file:

```
ListenPort=10051
```

To do that, you simply need to edit the `iptables` configuration file `/etc/sysconfig/iptables` and add the following line right on the head of the file:

```
-A INPUT -m state --state NEW -m tcp -p tcp --dport 10051 -j ACCEPT
```

Then, you need to restart your local firewall from root using the following command:

```
$ service iptables restart
```

The log file is generated at /var/log/zabbix/zabbix_proxy.log:

```
$ tail -n 40 /var/log/zabbix/zabbix_proxy.log
 62521:20150411:003816.801 **** Enabled features ****
 62521:20150411:003816.801 SNMP monitoring:        YES
 62521:20150411:003816.801 IPMI monitoring:        YES
 62521:20150411:003816.801 WEB monitoring:         YES
 62521:20150411:003816.801 VMware monitoring:      YES
 62521:20150411:003816.801 ODBC:                   YES
 62521:20150411:003816.801 SSH2 support:           YES
 62521:20150411:003816.801 IPv6 support:           YES
 62521:20150411:003816.801 **************************
 62521:20150411:003816.801 using configuration file: /etc/zabbix/zabbix_
proxy.conf
```

As you can quickly spot, the default configuration file is located at /etc/zabbix/zabbix_proxy.conf.

The only thing that you need to do is make the proxy known to the server and add monitoring objects to it. All these tasks are performed through the Zabbix frontend by just clicking on **Admin | Proxies** and then **Create**. This is shown in the following screenshot:

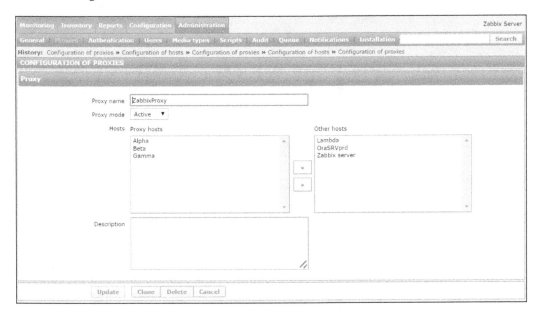

Please take care to use the same **Proxy name** that you've used in the configuration file, which, in this case, is **ZabbixProxy**; you can quickly check with:

```
$ grep Hostname= /etc/zabbix/zabbix_proxy.conf
# Hostname=
Hostname=ZabbixProxy
```

Note how, in the case of an **Active** proxy, you just need to specify the proxy's name as already set in `zabbix_proxy.conf`. It will be the proxy's job to contact the main server. On the other hand, a **Passive** proxy will need an IP address or a hostname for the main server to connect to, as shown in the following screenshot:

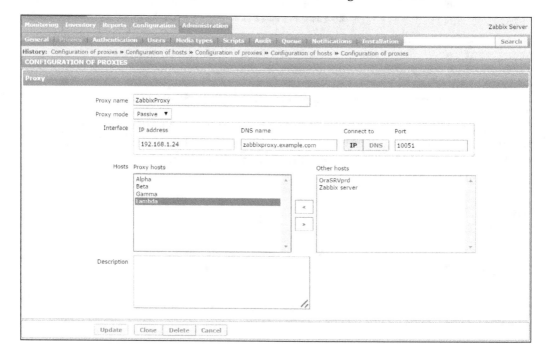

See the *Understanding the monitoring data flow with proxies* section for more details. You don't have to assign hosts to proxies at creation time or only in the proxy's edit screen. You can also do that from a host configuration screen, as follows:

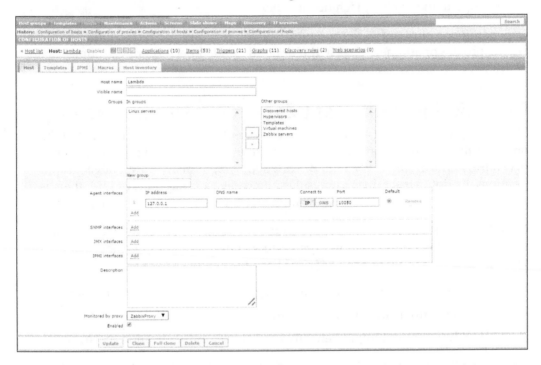

One of the advantages of proxies is that they don't need much configuration or maintenance; once they are deployed and you have assigned some hosts to one of them, the rest of the monitoring activities are fairly transparent. Just remember to check the number of values per second that every proxy has to guarantee, as expressed by the **Required performance** column in the proxies' list page:

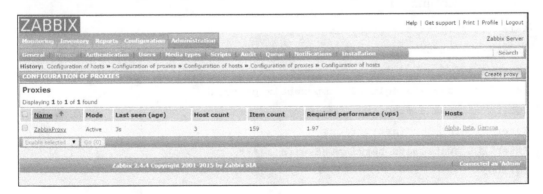

Values per second (VPS) is the number of measurements per second that a single Zabbix server or proxy has to collect. It's an average value that depends on the number of items and the polling frequency for every item. The higher the value, the more powerful the Zabbix machine must be.

Depending on your hardware configuration, you may need to redistribute the hosts among proxies or add new ones if you notice degraded performances coupled with high VPS.

Considering a different Zabbix proxy database

Nowadays, from Zabbix 2.4 the support for nodes has been discontinued, and the only distributed scenario available is limited to the Zabbix proxy; those proxies now play a truly critical role. Also, with proxies deployed in many different geographic locations, the infrastructure is more subject to network outages. That said, there is a case to consider which database we want to use for those critical remote proxies.

Now, SQLite3 is a good product as a standalone and lightweight setup, but if, in our scenario, the proxy we've deployed needs to retain a considerable amount of metrics, we need to consider the fact that SQLite3 has certain weak spots:

- The atomic-locking mechanism on SQLite3 is not the most robust ever
- SQLite3 suffers during high-volume writes
- SQLite3 does not implement any kind of user authentication mechanism

Apart from the point that SQLite3 does not implement any kind of authentication mechanism, the database files are created with the standard unmask, due to which, they are readable by everyone. In the event of a crash during high load it is not the best database to use.

Here is an example of the `sqlite3` database and how to access it using a third-party account:

```
$ ls -la /tmp/zabbix_proxy.db
-rw-r--r--. 1 zabbix zabbix 867328 Apr 12 09:52 /tmp/zabbix_proxy.db
]# su - adv
[adv@localhost ~]$ sqlite3 /tmp/zabbix_proxy.db
SQLite version 3.6.20
Enter ".help" for instructions
Enter SQL statements terminated with a ";"
sqlite>
```

Then, for all the critical proxies, it is advisable to use a different database. Here, we will use MySQL, which is a well-known database.

To install the Zabbix proxy with MySQL, if you're compiling it from source, you need to use the following command line:

```
$ ./configure --enable-proxy --enable-static --with-mysql --with-net-snmp --with-libcurl --with-ssh2 --with-openipmi
```

This should be followed by the usual:

```
$ make
```

Instead, if you're using the precompiled rpm, you can simply run from root:

```
$ yum install zabbix-proxy-mysql
```

Now, you need to start up your MySQL database and create the required database for your proxy:

```
$ mysql -uroot -p<password>
$ create database zabbix_proxy character set utf8 collate utf8_bin;
$ grant all privileges on zabbix_proxy.* to zabbix@localhost identified by '<password>';
$ quit;
$ mysql -uzabbix -p<password> zabbix_proxy < database/mysql/schema.sql
```

If you've installed using `rpm`, the previous command will be:

```
$ mysql -uzabbix -p<password> zabbix_proxy < /usr/share/doc/zabbix-proxy-mysql-2.4.4/create/schema.sql/schema.sql
```

Now, we need to configure `zabbix_proxy.conf` and add the proper value to those parameters:

```
DBName=zabbix_proxy
DBUser=zabbix
DBPassword=<password>
```

Please note that there is no need to specify `DBHost` as the socket used for MySQL.

Finally, we can start up our Zabbix proxy with the following command from root:

```
$ service zabbix-proxy start
Starting Zabbix proxy:                                    [  OK  ]
```

Understanding the Zabbix monitoring data flow

Before explaining the monitoring data flow of our Zabbix proxies, it is important to have at least an idea of the standard Zabbix monitoring data flow.

We can have at least four different kinds of data sources that can deliver items to the Zabbix server:

- The Zabbix agent
- The Zabbix sender `zabbix_send` command
- Custom-made third-party agents
- Zabbix proxy

The following diagram represents the simplified data flow followed by a Zabbix item:

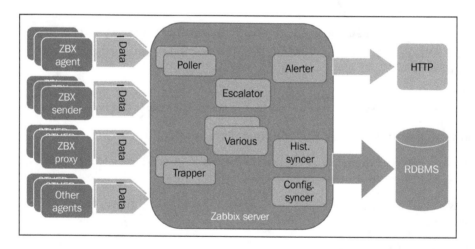

Be aware that this picture is a simplified, readable version of the full data flow, and that it includes many other small components that are summarized on the picture by the block called **various**. Then, basically on the left-hand side, we have all our possible data sources, and on the right-hand side, we have the GUI that represents the Zabbix web interface and, of course, the database that stores all the items. Now, in the next section, we will see how the dataflow on the Zabbix proxy detail is implemented.

Understanding the monitoring data flow with proxies

Zabbix proxies can operate in two different modes, active and passive. An active proxy, which is the default setup, initiates all connections to the Zabbix server, both to retrieve configuration information on monitored objects and to send measurements back to be further processed. You can tweak the frequency of these two activities by setting the following variables in the proxy configuration file:

```
ConfigFrequency=3600

DataSenderFrequency=1
```

Both the preceding values are in seconds. On the server side, in the zabbix_server. conf file, you also need to set the value of StartTrappers= to be higher than the number of all active proxies you have deployed. The trapper processes will have to manage all incoming information from proxies, nodes, and any item configured as an active check. The server will fork extra processes as needed, but it's advisable to pre-fork as many processes as you already know the server will use.

Back on the proxy side, you can also set HeartbeatFrequency so that after a predetermined number of seconds, it will contact the server even if it doesn't have any data to send. You can then check on the proxy availability with the following item, where proxy name, of course, is the unique identifier that you assigned to the proxy during deployment:

```
zabbix[proxy, "proxy name", lastaccess]
```

The item, as expressed, will give you the number of seconds since the last contact with the proxy, a value that you can then use with the appropriate triggering functions. A good starting point to fine-tune the optimal heartbeat frequency is to evaluate how long you can afford to lose contact with the proxy before being alerted, and consider that the interval is just over two heartbeats. For example, if you need to know whether a proxy is possibly down in less than 5 minutes, set the heartbeat frequency to 120 seconds and check whether the last access time was over 300 seconds. The following diagram depicts this discussion aptly:

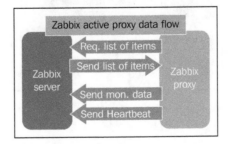

An active proxy is more efficient at offloading computing duties from the server as the latter will just sit idle, waiting to be asked about changes in configuration or to receive new monitoring data. The downside is that proxies will often be deployed to monitor secure networks, such as DMZs, and other segments with strict outgoing traffic policies. In these scenarios, it would be very difficult to obtain permission for the proxy to initiate contact with the server. And it's not just a matter of policies; DMZs are isolated as much as possible from internal networks for extremely good and valid reasons. On the other hand, it's often easier and more acceptable from a security point of view to initiate a connection from the internal network to a DMZ. In these cases, a passive proxy will be the preferred solution.

Connection- and configuration-wise, a passive proxy is almost the mirror image of the active version. This time, it's the server that needs to connect periodically to the proxy to send over configuration changes and to request any measurements the proxy may have taken. On the proxy configuration file, once you've set `ProxyMode=1` to signify that this is a passive proxy, you don't need to do anything else. On the server side, there are three variables you need to check:

- `StartProxyPollers=`:

  This represents the number of processes dedicated to manage passive proxies and should match the number of passive proxies you have deployed.

- `ProxyConfigFrequency=`:

  The server will update a passive proxy with configuration changes for the number of seconds you have set in the preceding variable.

- `ProxyDataFrequency=`:

  This is the interval, also in seconds, between two consecutive requests by the server for the passive proxy's monitoring measurements.

There are no further differences between the two modes of operation for proxies. You can still use the `zabbix[proxy, "proxy name", lastaccess]` item to check a passive proxy's availability, just as you did for the active one:

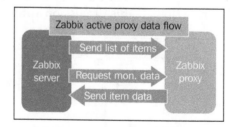

At the price of a slightly increased workload for the server, when compared to active proxies, a passive one will enable you to gather monitoring data from otherwise closed and locked-down networks. At any rate, you can mix and match active and passive proxies in your environment depending upon the flow requirements of specific networks. This way, you will significantly expand your monitoring solution both in its ability to reach every part of the network and in its ability to handle a large number of monitored objects, while at the same time keeping the architecture simple and easy to manage with a strong central core and many simple, lightweight yet effective satellites.

Monitoring Zabbix proxies

Since the proxy is the only component that allows us to split our Zabbix server workload and is also the only way that we have to split our network topology top-down, we need to keep the Zabbix proxy under our watchful eyes.

We've already seen how to produce an item to monitor them and their respective heartbeat; an this is not enough.

There are certain useful items that will help us, and all are contained in `Template App Zabbix Proxy`. It is important to have a look at it and definitely use it.

Unfortunately, there isn't an item that allows us to check how many items are still on the proxy queue to be sent.

This is the most obvious and critical check that you should have in place. This can be solved with the following query against the proxy database:

```
SELECT ((SELECT MAX(proxy_history.id) FROM proxy_history)-nextid) FROM
ids WHERE field_name='history_lastid'
```

This query will return the number of items that the proxy still needs to send to the Zabbix server. Then, the simple way to run this query against a SQLite3 database is to add the following `UserParameter` on the proxy side:

```
UserParameter=zabbix.proxy.items.sync.remaining,/usr/bin/sqlite3 /
path/to/the/sqlite/database "SELECT ((SELECT MAX(proxy_history.
id) FROM proxy_history)-nextid) FROM ids WHERE field_name='history_
lastid'" 2>&1
```

If you have to choose to use a more robust database behind your proxy, for instance MySQL, `UserParameter` will then be the following in the proxy agent configuration file:

```
UserParameter=zabbix.proxy.items.sync.remaining, mysql -u <your
username here> -p'<your password here>' <dbname> -e 'SELECT ((SELECT
MAX(proxy_history.id) FROM proxy_history)-nextid) FROM ids WHERE
field_name=history_lastid' 2>&1
```

Now, all you need to do is set an item on the Zabbix server side, with a relative trigger associated with it, that will track how your proxy is freeing its queue. This item is shown in the next screenshot:

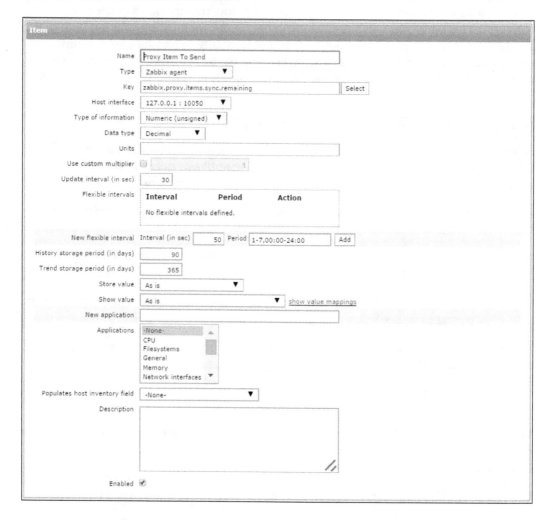

An example of the trigger that could be associated with this item can be:

```
{Hostname:zabbix.proxy.items.sync.remaining.min(10m)}>10000
```

This trigger will go on fire when the number in queue reaches the length of 10,000 items to send, which is a reasonable number; anyway, here you need to adjust this particular item to the number of hosts monitored that you have behind your proxy and the number of items that your proxy is acquiring.

Security considerations

One of the few drawbacks of the whole Zabbix architecture is the lack of built-in security at the Zabbix protocol level. While it's possible to protect both the web frontend and the Zabbix API by means of a standard SSL layer to encrypt communications by relying on different authorities for identification, there's simply no standard way to protect communication between the agents and the server, between proxies and the server, or among nodes. There's no standard way even when it comes to message authentication (the other party is indeed who it says it is), when it comes to message integrity (the data has not been tampered with), or when it comes to message confidentiality (no one else can read or understand the data).

If you've been paying attention to the configuration details of agents, proxies, and nodes, you may have noticed that all that a Zabbix component needs to know in order to communicate with another component is its IP address. No authentication is performed as relying on only the IP address to identify a remote source is inherently insecure. Moreover, any data sent is clear text as you can easily verify by running `tcpdump` (or any other packet sniffer):

```
$  zabbix_sender -v -z 10.10.2.9 -s alpha -k sniff.me -o "clear text
data"

$ tcpdump  -s0 -nn -q -A port 10051
00:58:39.263666 IP 10.10.2.11.43654 > 10.10.2.9.10051: tcp 113
E....l@.@.P..........'C..."^......V.......
.Gp|.Gp|{
      "request":"sender data",
      "data":[
            {
                "host":"alpha",
                "key":"sniff.me",
                " value":"clear text data"}]}
```

Certainly, simple monitoring or configuration data may not seem much, but at the very least, if tampered with, it could lead to false and unreliable monitoring.

While there are no standard counter measures to this problem, there are a few possible solutions to it that increase in complexity and effectiveness from elementary, but not really secure, to complex and reasonably secure. Keep in mind that this is not a book on network security, so you won't find any deep, step-by-step instructions on how to choose and implement your own VPN solution. What you will find is a brief overview of methods to secure the communication between the Zabbix components, which will give you a practical understanding of the problem, so you can make informed decisions on how to secure your own environment.

No network configuration

If, for any reason, you can do absolutely nothing else, you should, at the very least, specify a source IP for every Zabbix trapper item so that it wouldn't be too easy and straightforward to spoof monitoring data using the `zabbix_sender` utility. Use `macro {HOST.CONN}` in a template item so that every host will use its own IP address automatically:

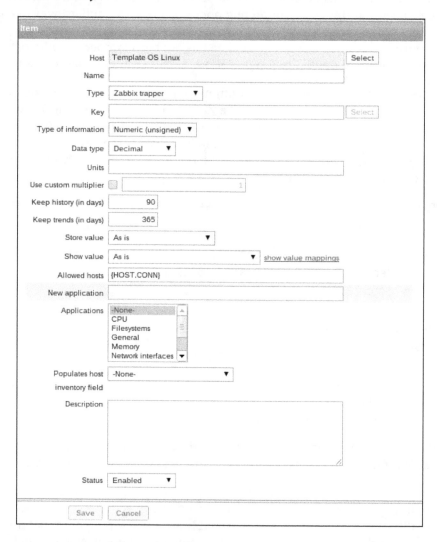

More importantly, make sure that remote commands are not allowed on agents. That is, `EnableRemoteCommands` in the `zabbix_agentd.conf` file must be set to `0`. You may lose a convenient feature, but if you can't protect and authenticate the server-agent communication, the security risk is far too great to even consider taking it.

Network isolation

Many environments have a management network that is separated and isolated from your production network via nonrouted network addresses and VLANs. Network switches, routers, and firewalls typically handle traffic on the production network but are reachable and can be managed only through their management network address. While this makes it a bit less convenient to access them from any workstation, it also makes sure that any security flaw in your components (consider, for example, a network appliance that has a faulty SSL implementation that you can't use, doesn't support SNMP v3, or has Telnet inadvertently left open) is contained in a separated and difficult-to-reach network. You may want to put all of the server-proxy and master-child communication on such an isolated network. You are just making it harder to intercept monitoring data and you may be leaving out the server-agent communication, but isolating traffic is still a sensible solution even if you are going to further encrypt it with one of the solutions outlined in the following sections.

On the other hand, you certainly don't want to use this setup for a node or proxy that is situated in a DMZ or another segregated network. It's far more risky to bypass a firewall through a management network than to have your monitoring data pass through the said firewall. Of course, this doesn't apply if your management network is also routed and controlled by the firewall, but it's strongly advised that you verify that this is indeed the case before looking into using it for your monitoring data.

Simple tunnels

So far, we haven't really taken any measures to secure and encrypt the actual data that Zabbix sends or receives. The simplest and most immediate way to do that is to create an ad hoc encrypted tunnel through which you can channel your traffic.

Secure Shell

Fortunately, **Secure Shell** (**SSH**) has built-in tunneling abilities, so if you have to encrypt your traffic in a pinch, you already have all the tools you need.

To encrypt the traffic from an active proxy to the server, just log on to the proxy's console and issue a command similar to the following one:

```
$ ssh -N -f user@zabbix.server -L 10053:localhost:10051
```

In the preceding command, `-N` means that you don't want the SSH client to execute any commands other than just routing the traffic; the `-f` option makes the SSH client go into the background (so you don't have to keep a terminal open or keep a start script executing forever); `user@zabbix.server` is a valid user (and the real hostname or IP address) on the Zabbix server, and `-L port:remote-server:port` sets up the tunnel. The first port number is what your local applications will connect to, while the following `host:port` combination specifies what host and TCP port the SSH server should connect to at the other end of the tunnel.

Now set your `Server` and `ServerPort` options in your `zabbix_proxy.conf` to `localhost` and `10053` respectively.

What will happen is that, from now on, the proxy will send data to port `10053` by itself, where there's an SSH tunnel session waiting to forward all traffic via the SSH protocol to the Zabbix server. From there, the SSH server will, in turn, forward it to a local port `10051` and, finally, to the Zabbix daemon. While all of the Zabbix components don't natively support data encryption for the Zabbix protocol, you'll still be able to make them communicate while keeping message integrity and confidentiality; all you will see on the network with such a setup will be standard, encrypted SSH traffic data on the TCP port `22`.

To make a Zabbix server contact a passive proxy via a tunnel, just set up a listening SSH server on the proxy (you should already have it in order to remotely administrate the machine) and issue a similar command as the one given earlier on the Zabbix server, making sure to specify the IP address and a valid user for the Zabbix proxy. Change the proxy's IP address and connection-port specifications on the web frontend, and you are done.

To connect to Zabbix nodes, you need to set up two such tunnels, one from the master to the child and one from the child to the master.

On the master, run the following command:

```
$ ssh -N -f user@zabbix.child -L 10053:localhost:10051
```

On the child, run the following command:

```
$ ssh -N -f user@zabbix.master -L 10053:localhost:10051
```

 Due the critical role covered by the SSH tunnel, it is a good practice to instruct the SSH client to send keep-alive packets to the server; an example of this usage is shown right after this tip.

```
ssh -o ServerAliveInterval=60 -N -f user@zabbix.[child|master] -L
10053:localhost:10051
```

In the above example, we've seen how to set keep-alive packets; the value of `ServerAliveInterval` is expressed in seconds and represents the frequency used to send packets to maintain alive the session. Also, it would be a good practice to monitor this channel, and if there are issues, to kill the broken SSH process and restart it.

> One of the ways to monitor whether an SSH tunnel is alive or not can be implemented adding the option:
>
> `ExitOnForwatdFailure=yes`
>
> This is specified in the command line. Doing that, we only need to monitor whether the process is alive as the SSH will exit if there are failures.

Stunnel

Similar functionalities can be obtained using the `stunnel` program. The main advantage of using `stunnel` over SSH is that, with `stunnel`, you have a convenient configuration file where you can set up and store all your tunneling configurations, while with SSH, you'll have to script the preceding commands somehow if you want the tunnels to be persistent across your machine's reboots.

Once installed, and once you have created the copies of the obtained SSL certificates that the program needs, you can simply set up all your port forwarding in the `/etc/stunnel/stunnel.conf` file. Considering, for example, a simple scenario with a Zabbix server that receives data from an active proxy and exchanges data with another node after having installed `stunnel` and SSL certificates on all three machines, you could have the following setup.

On the Zabbix server's `stunnel.conf` file, add the following lines:

```
[proxy]
accept = 10055
connect = 10051

[node - send]
accept = localhost:10057
connect = node.server:10057

[node - receive]
accept = 10059
connect = 10051
```

On the Zabbix proxy's `stunnel.conf`, add the following lines:

```
[server]
accept = localhost:10055
connect = zabbix.server:10055
```

On the other node's `stunnel.conf`, add the following lines:

```
[node - send]
accept = localhost:10059
connect = node.server:10059

[node - receive]
accept = 10057
connect = 10051
```

Just remember to update the host and port information for proxies and servers in their respective configuration files and web frontend forms.

As you can see, the problem with port-forwarding tunnels is that the more tunnels you set up, the more different ports you have to specify. If you have a large number of proxies and nodes or if you want to encrypt the agent data as well, all the port forwarding will quickly become cumbersome to set up and keep track of. This is a good solution if you just want to encrypt your data on an insecure channel among a handful of hosts, but if you want to make sure that all your monitoring traffic is kept confidential, you'll need to resort to a more complete VPN implementation.

A full-blown VPN

This is not the place to discuss the relative merits of different VPN implementations, but if you do use a VPN solution in your network, consider switching all Zabbix monitoring to your encrypted channel. Of course, unless you want the whole world to look at your monitoring data, this is practically mandatory when you link two nodes or a server and a proxy from distant geographical locations that are connected only through the Internet. In that case, you hopefully already have a VPN, whether a simple SSL one or a full-blown IPsec solution. If you don't have it, protecting your Zabbix traffic is an excellent reason to set up one.

These workarounds will protect your traffic and, in the best-case scenario, will provide basic host authentication, but keep in mind that until Zabbix supports some sort of security protocol on the application level, tunneling and encryption will only be able to protect the integrity of your monitoring data. Any user who gains access to a Zabbix component (whether it's a server, proxy, or agent) will be able to send bogus data over the encrypted channel, and you'll have no way to suspect foul play. So, in addition to securing all communication channels, you also need to make sure that you have good security at the host level. Starting from Zabbix 3.0, the dialogue will support encryption done with TLS, and the support will be given between the server, agent, and proxy. Anyway, this will be available only from Zabbix 3.0. Until then, we will need to continue to use the alternatives explained in this chapter.

Summary

In this chapter, we saw how to expand a simple, standalone Zabbix installation into a vast and complex distributed monitoring solution. By now, you should be able to understand how Zabbix proxies work, how they pass monitoring information around, what their respective strong points and possible drawbacks are, and what their impact in terms of hardware requirements and maintenance is.

You also learned about when and how to choose between an active proxy and a passive one, when there is the case to use a more robust database, such as MySQL, and more importantly, how to mix and match the two features into a tailor-made solution for your own environment.

Finally, you now have a clear understanding of how to evaluate possible security concerns regarding monitored data and what possible measures you can take to mitigate security risks related to a Zabbix installation.

In the next chapter, we will conclude with an overview on how to deploy Zabbix in a large environment by talking about high availability at the three levels: database, monitoring server, and web frontend.

High Availability and Failover

Now that you have a good knowledge of all the components of a Zabbix infrastructure, it is time to implement a highly available Zabbix installation. In a large environment, especially if you need to guarantee that all your servers are up and running, it is of vital importance to have a reliable Zabbix infrastructure. The monitoring system and Zabbix infrastructure should survive any possible disaster and guarantee business continuity.

High availability is one of the solutions that guarantee business continuity and provides a disaster recovery implementation; this kind of setup cannot be missed in this book.

This chapter begins with the definition of high availability, and it further describes how to implement an **HA** solution.

In particular, this chapter considers the three-tier setup that we described earlier:

- The Zabbix GUI
- The Zabbix server
- Databases

We have described how to set up and configure each one of the components on high availability. All the procedures presented in this chapter have been implemented and tested in a real environment.

In this chapter, we will cover the following topics:

- Understanding what high availability, failover, and service level are
- Conducting an in-depth analysis of all the components (the Zabbix server, the web server, and the RDBMS server) of our infrastructure and how they will fit into a highly available installation
- Implementing a highly available setup of our monitoring infrastructure

Understanding high availability

High availability is an architectural design approach and associated service implementation that is used to guarantee the reliability of a service. Availability is directly associated with the uptime and usability of a service. This means that the downtime should be reduced to achieve an agreement on that service.

We can distinguish between two kinds of downtimes:

- Scheduled or planned downtimes
- Unscheduled or unexpected downtimes

To distinguish between scheduled downtimes, we can include:

- System patching
- Hardware expansion or hardware replacement
- Software maintenance
- All that is normally a planned maintenance task

Unfortunately, all these downtimes will interrupt your service, but you have to agree that they can be planned into a maintenance window that is agreed upon.

The unexpected downtime normally arises from a failure, and it can be caused by one of the following reasons:

- Human error
- Hardware failure
- Software failure
- Physical events

Unscheduled downtimes also include power outages and high-temperature shutdown, and all these are not planned; however, they cause an outage. Hardware and software failure are quite easy to understand, whereas a physical event is an external event that produces an outage on our infrastructure. A practical example can be an outage that can be caused by lightning or a flood that leads to the breakdown of the electrical line with consequences on our infrastructure. The availability of a service is considered from the service user's point of view; for example, if we are monitoring a web application, we need to consider this application from the web user's point of view. This means that if all your servers are up and running, but a firewall is cutting connections and the service is not accessible, this service cannot be considered available.

Understanding the levels of IT service

Availability is directly tied with service level and is normally defined as a percentage. It is the percentage of uptime over a defined period. The availability that you can guarantee is your service level. The following table shows what exactly this means by considering the maximum admitted downtime for a few of the frequently used availability percentages:

Availability percentage	Max downtime per year	Max downtime per month	Max downtime per week
90% called *one nine*	36.5 days	72 hours	16.8 hours
95%	18.25 days	36 hours	8.4 hours
99% called *two nines*	3.65 days	7.20 hours	1.68 hours
99.5%	1.83 days	3.60 hours	50.4 minutes
99.9% called *three nines*	8.76 hours	43.8 minutes	10.1 minutes
99.95%	4.38 hours	21.56 minutes	5.04 minutes
99.99% called *four nines*	52.56 minutes	4.32 minutes	1.01 minutes
99.999% called *five nines*	5.26 minutes	25.9 seconds	6.05 seconds
99.9999% called *six nines*	31.5 seconds	2.59 seconds	0.605 seconds
99.99999% called *seven nines*	3.15 seconds	0.259 seconds	0.0605 seconds

 Uptime is not a synonym of availability. A system can be up and running but not available; for instance, if you have a network fault, the service will not be available, but all the systems will be up and running.

The availability must be calculated end to end, and all the components required to run the service must be available. The next sentence may seem a paradox; the more hardware you add and the more failure points you need to consider, the greater the difficulty in implementing an efficient solution. Also, an important point to consider is how easy the patching of your HA system and its maintenance will be. A truly highly available system implies that human intervention is not needed; for example, if you need to agree to a *five nines* service level, the human (your system administrator) will have only one second of downtime per day, so here the system must respond to the issue automatically. Instead, if you agree to a *two nines* **service level agreement (SLA)**, the downtime per day can be of 15 minutes; here, the human intervention is realistic, but unfortunately this SLA is not a common case. Now, while agreeing to an SLA, the mean time to recovery is an important factor to consider.

Mean Time To Recovery (MTTR) is the mean time that a device will take to recover from a failure.

The first thing to do is to keep the architecture as simple as possible and reduce the number of actors in play to a minimum. The simpler the architecture, the less the effort required to maintain, administer, and monitor it. All that the HA architecture needs is to avoid a single point of failure, and it needs to be as simple as possible. For this reason, the solution presented here is easy to understand, tested in production environments, and quite easy to implement and maintain.

 Complexity is the first enemy of high availability.

Unfortunately, a highly available infrastructure is not designed to achieve the highest performance possible. This is because it is normal for an overhead to be introduced to keep two servers updated, and a highly available infrastructure is not designed for maximum throughput. Also, there are implementations that consider using the standby server as a read-only server to reduce the load on a primary node, using then an unused/inactive server.

 A highly available infrastructure is not designed to achieve maximum performance or throughput.

Some considerations about high availability

Every HA architecture has common problems to solve or common questions to respond to:

- How the connection can be handled
- How the failover can be managed
- How the storage is shared or replicated to other sites

There are some production-stable and widely used solutions for each one of those questions. Let's study these questions in detail:

- How the connection can be handled

    One of the possible answers to this question is just one word — **VIP (Virtual IP)**. Basically, every software component needs to communicate or is interconnected with different logical layers, and those components are often deployed on different servers to divide and equalize the workload. Much of the communication is TCP/IP-based, and here the network protocol gives us a hand.

    It is possible to define a VIP that is assigned to the active servers and all the software required to be configured to use that address. So if there is a failover, the IP address will follow the service and all the clients will continue to work. Of course, this solution can't guarantee that there isn't downtime at all, but it will be limited by time and will be for a short period of time. From an administration point of view, apart from checking the failover, the administrator doesn't need to reconfigure anything.

- How the failover can be managed

    The answer to this question is: use a resource manager. You need to think of a smart way to move a faulty service to the standby node that is independent of SLA as soon as possible. To achieve the minimum downtime possible, you need to automate the service failover on the standby node and give the business continuity. The fault needs to be found as soon as possible when it happens.

- How the storage is shared or replicated to the other site

This last question can be implemented with different actors, technologies, and methodologies. You can use a shared disk, a replicated **Logical Unit Number (LUN)** between two storages, or a replicated device with software. Unfortunately, using a replicated LUN between two storages is quite expensive. This software should be closer to the kernel and should be working on the lowest layer possible to be transparent from the operating system's perspective, thereby keeping things easy to manage.

Automating switchover/failover with a resource manager

The architecture that you are going to implement needs a component to automate switchover or failover; basically, as said earlier, it requires a resource manager.

One of the resource managers that is widely used and is production mature is **Pacemaker**. Pacemaker is an open source, high-availability resource manager designed for small and large clusters. Pacemaker is available for download at `http://clusterlabs.org/`.

Pacemaker provides interesting features that are really useful for your cluster, such as:

- Detecting and recovering server issues at the application level
- Supporting redundant configurations
- Supporting multiple node applications
- Supporting startup/shutdown ordering applications

Practically, Pacemaker replaces you and is automated and fast. Pacemaker does the work that a Unix administrator normally does in the event of a node failure. It checks whether the service is no more available and switches all the configured services on the spare node; plus, it does all this work as quickly as possible. This switchover gives us the time required to do all the forensic analysis while all the services are still available. In another context, the service would be simply unavailable.

There are different solutions that provide cluster management. Red Hat Cluster Suite is a popular alternative. It is not proposed here as it is not really completely tied to Red Hat; however, it is definitely developed with this distribution in mind.

Replicating the filesystem with DRBD

Distributed Replicated Block Device (DRBD) has some features that are the defining points of this solution:

- This is a kernel module
- This is completely transparent from the point of view of RDBMS
- This provides realtime synchronization
- This synchronizes writes on both nodes
- This automatically performs resynchronization
- This practically acts like a networked RAID 1

The core functionality of DRBD is implemented on the kernel layer; in particular, DRBD is a driver for a virtual block device, so DRBD works at the bottom of the system I/O stack.

DRBD can be considered equivalent to a networked RAID 1 below the OS's filesystem, at the block level.

This means that DRBD synchronization is synced to the filesystem. The worst-case scenario and more complex to handle is a filesystem replication for a database. In this case, every commit needs to be acknowledged on both nodes before it happens, and all the committed transactions are written on both nodes; DRBD completely supports this case.

Now, what happens when a node is no longer available? It's simple; DRBD will operate exactly as a degraded RAID 1 would. This is a strong point because, if your Disaster Recovery site goes down, you don't need to do anything. Once the node reappears, DRBD will do all the synchronization work for us, that is, rebuilding and resynchronizing the offline node.

Implementing high availability on a web server

Now that you know all the software components in play, it's time to go deep into a web server HA configuration. This proposed design foresees Apache, bonded to a virtual IP address, on top of two nodes. In this design, the HTTPD or, better, Apache is on top of an active/passive cluster that is managed by Corosync/Pacemaker.

It is quite an easy task to provide a highly available configuration for the Zabbix GUI because the web application is well defined and does not produce or generate data or any kind of file on the web server. This allows you to have two nodes deployed on two different servers — if possible, on two distant locations — implementing a highly available fault-tolerant disaster-recovery setup. In this configuration, since the web content will be *static*, in the sense that it will not change (apart from the case of system upgrade), you don't need a filesystem replication between the two nodes. The only other component that is needed is a resource manager that will detect the failure of the primary node and coordinate the failover on the secondary node. The resource manager that will be used is Pacemaker/Corosync.

The installation will follow this order:

1. Installing the HTTPD server on both nodes.
2. Installing Pacemaker.
3. Deploying the Zabbix web interface on both nodes.
4. Configuring Apache to bind it on VIP.
5. Configuring Corosync/Pacemaker.
6. Configuring the Zabbix GUI to access RDBMS (on VIP of PostgreSQL).

The following diagram explains the proposed infrastructure:

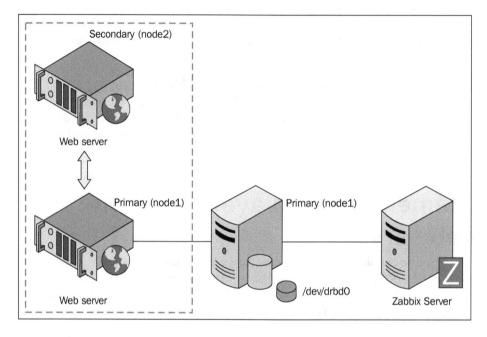

Configuring HTTPD HA

Pacemaker is a sophisticated cluster resource manager that is widely used with a lot of features. To set up Pacemaker, you need to:

- Install Corosync
- Install Pacemaker
- Configure and start Corosync

It is time to spend a couple of lines on this part of the architecture. **Corosync** is a software layer that provides the messaging service between servers within the same cluster.

Corosync allows any number of servers to be a part of the cluster using different fault tolerant configurations, such as Active-Active, Active-Passive, and N+1. Corosync, in the middle of its tasks, checks whether Pacemaker is running and practically bootstraps all the process that is needed.

To install this package, you can run the following command:

```
$ yum install pacemaker corosync
```

Yum will resolve all dependencies for you; once everything is installed, you can configure Corosync. The first thing to do is copy the sample configuration file available at the following location:

```
$ cp /etc/corosync/corosync.conf.example /etc/corosync/corosync.conf
```

To configure Corosync, you need to choose an unused multicast address and a port:

```
$ export MULTICAST_PORT=4000
```

```
$ export MULTICAST_ADDRESS=226.94.1.1
```

```
$ export BIND_NET_ADDRESS=`ip addr | grep "inet " |grep brd |tail -n1 |
awk '{print $4}' | sed s/255/0/`
```

```
$ sed -i.bak "s/.*mcastaddr:.*/mcastaddr:\ $MULTICAST_ADDRESS/g" /etc/
corosync/corosync.conf
```

```
$ sed -i.bak "s/.*mcastport:.*/mcastport:\ $MULTICAST_PORT/g" /etc/
corosync/corosync.conf
```

```
$ sed -i.bak "s/.*bindnetaddr:.*/bindnetaddr:\ $BIND_NET_ADDRSS/g" /etc/
corosync/corosync.conf
```

> Please take care to allow the multicast traffic through the 4000 port running this command from root:
>
> ```
> iptables -I INPUT -p udp -m state --state NEW -m
> multiport --dports 4000 -j ACCEPT
> ```
>
> Follow up the preceding steps with:
>
> ```
> service iptables save
> ```

Now you need to tell Corosync to add the Pacemaker service and create the /etc/ corosync/service.d/pcmk file with the following content:

```
service {
# Load the Pacemaker Cluster Resource Manager
name: pacemaker
ver: 1
}
```

At this point, you need to propagate the files you just configured on node2:

```
/etc/corosync/corosync.conf
/etc/corosync/service.d/pcmk
```

After that, you can start Corosync and Pacemaker on both nodes:

```
$ /etc/init.d/corosync start
```

```
$ /etc/init.d/pacemaker start
```

Check the cluster status using the following command:

```
$ crm_mon
```

Examine the configuration using the following command:

```
$ crm configure show
```

Understanding Pacemaker and STONITH

Shoot The Other Node In The Head (STONITH) can introduce a weak point in this configuration; it can cause a split-brain scenario, especially if servers are in two distant locations where numerous causes that can prevent communication between them. The split-brain scenarios happen when each node believes that the other is broken and that it is the first node. Then, when the second reboot occurs, it shoots the first and so on. This is also known as the STONITH death match.

There are basically three issues that can cause one node to STONITH the other:

- The nodes are alive but unable to communicate with each other
- A node is dead
- An HA resource failed to stop

The first cause can be avoided by ensuring redundant communication paths and by handling the multicast properly. This involves the whole network infrastructure, and if you buy a network service from a vendor, you cannot expect safety or trust, and multicasts will not be well managed. The second cause is obvious, and it is unlikely that the node causes the STONITH death match.

The third cause is not easy to understand. This can be clarified with an example. Basically, an HA resource is started on a node. If it is started, the resource will be monitored indefinitely; if the start fails, the resource will be started and stopped and then restarted in either the current node or the second node. If the resource needs to be stopped and the stop happens, the resource is restarted on the other node. Now, if the stop fails, the node will be fenced STONITH because it is considered the safe thing to do.

> If the HA resource can't be stopped and the node is fenced, the worse action is killing the whole node. This can cause data corruption on your node, especially if there is an ongoing transactional activity, and this needs to be avoided. It's less dangerous if the HA service is a resource, such as an HTTP server that provides web pages (without transactional activity involved); however, this is not safe.

There are different ways to avoid the STONITH death match, but we want the proposed design to be as easy as possible to implement, maintain, and manage, so the proposed architecture can live without the STONITH actor that can introduce issues if not managed well and configured.

 Pacemaker is distributed with STONITH enabled. STONITH is not really necessary on a two-node cluster setup.

To disable STONITH, use the following command:

```
$ crm configure property stonith-enabled="false"
```

Pacemaker – is Quorum really needed?

Quorum refers to the concept of voting; it means each node can vote with regard to what can happen. This is similar to democracy, where the majority wins and implements decisions. For example, if you have a three-node (or more) cluster and one of the nodes in the pool fails, the majority can decide to fence the failed node.

With the Quorum configuration, you can also decide on a no-Quorum policy; this policy can be used for the following purposes:

- **Ignore**: No action is taken if a Quorum is lost
- **Stop** (default option): This stops all resources on the affected cluster node
- **Freeze**: This continues running all the existing resources but doesn't start the stopped ones
- **Suicide**: This can fence all nodes on the affected partition

All these considerations are valid if you have a three-node or more (nodes) configuration. Quorum is enabled by default on most configurations, but this can't be applied to two-node clusters because there is no majority to elect the winner and get a decision.

The following command needs to be disabled to apply the `ignore` rule:

```
$ crm configure property no-quorum-policy=ignore
```

Pacemaker – the stickiness concept

It is obviously highly desirable to prevent healthy resources from being moved around the cluster. Moving a resource always requires a period of downtime that can't be accepted for a critical service (such as the RDBMS), especially if the resource is healthy. To address this, Pacemaker introduces a parameter that expresses how much a service prefers to stay running where it is actually located. This concept is called **stickiness**. Every downtime has its cost, which is not necessarily represented by an expense that is tied to the little downtime period needed to switch the resource to the other node.

Pacemaker doesn't calculate this cost associated with moving resources and will do so to achieve the optimal resource placement.

On a two-node cluster, it is important to specify the stickiness; this will simplify all the maintenance tasks. Pacemaker can't decide on switching the resource to a maintenance node without disrupting the service.

Note that Pacemaker's optimal resource placement does not always agree with what you would want to choose. To avoid this movement of resources, you can specify a different stickiness for every resource:

```
$ crm configure property default-resource-stickiness="100"
```

It is possible to use INFINITY instead of a number on the stickiness properties. This will force the cluster to stay on that node until it's dead, and once the INFINITY node comes up, all will migrate back to the primary node:

```
$ crm configure property default-resource-
stickiness="INFINITY"
```

Pacemaker – configuring Apache/HTTPD

The Pacemaker resource manager needs to access the Apache server's status to know the status of HTTPD. To enable access to the server's status, you need to change the /etc/httpd/conf.d/httpd.conf file as follows:

```
<Location /server-status>
    SetHandler server-status
    Order deny,allow
    Deny from all
    Allow from
127.0.0.1 <YOUR-NETWOR-HERE>/24
</Location>
```

For security reasons, it makes sense to deny access to this virtual location and permit only your network and the localhost (127.0.0.1).

Once this is done, we need to restart Apache by running the following command from root:

```
$ service httpd restart
```

This kind of configuration foresees two web servers that will be called www01 and www02 to simplify the proposed example. Again, to keep the example as simple as possible, you can consider the following addresses:

- www01 (eth0 192.168.1.50 eth1 10.0.0.50)
- www02 (eth0 192.168.1.51 eth1 10.0.0.51)

Now the first step to perform is to configure the virtual address using the following commands:

```
$ crm configure
crm(live)configure#
primitive vip ocf:heartbeat:IPaddr2 \
> params ip="10.0.0.100"
# please note that 10.0.0.100 is the pacemaker ip address
> nic="eth1" \
> cidr_netmask="24" \
> op start interval="0s" timeout="50s" \
> op monitor interval="5s" timeout="20s" \
> op stop interval="0s" timeout="50s"
crm(live)configure#
show
# make sure
node www01.domain.example.com
node www02.domain.example.com
primitive vip ocf:heartbeat:IPaddr2 \
        params ip="10.0.0.100" nic="eth1" cidr_netmask="24" \
        op start interval="0s" timeout="50s" \
        op monitor interval="5s" timeout="20s" \
        op stop interval="0s" timeout="50s"
property $id="cib-bootstrap-options" \
```

```
              dc-version="1.1.2-f059ec7cedada865805490b67ebf4a0b963bccfe" \

              cluster-infrastructure="openais" \

              expected-quorum-votes="2" \

              no-quorum-policy="ignore" \

              stonith-enabled="false"
rsc_defaults $id="rsc-options" \

              resource-stickiness="INFINITY" \

              migration-threshold="1"


crm(live)configure# commit
crm(live)configure# exit
```

Using `commit`, you can enable the configuration. Now, to be sure that everything went fine, you can check the configuration using the following command:

```
$ crm_mon
```

You should get an output similar to the following one:

```
============
Last updated: Fri Jul 10 10:59:16 2015
Stack: openais
Current DC: www01.domain.example.com  - partition WITHOUT quorum
Version: 1.1.2-f059ec7cedada865805490b67ebf4a0b963bccfe
2 Nodes configured, , unknown expected votes
1 Resources configured.
============


Online: [ www01.domain.example.com  www02.domain.example.com  ]


vip       (ocf::heartbeat:IPaddr2):       Started www01.domain.example.com
To be sure that the VIP is up and running you can simply ping it
$ ping 10.0.0.100

PING 10.0.0.100 (10.0.0.100) 56(84) bytes of data.
64 bytes from 10.0.0.100: icmp_seq=1 ttl=64 time=0.012 ms
64 bytes from 10.0.0.100: icmp_seq=2 ttl=64 time=0.011 ms
64 bytes from 10.0.0.100: icmp_seq=3 ttl=64 time=0.008 ms
64 bytes from 10.0.0.100: icmp_seq=4 ttl=64 time=0.021 ms
```

Now you have the VIP up and running. To configure Apache in the cluster, you need to go back to the CRM configuration and tell Corosync that you will have a new service, your HTTPD daemon, and that it will have to group it with the VIP. This group will be called "web server".

This configuration will tie the VIP and the HTTPD, and both will be up and running on the same node. We will configure the VIP using the following commands:

```
$ crm configure
crm(live)configure# primitive httpd ocf:heartbeat:apache \
> params configfile="/etc/httpd/conf/httpd.conf" \
> port="80" \
> op start interval="0s" timeout="50s" \
> op monitor interval="5s" timeout="20s" \
> op stop interval="0s" timeout="50s"

crm(live)configure# group webserver vip httpd

crm(live)configure# commit

crm(live)configure# exit
```

Now you can check your configuration using the following command:

```
$ crm_mon
============
Last updated: Fri Jul 10 10:59:16 2015
Stack: openais
Current DC: www01.domain.example.com - partition WITHOUT quorum
Version: 1.1.2-f059ec7cedada865805490b67ebf4a0b963bccfe
2 Nodes configured, unknown expected votes
1 Resources configured.
============


Online: [ www01.domain.example.com www02.domain.example.com ]


Resource Group: webserver
     vip          (ocf::heartbeat:IPaddr2):      Started www01.domain.
example.com
     httpd        (ocf::heartbeat:apache):       Started www01.domain.
example.com
```

 Note that since you are not using Quorum, you need to make sure that the crm_mon display: partition WITHOUT Quorum and unknown expected votes are normal.

Configuring the Zabbix server for high availability

A high-availability cluster for a Zabbix server is easier to configure compared to Apache or a database server. Whether it's a standalone server or a node that is a part of a distributed setup, the procedure is exactly the same, as shown in the following diagram:

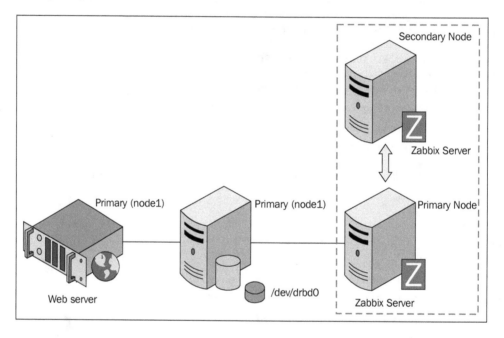

Once you have installed Corosync and Pacemaker on the two nodes (see the previous sections for details), you will also install Zabbix on the nodes that will make the cluster. You will then need to configure Zabbix to listen to the virtual IP address that you have identified for the cluster. To do so, change both SourceIP and ListenIP to the appropriate value in the zabbix_server.conf configuration file:

```
SourceIP=10.10.1.9
ListenIP=10.10.1.9
```

Needless to say, change the IP value to the one that you have reserved as a virtual IP for the Zabbix cluster and that is appropriate for your environment.

You can now proceed to disable STONITH using the following command:

```
$ crm configure property stonith-enabled="false"
```

If you have just two nodes, you also need to disable Quorum; otherwise, the cluster won't know how to obtain a majority:

```
$ crm configure property no-quorum-policy=ignore
```

And finally, set the service stickiness high enough so that you don't have a service going back and forth between the nodes and it stays where it is unless you manually move it or the active node goes down:

```
$ crm configure property default-resource-stickiness="100"
```

Much like the Apache/HTTPD cluster configuration, you now need to define a primitive for the virtual IP:

```
$ crm configure primitive Zbxvip ocf:heartbeat:IPaddr2 \
params ip="10.10.1.9" iflabel="httpvip" \
op monitor interval="5"
```

For the Zabbix server, define the primitive using the following command:

```
$ crm configure primitive Zabbix lsb::zabbix_server \
op monitor interval="5"
```

Just as in the previous section, all that is now left to do is group the primitives together, set up colocation, and service StartOrder—and you are done:

```
$ crm configure group Zbx_server Zbxvip Zabbix meta target-role="Started"
$ crm configure colocation Ip_Zabbix inf: Zbxvip Zabbix
$ crm configure order StartOrder inf: Zbxvip Zabbix
```

As you can see, the simpler the components, the easier it is to set them up in a cluster configuration using Pacemaker. While it is still fairly easy and simple, things start to change when you turn to configure the most critical part of any high-availability setup: the database and data storage.

Implementing high availability for a database

Implementing high availability for a database is not an easy task. There are a lot of ways to implement a high-availability configuration using different software and complexity.

The architecture proposed here is fully redundant; it is one of the possible solutions that are widely used in large environments. You need two database servers and two installations of the same software and operating system to implement this solution. Obviously, since servers are twins and tied together, they need to have the same software, have the same release patch, and basically, be identical.

Since we are going to have two different servers, it is clear that the data needs to be replicated between them; this implies that your server needs to be interconnected with a dedicated network connection that is capable of providing the needed throughput.

In this design, your server can be placed in the same location or in two different data centers that provide a reliable disaster-recovery solution. In this case, we are going to provide a highly available design.

There are different ways to provide data replication between two servers. They are as follows:

- Filesystem replication
- Shared disk failover
- Hot/warm standby using PITR
- Trigger-based master-standby replication
- Statement-based replication middleware
- Asynchronous multimaster replication
- Synchronous master replication

There are positive and negative sides to each one of them. Among all these options, we can exclude all the solutions that are trigger-based because all of them introduce an overhead on the master node. Also, adding a user-lever layer can be imprecise/inexact.

Between these options, there are a few solutions that permit a low or really low mean time to recovery and are safe from data loss. The following solutions guarantee that, if there is a master failure, there will no data loss:

- Shared disk failover
- Filesystem replication
- Statement-based replication middleware

A solution that adopts a shared disk failover cluster implies the use of a shared SAN. This means that if you want to place your server on a separate server farm in a different location, this system will be really expensive.

If the solution adopts a warm and hot standby using **Point-In-Time Recovery (PITR)** and your node goes down, you need enough free space to handle and store all the transaction log files generated. This configuration, by design, needs a secondary database (identical to the master node) that is a warm standby and waits for the log transaction. Once the transaction has arrived, the RDBMS needs to apply the transaction on your secondary node.

In this case, if the secondary node goes down, we need to be warned because the primary database will produce the archived log files that are not shipped, and this can bring your infrastructure to a halt. In a large environment, the transactional activity is normally heavy, and if the fault happens to be out of the normal working hours, this HA configuration needs to be handled.

Another way is the PostgreSQL synchronous replication. If the secondary node goes down, this configuration would need a reload to prevent the hanging of the transaction from hanging.

Trigger-based configurations are heavy and dangerous because they imply that a trigger can go on firing every insert and replicate the same insert on the secondary node by introducing a feasible overhead. Partitioning with inheritance is not supported well by this method. Also, this method does not give us a warranty against data loss when the master fails.

Infrastructures that include a second standby database introduce a second actor, that is, if the database is down or unreachable, it shouldn't cause a master to hang. Nowadays, with PostgreSQL 9.1, synchronous replication is a viable solution. These configurations unfortunately add certain constraints: the transmission must be acknowledged before the commit happens, and the transmission doesn't guarantee that you will get a reply.

This practically means that if the secondary node goes down, the primary database will hang until the slave receives the transaction and notifies back to the master that this one has been acquired. The result is that a primary node can hang for an indefinite period of time, and this practically doubles the risk of downtime.

An issue on the slave's node shouldn't impact the primary node. This practically doubles the risk of downtime and is not acceptable in the context of high availability.

Clustering of PostgreSQL

The cluster presented here is simple and designed to have as few actors in play as possible but with the high-availability design in mind.

The architecture shown in the following diagram is efficient. It has a minimum number of actors in play and is easy to monitor, maintain, and upgrade:

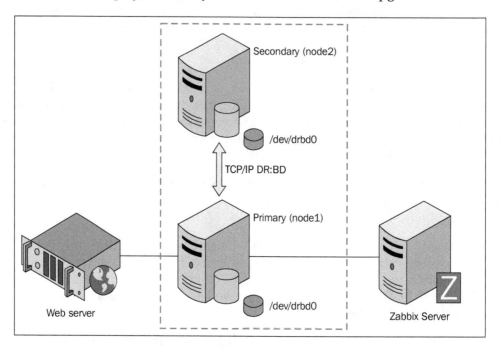

Mirrored logical volume with LVM and DRDB

LVM2 is the Linux implementation of **Logical Volume Manager (LVM)** on the Linux logical device mapper framework. LVM2, apart from the name, doesn't have anything in common with the previous one.

The basic concepts of LVM2 are as follows:

- **Physical Volume (PV)**: This is the actual physical partition or storage system on which the LVM system is built.

- **Volume Group (VG)**: This is the basic administrative unit. It may include one or more PVs. Every VG has a unique name and can be extended at runtime by adding additional PVs or enlarging the existing PV.

- **Logical Volume (LV)**: This is available as a regular block device to the Linux kernel, and its components can be created at runtime within the available volume groups. Logical volumes can be resized when online and also moved from one PV to another PV if they are on the same VG.

- **Snapshot Logical Volume (SLV)**: This is a temporary point-in-time copy of an LV. The strong point is that if the size is really big (several hundred gigabytes), the space required is significantly less than the original volume.

 The partition-type Linux LVM that owns the signature **0x8E** is used exclusively for LVM partitions. This, however, is not required. LVM indeed recognizes the PV group by a signature written on the PV initialization.

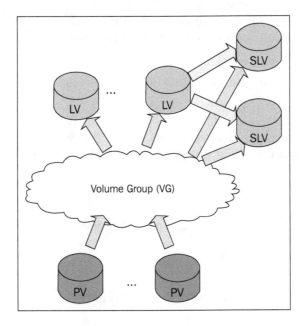

Since a logical volume, once created, is simply seen as a block device, you can use DRBD on it.

Prerequisite tasks to start with DRBD on LVM

While setting up DRBD on LVM, there are certain basic steps to bear in mind:

- LVM needs to know about your DRBD devices
- LVM caching needs to be disabled
- Remember to update `initramfs` with the new kernel device map

LVM, by default, scans all block devices founded on /dev while looking for PV signatures; hence, we need to set an appropriate filter on /etc/lvm/lvm.conf:

```
filter = ["a|sd.*|", "a|drbd.*|", "r|.*|"]
```

This filter accepts all the SCSI and DRBD disks. Now, we need to rescan all your volume groups with the following command:

```
# vgscan
```

It is important that you remember to disable LVM caching because DRBD disks will disappear in the event of a failure. This is normal when we face a fault, and if caching is not disabled, it is possible that you will see the disk as available when in reality it is not.

This is done by adding the following line in /etc/lvm/lvm.conf:

```
write_cache_state = 0
```

Now that the cache has been disabled, it is possible that we still have a portion or piece of cache on your disks that was generated previously. We need to clean up the following location:

```
/etc/lvm/cache/.cache
```

Now it's better to regenerate the kernel device map files with the following command:

```
# update-initramfs -u
```

Now it is possible for us to go ahead with the configuration.

Creating a DRBD device on top of the LVM partition

Now that your caching is disabled and the LVM is properly configured, we need to create your PV. To initialize your SCSI partitions as physical volumes, we run the following commands from the root account:

```
$ pvcreate /dev/sda1
  Physical volume "/dev/sda1" successfully created
$ pvcreate /dev/sdb1
  Physical volume "/dev/sdb1" successfully created
```

The given output tells us that the volume has been initialized. Now you can create a low-level VG, vgpgdata:

```
$ vgcreate vgpgdata /dev/sda1 /dev/sda2
  Volume group "vgpgdata" successfully created
```

Finally, you can create your volume or a better logical volume that will be used as DRBD's block device:

```
$ lvcreate --name rpgdata0 --size 10G local
  Logical volume "rpgdata0" created
```

All these steps need to be repeated in the same order on both your nodes. Now you need to install DRBD on both nodes using the following command:

```
$ yum install drbd kmod-drbd
```

> To install DRBD, it is important to have the EXTRAS repositories enabled.

Now edit the `drbd.conf` file located in `/etc/drbd.conf` and create the `rpgdata0` resource as follows:

```
resource rpgdata0 {
  device /dev/drbd0;
  disk /dev/local/rpgdata0;
  meta-disk internal;
  on <host1> { address <address_host1>:<port>; }
  on <host2> { address <address_host2>:<port>; }
}
```

> Replace `host1`, `host2`, `address_host1`, and `address_host2` with the two hostnames and their respective network addresses.

Make sure that you have copied the `drbd.conf` file on both nodes before proceeding with the next section. Disable automatic start for DRBD because it will be managed by Pacemaker:

```
$ chkconfig drbd off
```

Enabling resources in DRBD

Now, before we initialize our DRBD service, it is important to do a bit of server-side configuration. Here, SELinux can cause quite a few issues, so the best approach with RedHat 6.X is to disable SELinux.

To disable or set SELinux to permissive, you need to edit the configuration file `/etc/sysconfig/selinux` by setting the SELinux option as follows:

```
SELINUX=permissive
```

This needs to be done on both nodes; once done, you need to reboot and can check whether the status has been properly retrieved with this command from root:

```
# sestatus
SELinux status:              enabled
SELinuxfs mount:             /selinux
Current mode:                permissive
Mode from config file:       permissive
Policy version:              24
Policy from config file:     targeted
```

Here, we see that `Current mode` is set to `permissive`.

Now it is time to add an iptables rule to allow connectivity across port `7788` by adding the following rule to our iptable. We can directly edit the `/etc/sysconfig/iptables` file by adding the following line:

```
-A INPUT -m stat -state NEW -m tcp -p tcp --dport 7788 -j ACCEPT
```

Then, we need to restart iptables with:

```
# service iptables restart
iptables: Setting chains to policy ACCEPT: nat mangle filte[  OK  ]
iptables: Flushing firewall rules:                          [  OK  ]
iptables: Unloading modules:                                [  OK  ]
iptables: Applying firewall rules:                          [  OK  ]
```

Now that the configuration file has been copied on all your nodes and we've finished with SELinux and iptables, it is time to initialize the device and create the required metadata.

This initialization process needs to be executed on both nodes and can be run from root using the following command:

```
$ drbdadm create-md rpgdata0
v08 Magic number not found
Writing meta data...
initialising activity log
NOT initializing bitmap
New drbd meta data block successfully created.
```

 This is the initialization process and needs to be executed only on a new device.

Now you can enable the `rpgdata0` resource:

```
$ drbdadm up rpgdata0
```

The process can be observed by looking at the `/proc` virtual filesystem:

```
$ tail /proc/drbd
version: 8.4.1 (api:1/proto:86-100)
GIT-hash: 91b4c048c1a0e06837625f65d312b38d47abara80 build by buildsystem@
linbit, 2013-02-20 12:58:48
 0: cs:Connected ro:Secondary/Secondary ds:Inconsistent/Inconsistent C
r-----
    ns:0 nr:0 dw:0 dr:0 al:0 bm:0 lo:0 pe:0 ua:0 ap:0 ep:1 wo:b
oos:524236
```

> The `Inconsistent/Inconsistent` state here, at this point,
> is normal. You need to specify which node is the master and
> which will be the source of this synchronization.

At this point, DRBD has allocated the disk and network and is ready to begin the synchronization.

Defining a primary device in DRDB

The primary promotion is quite easy; you need go to the primary node and run the following command:

```
$ drbdadm primary rpgdata0
```

Now the server on which you run this command becomes the master of the replication server, and you can create the PV on that new device. So, on the master node, you need to run the following command:

```
$ pvcreate /dev/drbd0
Physical volume "/dev/drbd0" successfully created
```

Create your VG, which, in this example, will be `secured_vg_pg`:

```
$ vgcreate secured_vg_pg /dev/drbd0
Volume group "secured_vg_pg" successfully creatced
```

Finally, it is possible to create an LV on that PV using the following command:

```
$ lvcreate -L 6G -n secured_lv_pg secured_vg_pg
```

In this example, we reserved a space for snapshots; so, if you ever want one, you have enough space for that. Finally, it is possible to set up the filesystem.

Creating a filesystem on a DRBD device

Now it is important to check whether the DRBD service is disabled from the startup and shutdown lists because this service will be managed directly from Pacemaker. Once you disable the service, it is possible to create the filesystem on the new device but before that, it is important to do the following:

- Create a mountpoint
- Create a filesystem
- Mount the filesystem and make it available

You can create your own mountpoint, but this step-by-step installation will use /db/pgdata:

```
$ mkdir -p -m 0700 /db/pgdata
```

Now, there are different filesystems supported by most of the distributions; RedHat 6.0 completely supports XFS. XFS has an important feature that permits parallel access to the filesystem. It supports parallel read/write. XFS allows us to write the same files from multiple threads concurrently; this, obviously, is a big improvement for a large database table, and it also reduces the contention on filesystems.

To install XFS and the relative utils, use the following command:

```
$ yum install xfsprogs
```

> XFS allows write access to the same file for multiple thread concurrency; this is interesting, especially in DRBD use, where contention on filesystems becomes an important factor.

Once installed and available, you can format the logical volume using the following command:

```
$ mkfs.xfs /dev/secured_vg_pg/secured_lv_pg
```

> Once created, the filesystem can't be reduced but only enlarged using the xfs_growfs command.

Now you can mount the filesystem using the following command:

```
$ mount -t xfs -o noatime,nodiratime,attr2 /dev/secured_vg_pg/secured_lv_
pg /db/pgdata
```

 Do not forget to add this partition on `automount` (`fstab`); otherwise, you will lose your partition after a reboot.

Everything can be changed to your PostgreSQL process owner, usually `postgres`:

```
$ chown postgres:postgres /db/pgdata
```

```
$ chmod 0700 /db/pgdata
```

 The filesystem creation steps need to be done only on the primary node.

Now the filesystem is mounted, formatted, and ready for PostgreSQL.

Pacemaker clusters – integrating DRBD

Pacemaker makes DRBD extremely powerful in a really wide variety of scenarios. There are some attention points that have already been discussed when we presented Pacemaker/Corosync. These points are as follows:

- Disable STONITH
- Disable Quorum
- Enable stickiness

As discussed earlier in this chapter, it is really important to avoid split-brain scenarios and STONITH death matches. Just as a reminder, to disable STONITH, you can run the following command:

```
$ crm configure property stonith-enabled="false"
```

Since this again is a two-node cluster, it is strongly recommended that you disable Quorum. The command that permits us to do this is as follows:

```
$ crm configure property no-quorum-policy=ignore
```

Now, it is preferred that stickiness be enabled. This argument has been discussed earlier in the chapter. Anyway, as a quick reminder, we can say that, by enabling stickiness, we have a guarantee of a preferred node over another. This will help you to keep your cluster on one side and have a preferred site where everything should run. The command for this is as follows:

```
$ crm configure property default-resource-stickiness="100"
```

Enabling the DRBD configuration

This section explains how to enable the DRBD-backend service in your Pacemaker cluster. There are a few steps to be followed:

- Add DRDB to Pacemaker
- Add and define the master/slave resource

You need to have a `master/slave` resource that controls which node is primary and which one is secondary. This can be done with the following command:

```
$ crm configure primitive drbd_pg ocf:linbit:drbd \
params drbd_resource="rpgdata0" \
op monitor interval="15" \
op start interval="0" timeout="240" \
op stop interval="0" timeout="120"
```

Once done, you need to set up a resource that can promote or demote the DRBD service on each node. Keep in mind that the service needs to run on both the nodes at all times with a different state, thus defining a master/slave resource as follows:

```
$ crm configure ms ms_drbd_pg drbd_pg \
meta master-max="1" master-node-max="1" clone-max="2" \
clone-node-max="1" notify="true"
```

Pacemaker – the LVM configuration

Now you need to configure Pacemaker to:

- Manage the LVM
- Manage the filesystem

Because of the design and working of DRBD, the actual active volume will be invisible on the secondary node. On the secondary node, you can't mount or handle this volume. Having said that, you need to help DRBD to find devices:

```
$ crm configure primitive pg_lvm ocf:heartbeat:LVM \
params volgrpname="secured_vg_pg" \
op start interval="0" timeout="30" \
op stop interval="0" timeout="30"
```

With the preceding configuration, Pacemaker will search for a usable volume on DRBD devices and will be available using the DRBD resource promotion. Since the filesystem adopted on DRBD devices is XFS, you need to define how to mount and handle this device:

```
$ crm configure primitive pg_fs ocf:heartbeat:Filesystem \
params device="/dev/secured_vg_pg/secured_lv_pg" directory="/db/pgdata" \
options="noatime,nodiratime" fstype="xfs" \
op start interval="0" timeout="60" \
op stop interval="0" timeout="120"
```

Since LVM is the last layer on this configuration, you can take advantage of snapshot capabilities and a good level of isolation.

Pacemaker – configuring PostgreSQL

Now you can add the PostgreSQL configuration to the cluster.

> PostgreSQL installation is not covered here because it is already discussed in *Chapter 1, Deploying Zabbix*.

The following lines add a primitive to Pacemaker that will set a PostgreSQL health check every 30 seconds and define a timeout of 60 seconds to retrieve the response:

```
$ crm configure primitive pg_lsb lsb:postgresql \
op monitor interval="30" timeout="60" \
op start interval="0" timeout="60" \
op stop interval="0" timeout="60"
```

> This command extends the start and stop timeout because it will handle big databases. It can also happen that Pacemaker may be required to give time to complete a checkpoint on shutdown and a recovery on startup.

Pacemaker uses those parameters in a primary manner to determine whether PostgreSQL is available or not.

Pacemaker – the network configuration

Up until now, you haven't configured a predefined IP address for PostgreSQL. Since it doesn't make sense to have different addresses in the event of a switchover or failover, you need to set up a virtual IP that will follow your service. This prevents any change of configuration for all your clients. You can use a cluster name or an IP address. For that, you need to issue the following lines:

```
$ crm configure primitive pg_vip ocf:heartbeat:IPaddr2 \
params ip="192.168.124.3" iflabel="pgvip" \
op monitor interval="5"
NOTE: change the address 192.168.124.3 with your own.
```

Here, it is not specified that the ARP address, `IPaddr2`, will automatically send five ARP packets, and this value can be increased if necessary.

Pacemaker – the final configuration

Now you have all the required components ready to be tied together in a group that will contain all your resources. The group is `PGServer`:

```
$ crm configure group PGServer pg_lvm pg_fs pg_lsb pg_vip
$ crm configure colocation col_pg_drbd inf: PGServer ms_drbd_pg:Master
```

The `Master` server specifies that your `PGServer` group depends on the master/slave setup reporting a master status that happens exclusively on an active node. It is also true that the `PGServer` group depends on the DRBD master.

Now it is important to specify the right order to start and shutdown all the services. We will use the following command to do so:

```
$ crm configure order ord_pg inf: ms_drbd_pg:promote PGServer:start
```

> The `:promote` and `:start` options are fundamental; they mean that once `ms_drdb_pg` is promoted, `PGServer` will start. With this precise order of events, if you omit `:start`, Pacemaker can choose the start/stop order, and it might end up in a broken state.

Cluster configuration – the final test

Finally, the cluster is ready! What do we do next? It is simple! You can break your own cluster, play with the configuration, and verify that all is fine before we go live with this new infrastructure.

The faults that need to be tested are as follows:

- The node goes offline
- Manual failover of the cluster
- Primary crash
- Secondary crash
- Forceful synchronization of all the data

Run the following command:

```
$ crm node standby HA-node2
```

If all is fine, crm_mon will respond with the following:

```
Node HA-node2: standby
Online: [ HA-node1 ]
```

You can easily fix this state by firing the following command:

```
$ crm node online HA-node2
```

Until now, it has been quite easy. Now you can try a failover of the whole cluster using the following command:

```
$ crm resource migrate PGServer HA-node2
```

 You can migrate PGServer to the second node. If that becomes unavailable, Pacemaker will move to the primary node until the secondary return. This is because the migrate command will give a higher score to the named node, and this will win against your specified stickiness.

The server can be migrated back with the following:

```
$ crm resource unmigrate PGServer
```

Now you can switch off the secondary node and Pacemaker will respond with the following:

```
Online: [ HA-node1 ]
OFFLINE: [ HA-node2 ]
Master/Slave Set: ms_drbd_pg [drbd_pg]
Masters: [ HA-node1 ]
Stopped: [ drbd_pg:1 ]
```

After that, you can start up the secondary node again. Now switch off the secondary node and Pacemaker will respond with the following:

```
Online: [ HA-node1 HA-node2 ]
Master/Slave Set: ms_drbd_pg [drbd_pg]
Masters: [ HA-node1 ]
Slaves: [ HA-node2 ]
```

Now, as a final test, you can invalidate all the data on the secondary node with the following command:

```
$ drbdadm invalidate-remote all
```

Alternatively, from the secondary node, you can run the following command:

```
$ drbdadm invalidate all
```

This will force DRBD to consider all the data on the secondary node out of sync. Therefore, DRBD will resync all the data on the secondary node before getting it from the primary node.

DRBD performance and optimization

There are certain aspects that can be improved and that should be considered when you implement a DRBD cluster. There are some optimizations that can be applied. You need to consider that if your database, or more specifically, the second node of the DRBD cluster, is in a different location that is far away from your data center, the network bandwidth can have efficient synchronization, which plays a fundamental role. Another thing that needs to be considered on a disaster recovery site is the bandwidth and its cost. It is also important to calculate and understand how much data is required and the transfer rate that we can reach or need.

DRBD efficient synchronization

Synchronization is a distinct process and can't be considered on the same lines as device replication. While replication happens only the first time you start up the device, synchronization and resynchronization as well are decoupled from incoming writes. On the proposed architecture, synchronization is necessary when:

- The link has been interrupted
- The server has a fault on the primary node
- The server has a fault on the secondary node

DRBD doesn't synchronize blocks sequentially and not in the order they were originally written.

> While synchronization is ongoing, during the process you will have partly obsolete data and partly updated data on the disk.

The service will continue to run on the primary node while the background synchronization is in progress. Since this configuration has an LVM layer on top of DRBD, it is possible to use snapshots during the synchronization; this is a strong point of this architecture. While synchronization is ongoing, you are in a delicate phase because there is a single point of failure; only the primary node is working fine, and if something happens here, you might completely lose all the data and the secondary node might contain bad data. This critical situation can be mitigated with the LVM snapshot.

> The use of snapshots before beginning synchronization can give you hands-on experience in that situation because data on the secondary node is consistent and valid but not recently updated. Enabling snapshots before beginning synchronization will reduce the **Estimated Time to Repair (ETR)**, which is also known as **Recovery Time Objective (RTO)**.

To automate the snapshot, you can add the following lines to your DRBD configuration:

```
resource RESOURCE_NAME {
  handlers {
    before-resync-target "/usr/lib/drbd/snapshot-resync-target-lvm.
sh";
    after-resync-target "/usr/lib/drbd/unsnapshot-resync-target-lvm.
sh";
  }
}
```

The `snapshot-resync-target-lvm.sh` script is called before we begin the synchronization, and the `unsnapshot-resync-target-lvm.sh` script will remove the snapshot once the synchronization is complete.

 If the script fails, the synchronization will not commence.

To optimize the synchronization support for DRBD, a checksum-based synchronization is required. A checksum-based synchronization is more efficient in the sense that brute force overwrites and blocks synchronization, which is not enabled by default. With these features enabled, DRBD reads blocks before synchronizing them and calculating a hash of the contents. It compares the hash calculated with the same data obtained from the same sector on the out-of-sync secondary node, and if the hash matches, DRBD omits rewriting these blocks.

To enable this feature, you need to add the following lines on the DRBD configuration:

```
resource <resource>
  net {
    csums-alg <algorithm>;
  }
  ...
}
```

The `<algorithm>` tag is any message digest supported from the kernel cryptographic API, usually one among `sha1`, `md5`, and `crc32c`.

 If this change is done on an existing resource, you need to copy the changed `drbd.conf` file on the secondary client and thereafter run:

drbdadm adjust <resource>

Enabling DRBD online verification

Online verification enables a block-by-block data integrity check in a very efficient way. This is particularly interesting for efficiency in bandwidth usage; additionally, it doesn't interrupt or break redundancy in any way.

 Online verification is a CPU-intensive process; it will impact the CPU load.

DRDB, with this functionality, will calculate a cryptographic digest of every block on the first node, and then this hash is sent to the peer node that will do the same check. If the digest differs, the block will be marked out of sync and DRBD will retransmit only the marked blocks. This feature is not enabled by default and can be enabled by adding the following lines in `drbd.conf`:

```
resource <resource>
  net {
    verify-alg <algorithm>;
  }
  ...
}
```

Also, here `<algotithm>` can be any digest supported by the cryptographic API, usually by `sha1`, `md5`, or `crc32c`. Once configured, it is possible to run online verification with the following command:

$ drbdadm verify <resource>

> Since the check introduced will ensure that both nodes are perfectly in sync, it is advised that you schedule a weekly or a monthly check within crontab.

If you have an out-of-sync block, it is possible to resync it simply with the following command:

$ drbdadm disconnect <resource>

$ drbdadm connect <resource>

DRBD – some networking considerations

When you use a block-based filesystem over DRBD, it is possible to improve the transfer rate, enlarging **Maximum Transmission Unit** (**MTU**) to higher values.

A block-based filesystem will have a noticeable improvement. Block-based filesystems include EXT3, ReiserFS, and GFS. The filesystem proposed here on this architecture is extent-based and is not expected to see high improvement by enabling the jumbo frame.

DRBD permits us to set up the synchronization rate. Normally, DRBD will try to synchronize the data on the secondary node as quickly as possible to reduce the inconsistent data time. Anyway, you need to prevent the degrading of a performance that is caused by the bandwidth consumed for the synchronization.

Make sure that you set up this parameter in relation to the bandwidth available; for instance, it doesn't make any sense to set up a rate that is higher than the maximum throughput.

The maximum bandwidth used from the background process of resynchronization is limited by a parameter rate expressed in bytes; so, 8192 means 8 MiB. To fix the rate, you can change the DRBD configuration file by adding in the following code:

```
resource <resource>
  disk {
    resync-rate 50M;
    ...
  }
...
}
```

 The rule to calculate the right rate and the resync rate is MAX_ALLOWED_BANDWIDTH * 0.3. It means that we are going to use 30 percent of the maximum bandwidth available.

The sync rate follows exactly the same rule and can be specified as well on the drbd.conf file:

```
resource <resource>
  syncer {
    rate 50M;
    ...
  }
...
}
```

 The syncer rate can be temporarily modified with the following command:

drbdsetup /dev/drbdnum syncer -r 120M

The resync rate can be temporarily changed with the following command:

drbdadm disk-options --resync-rate=110M <resource>

Both these rates can be reverted with the following command:

drbdadm adjust resource

DRBD gives us other interesting parameters to fine-tune the system and optimize performance; of course, those that follow are not solutions to all the throughput issues. They can vary from system to system, but it is useful to know that they exist, and you can get some benefit from them.

In particular, there are two parameters. They are as follows:

- `max-buffers`
- `max-epoch-time`

The first property (`max-buffers`) represents the maximum number of buffer DRBDs. The second property (`max-epoch-time`) represents the maximum number of write requests permitted between two write barriers. Both can be changed inside the `drbd.conf` file:

```
resource <resource> {
  net {
    max-buffers 8000;
    max-epoch-size 8000;
    . . .
  }
  . . .
}
```

> The default value for both is 2,048, but both can be changed to 8,000. This is a reasonable value for most of the modern RAID-SCSI controllers.

There is another network optimization that can be done. Change the send buffer of the TCP/IP. By default, this value is set to 128 K, but if you are in a high-throughput network, such as a gigabit network, it make sense to increase this value to 512 K.

```
resource <resource> {
  net {
    sndbuf-size 512K;
    . . .
  }
  . . .
}
```

> If you set these properties to `0`, the DRBD will use the auto-tuning feature, thus adapting the TCP to send the buffer to the network.

To close this optimization section, it is important to say that DRBD manages certain other parameters:

- `no-disk-barrier`
- `no-disk-flushes`
- `no-disk-drain`

My personal advice is that you stay away from them if you don't really know what kind of hardware you have. Set them to represent a *big iron* on the system RAID. These parameters disable the write barriers, disk flush, and drain. Usually, all these features are managed directly from the controller. It doesn't make any sense to enable DRBD to manage them.

Summary

In this chapter, you learned some fundamental concepts about high availability and service clustering. You also learned how to apply them to the Zabbix server architecture using the open source Pacemaker service manager suite and filesystem replication with DRBD. We also taught you the value of keeping things light and simple by choosing as few nodes as possible while maintaining a robust, redundant architecture. This completes the first part of the book that was focused on choosing the optimal Zabbix solution for an environment of any size. By choosing the right hardware, supporting software (refer to the *Distributed monitoring* section in *Chapter 1, Deploying Zabbix*), and high availability for the most sensitive components, you should now have Zabbix installed that is perfectly tailored to your needs and environment.

In the rest of the book, we will focus on using this setup to actually monitor your network and servers and make use of the data collected beyond simple alerts. The next chapter will focus on data collection and use many of Zabbix's built-in item types to obtain monitoring data from a number of simple, complex, or aggregated sources.

4
Collecting Data

Now that you have a Zabbix installation that is properly sized for your environment, you will want to actually start monitoring it. While it's quite easy to identify which hosts and appliances, physical or otherwise, you may want to monitor, it may not be immediately clear what actual measurements you should take on them. The metrics that you can define on a host are called items, and this chapter will discuss their key features and characteristics. The first part will be more theoretical and will focus on the following:

- Items as metrics, not for status checks
- Data flow and directionality for items
- Trapper items as a means to control the data flow

We will then move to a more practical and specific approach and will discuss how to configure items to gather data from the following data sources:

- Databases and ODBC sources
- Java applications, the JMX console, and SNMP agents
- SSH monitoring
- IMPI items
- Web page monitoring
- Aggregated and calculated items

Gathering items as raw data

One of the most important features that sets Zabbix apart from most other monitoring solutions is that its main mode of interaction with the monitored objects is focused on gathering raw data as opposed to alerts or status updates. In other words, many monitoring applications have the workflow (or variation) as shown in the following diagram:

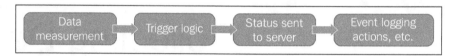

That is, an agent or any other monitoring probe is asked to not only take a measurement, but also incorporate a kind of status decision about the said measurement before sending it to the main server's component for further processing.

On the other hand, the basic Zabbix workflow is subtly, but crucially, different, as shown in the following diagram:

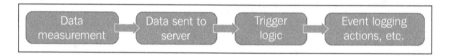

Here, an agent or monitoring probe is tasked with just the measurement part, and then it sends the said measurement to the server component for storage and eventually for further processing.

The data is not associated with a specific trigger decision (pass/fail, ok/warning/ error, or any other variation) but is kept on the server as a single data point or measurement. Where applicable, that is, for numeric types, it's also kept in an aggregate and trending format as minimum, maximum, and average, over different periods of time. Keeping data separated from the decision logic, but all in a single place, gives Zabbix two distinct advantages.

The first one is that you can use Zabbix to gather data on things that are not directly related to the possible alerts and actions that you have to take, but related to the overall performance and behavior of a system. A classic example is that of a switch with many ports. You may not be interested in being alerted about anomalous traffic on every single port (as it may also be difficult to exactly define anomalous traffic on a single port with no contextual information), but you may be interested in gathering both port-level and switch-level traffic measurement in order to establish a baseline, evaluate possible bottlenecks, or plan for an expansion of your network infrastructure. Similar cases can be made about the CPU and core usage, storage capacity, number of concurrent users on a given application, and much more. At its simplest, Zabbix could even be used to gather the usage data and visualize it in different graphs and plots, without even touching its powerful trigger and correlation features, and still prove to be an excellent investment of your time and resources.

Speaking of triggering, the second big advantage of having a full, central database of raw data as opposed to a single measurement (or at best, just a handful of measurements of the same item) is that, for every trigger and decision logic need that you may have, you can leverage the whole measurement database to exactly define the kind of event that you want to monitor and be alerted about. You don't need to rely on a single measurement; you don't even need to rely on the latest measurement, plus a few of the previous ones of the same item or limit yourself to items from the same host. In fact, you can correlate anything with anything else in your item history database. This is a feature that is so powerful that we have dedicated an entire chapter to it, and you can go directly to the next one if that's what you want to read about. It would suffice to say that all this power is based on the fact that Zabbix completely separates its data-gathering functions from its trigger logic and action functions. All of this is based on the fact that measurements are just measurements and nothing else.

So, in Zabbix, an item represents a single metric—a single source of data and measurements. There are many kinds of native Zabbix items even without considering the custom ones that you can define using external scripts. In this chapter, you will learn about some of the less obvious but very interesting ones. You will see how to deal with databases, how to integrate something as alien as SNMP traps to the Zabbix mindset, how to aggregate the existing items together to represent and monitor clusters, and more. As you lay a solid foundation, with sensible and strategic item definition and data gathering, you will be able to confidently rely on it to develop your event management and data visualization functions, as you will see in the following chapters.

Understanding the data flow for Zabbix items

A Zabbix item can be understood by its bare essentials—an identifier, data type, and associated host. These are the elements that are generally more useful for the rest of Zabbix's components. The identifier (that's usually the name and the associated item key) and the associated host are used to distinguish a single item among the thousands that can be defined in a monitoring environment. The data type is important so that Zabbix knows how to store the data, how to visualize it (text data won't be graphed, for example), and most importantly, what kind of functions can be applied to it in order to model triggers and the process further.

> The item's name is a descriptive label that is meant to be easily read, while the item's key follows a specific syntax and defines exactly the metric that we want to measure.

Two other very important elements that are common to all the items are the history (and trends) retention period and item type. We already saw in *Chapter 1, Deploying Zabbix,* how history retention directly affects the size of the monitoring database, how to estimate it, and how to strike a balance between the performance and data availability. On the other hand, the item type is essential as it tells Zabbix how the item data is actually going to be made available to the server, which, in other words, means how Zabbix is going to collect the data: through an agent, an SNMP query, an external script, and so on.

As you probably already know, there's a fair number of different item types. While it's fairly easy to understand the difference between an SSH item and an ODBC one, it's also important to understand how the data is passed around between the server and its probes and whether they are a Zabbix agent, a server-side probe, or an external check of some kind. To this end, we'll first concentrate on the Zabbix agent and the difference between a passive item and an active item.

First of all, the active and passive concepts have to be understood from the agent's point of view and not the server's. Furthermore, they serve to illustrate the component that initiates a connection in order to send or receive configuration information and monitor data, as shown in the following diagram:

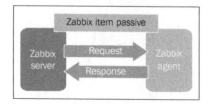

So, a standard Zabbix item is considered passive from the agent's point of view. This means that it's the server's job to ask the agent, at the time intervals defined for the item, to get the desired measurement and report it back immediately. In terms of network operations, a single connection is initiated and brought down by the server while the agent is in the listening mode.

At the other end, in the case of a Zabbix active item, it's the agent's job to ask the server what monitoring data it should gather and at what intervals. It then proceeds to schedule its own measurements and connects back to the server to send them over for further processing. In terms of network operations, the following are the two separate sessions involved in the process:

- The agent asks the server about items and monitoring intervals
- The agent sends the monitoring data it collected to the server

Unlike standard passive items, you'll need to configure an agent so that it knows which server it should connect to for the purpose of configuration and data exchange. This is, of course, defined in the `zabbix_agentd.conf` file for every agent; just set `ServerActive` as the hostname or the IP address of your Zabbix server, and set `RefreshActiveChecks` to the number of seconds the agent should wait before checking whether there are any new or updated active item definitions. The following diagram shows this:

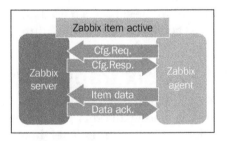

Apart from the network connection initiation, the main difference between a passive item and an active item is that, in the latter, it's impossible to define flexible monitoring intervals. With a passive item, you can define different monitoring intervals based on the time of the day and the day of the week. For example, you could check the availability of an identity management server every minute during office hours and every 10 minutes during the night. On the other hand, if you use an active item, you are stuck with just one option to monitor the intervals.

You may also have noticed a more-than-passive resemblance between the Zabbix active and passive items, and the resemblance between the functionality and features of the Zabbix active and passive proxies.

In fact, you can choose between the active and passive items in much the same way, and for the same reasons you choose between an active or passive proxy in *Chapter 2, Distributed Monitoring*, to offload some of the server's scheduling jobs and to work around the restrictions and limitations of your network and the routing or firewall configuration.

There is, of course, one main difference between proxies and agents. It's not the fact that a proxy can gather monitoring data from many different hosts, while an agent is theoretically (but not practically, it's certainly possible to stretch its functionality using custom items that rely on scripts or external applications) limited to monitoring just the host it's installed on.

The main difference when it comes to the data flow is that the mode of operation of a proxy is applied to all the hosts and items that the proxy manages. In fact, it doesn't care about the nature of the items a proxy has to monitor. However, when an active proxy gathers its data (whether with active or passive agent items, external scripts, SNMP, SSH, and so on), it will always initiate all connections to the server. The same goes for a passive proxy; it doesn't matter whether all the items it has to monitor are active agent items. It will always wait for the main server for updates on configuration and measurement requests.

On the other hand, an active or passive item is just an item of many. A host can be defined by a mix of active and passive items; so, you can't assume that an agent will always initiate all its connections to the server. To do that, all of the items that rely on the agent have to be defined as active, including the future ones.

Understanding Zabbix trapper items

An extreme version of an active item that still relies on the Zabbix agent protocol is the Zabbix **trapper item**. Unique among all other item types, a trapper item does not have a monitoring interval defined at the server level. In other words, a server will know whether a Zabbix trapper item is defined, its data type, the host it's associated with, and the retention period for both history and trends. But it will never schedule a check for the item nor pass the scheduling and monitoring interval information to any proxy or agent. So, it's up to the specific probe to be scheduled in some way and then send the information about the gathered data to the server.

Trapper items are, in some respects, the opposite of Zabbix's external checks from a data flow's point of view. As you probably already know, you define an external check item type when you want the server to execute an external script to gather measurements instead of asking an agent (Zabbix, SNMP, or others). This can exact an unexpected toll on the server's performance as it has to fork a new process for every external script it has to execute and then wait for the response. As the number of external scripts grows, it can significantly slow down the server operations to the point of accumulating a great number of overdue checks while it's busy executing scripts. An extremely simple and primitive, yet effective, way to work around this problem (after reducing the number of external scripts as much as possible, of course) is to convert all external check items to trapper items, schedule the execution of the same scripts used in the external checks through the crontab or any other scheduling facility, and modify the scripts themselves so that they use zabbix_sender to communicate the measured data to the server. When we talk about the Zabbix protocol in *Chapter 8, Handling External Scripts*, you'll see quite a few examples of this setup.

The data flow overview

This is a rundown of item types, classified with the connection type, with a proposed alternative if you want, for any reason, to turn it around. As you can see, Zabbix Trapper is often the only possible, albeit clunky or clumsy, alternative if you absolutely need to reverse a connection type. Note that, in the following table, the term Passive means that the connection is initiated by the server, and Active means that the connection is initiated by whatever probe is used. While this may seem counterintuitive, it's in fact incoherent with the same terms as applied to proxies and agents, as shown in the following table:

Item Type	Direction	Alternative
Zabbix agent	Passive	Zabbix agent(active)
Zabbix agent (active)	Active	Zabbix agent
Simple check	Passive	Zabbix trapper
SNMP agent	Passive	Zabbix trapper (SNMP traps are completely different in nature)
SNMP trap	Active	N/A
Zabbix internal	N/A (data about the server monitoring itself)	N/A
Zabbix trapper	Active	Depends on the nature of the monitored data
Zabbix aggregate	N/A (uses data already available in the database)	N/A
External check	Passive	Zabbix trapper

Item Type	Direction	Alternative
Database monitor	Passive	Zabbix trapper
IPMI agent	Passive	Zabbix trapper
SSH agent	Passive	Zabbix trapper
TELNET agent	Passive	Zabbix trapper
JMX agent	Passive	Zabbix trapper
Calculated	N/A (uses data already in the database)	N/A

In the next few paragraphs, we'll dive deeper into some of the more complex and interesting item types.

Database monitoring with Zabbix

Zabbix offers a way to query any database using SQL queries. The result retrieved from the database is saved as the item value and can have, as usual, triggers associated with it. This functionality is useful in many applications. This gives you a way to monitor the user currently connected to a database, the number of users connected to your web portal, or simply retrieve metrics from the DBMS engine.

Delving into ODBC

ODBC is a layer—a translation layer between **Database Management Systems (DBMS)** and the application. The application uses the ODBC function through the linked ODBC driver manager. The ODBC driver has been implemented and developed in concert with most of the DBMS vendors to enable their database to interoperate with this layer. The configuration file specifies the driver to load all the connection parameters for each **Data Source Name (DSN)**, and all the DSNs are enumerated and defined inside this file. DSN also gives the functionality to present the entire database in a human-readable format. The DSN file needs to be protected. In the proposed setup, it is advisable to use a different Unix account for your Zabbix server, which will make things easy. As there is only one Zabbix server, the only user that needs to access this file is the Zabbix server user. This file should be owned by this user and made unreadable to others. DSNs are contained in the odbc.ini file in the ect folder. This file will contain all the DSNs for all the different databases to which we want to connect. Take care to protect this file, and prevent other people from accessing this file because it can contain passwords.

There are two open source versions of ODBC available—**unixODBC** and **iODBC**. Zabbix can use both of them, but before you can use them, the first thing to do is enable Zabbix to use ODBC and install the unixODBC layer. There are two ways to do that: one is with the package manager, and the other one is to go through the old way of downloading and compiling it from the source (currently, the latest stable version is 2.3.2):

```
$ wget ftp://ftp.unixodbc.org/pub/unixODBC/unixODBC-2.3.2.tar.gz
$ tar zxvf unixODBC-2.3.2.tar.gz
$ cd unixODBC-2.3.2
$ ./configure --prefix=/usr --sysconfdir=/etc
$ make
$ make install
```

If you are on a 64-bit system, you have to specify the 64-bit version of libraries with `--libdir`, as follows:

```
./configure --prefix=/usr --sysconfdir=/etc --libdir=/
usr/lib64
```

The default locations are `/usr/bin` for binary and `/usr/lib` or `/usr/lib64` for libraries depending on the version you have installed.

If you're looking to install unixODBC via the package manager, you need to run the following command from root:

```
$ yum -y install unixODBC unixODBC-devel
```

Installing database drivers

unixODBC supports a wide and almost complete list of databases. Most of the following widely diffused databases are supported:

- MySQL
- PostgreSQL
- Oracle
- DB2
- Sybase
- Microsoft SQL Server (via FreeTDS)

The complete list of databases supported by unixODBC is available at `http://www.unixodbc.org/drivers.html`.

MySQL ODBC drivers

Now, if you have previously installed unixODBC via the package manager, you can follow the same procedure, for example, on Red Hat with the following command:

```
$ yum install mysql-connector-odbc
```

Otherwise, they are also available as a packet; you only need to download the package, for example, `mysql-connector-odbc-5.1.13-linux-glibc2.5-x86-64bit.tar.gz`.

Then, decompress the package and copy the contents in the `/usr/lib/odbc` and `/usr/lib64/odbc/` directories as follows:

```
$ tar xzf mysql-connector-odbc-5.1.13-linux-glibc2.5-x86-64bit.tar.gz
$ mkdir /usr/lib64/odbc/
$ cp /usr/src/ mysql-connector-odbc-5.1.13-linux-glibc2.5-x86-64bit/lib/*
/usr/lib64/odbc/
```

Now you can check whether all the needed libraries are present on your system using the `ldd` command.

This can be done on a 32-bit system with the following command:

```
$ ldd /usr/lib /libmyodbc5.so
```

This can be done on a 64-bit system using the following command:

```
$ ldd /usr/lib64 /libmyodbc5.so
```

If nothing is marked as `Not Found`, this means that all the needed libraries are found and you can go ahead; otherwise, you need to check what is missing and fix it.

All the installed ODBC database drivers are listed in `/etc/obcinst.ini`; this file, for MySQL 5, should contain the following:

```
[mysql]
Description = ODBC for MySQL
Driver      = /usr/lib /libmyodbc5.so
Setup       = /usr/lib/libodbcmyS.so
```

A 64-bit system should contain the following:

```
[mysql]
Description = ODBC for MySQL
Driver64        = /usr/lib64/libmyodbc5.so
Setup64         = /usr/lib64/libodbcmyS.so
```

For all the available ODBC options, refer to the official documentation available at `http://dev.mysql.com/doc/refman/5.1/en/connector-odbc-info.html`.

Data sources are defined in the `odnc.ini` file. You need to create a file with the following content:

```
[mysql-test]
# This is the driver name as specified on odbcinst.ini
Driver = MySQL5
Description = Connector ODBC MySQL5
Database = <db-name-here>
USER= <user-name-here>
Password = <database-password-here>
SERVER = <ip-address-here>
PORT = 3306
```

It is possible to configure ODBC to use a secure SSL connection, but you need to generate a certificate and configure both the sides (ODBC and server) to enable that. Refer to the official documentation for this.

PostgreSQL ODBC drivers

In order to access a PostgreSQL database via ODBC, you need to install the appropriate drivers. They will be used by the Zabbix server to send the queries to any PostgreSQL database via the ODBC protocol.

The official ODBC drivers for PostgreSQL are available at `http://www.postgresql.org/ftp/odbc/versions/src/`.

Perform the following steps to work with the PostgreSQL database:

1. You can download, compile, and install the psqlODBC driver with the following commands:

   ```
   $ tar -zxvf psqlodbc-xx.xx.xxxx.tar.gz
   $ cd psqlodbc-xx.xx.xxxx
   $ ./configure
   $ make
   $ make install
   ```

2. The configuring script accepts different options; some of the most important ones are as follows:

```
--with-libpq=DIR postgresql path
--with-unixodbc=DIR path or direct odbc_config file (default:yes)
--enable-pthreads= thread-safe driver when available (not on all
platforms)
```

3. Alternatively, you can even choose the rpm packages here and then run the following command:

```
$ yum install postgresql-odbc
```

4. Having compiled and installed the ODBC driver, you can create the /etc/ obcinst.ini file, or if you have installed the rpm, just check that the file exists with the following content:

```
[PostgreSQL]
Description       = PostgreSQL driver for Linux
Driver            = /usr/local/lib/libodbcpsql.so
Setup             = /usr/local/lib/libodbcpsqlS.so
Driver64          = /usr/lib64/psqlodbc.so
Setup64           = /usr/lib64/libodbcpsqlS.so
```

5. Now, odbcinst can be invoked by passing your template to that command.

```
$ odbcinst -i -d -f template_filepsql
```

 ODBC supports encrypted logins with md5 but not with crypt. Bear in mind that *only* the login is encrypted after login. ODBC sends all the queries in plain text. As of Version 08.01.002, psqlODBC supports SSL encrypted connections, which will protect your data.

6. As the psqlODBC driver supports threads, you can alter the thread serialization level for each driver entry. So, for instance, the content of odbcinst.ini will be as follows:

```
[PostgreSQL]
Description       = PostgreSQL driver for Linux
Driver            = /usr/local/lib/libodbcpsql.so
Setup             = /usr/local/lib/libodbcpsqlS.so
Threading         = 2
```

7. Now you need to configure the odbc.ini file. You can also use odbcinst here, providing a template or simply a text editor, as follows:

```
$ odbcinst -i -s -f template_file
```

8. You should have inside your `odbc.ini` file something similar to the following:

```
[PostgreSQL]
Description         = Postgres to test
Driver              = /usr/local/lib/libodbcpsql.so
Trace               = Yes
TraceFile           = sql.log
Database            = <database-name-here>
Servername          = <server-name-or-ip-here>
UserName            = <username>
Password            = <password>
Port                = 5432
Protocol            = 6.4
ReadOnly            = No
RowVersioning       = No
ShowSystemTables    = No
ShowOidColumn       = No
FakeOidIndex        = No
ConnSettings        =
```

Oracle ODBC drivers

Oracle is another widely used database and provides an ODBC driver as well. The following is a description of how to install Oracle's ODBC because at `http://www.unixodbc.org`, there isn't much information about it.

1. The first thing to do is get the instant client from the Oracle website. Oracle provides some of the instant client packets as `rpm` and `tar.gz`, as shown in the following commands:

   ```
   $ rpm -I oracle-instantclient11.2-basic-11.2.0.1.0-1.i386.
   rpm oracle-instantclient11.2-odbc-11.2.0.1.0-1.i386.rpm oracle-
   instantclient11.2-sqlplus-11.2.0.1.0-1.i386.rpm
   ```

2. Then, you need to configure some environment variables as follows:

   ```
   $ export ORACLE_HOME=/usr/lib/oracle/11.2/client
   ```

   ```
   $ export ORACLE_HOME_LISTNER=/usr/lib/oracle/11.2/client/bin
   ```

   ```
   $ export LD_LIBRARY_PATH=$LD_LIBRARY_PATH :/usr/lib/oracle/11.2/
   client/lib
   ```

   ```
   $ export SQLPATH=/usr/lib/oracle/11.2/client/lib
   ```

   ```
   $ export TNS_ADMIN=/usr/lib/oracle/11.2/client/bin
   ```

3. Now, you need to configure the `/etc/odbcinst.ini` file. This file should have the following content:

    ```
    [Oracle11g]
    Description = Oracle ODBC driver for Oracle 11g
    Driver      = /usr/lib/oracle/11.2/client/lib/libsqora.so.11.1
    ```

4. In the `odbc.ini` file, the relative DSN entry needs to be configured as follows:

    ```
    [ORCLTEST]
    Driver     = Oracle 11g ODBC driver
    ServerName = <enter-ip-address-here>
    Database   = <enter-sid-here>
    DSN        = ORCLTEST
    Port       = 1521
    ```

5. You can test the connection as usual with the following command:

    ```
    $ isql -v ORCLTEST

    +---------------------------------------+
    | Connected!                            |
    |                                       |
    | sql-statement                         |
    | help [tablename]                      |
    | quit                                  |
    +---------------------------------------+
    ```

6. Now your ODBC connection is fine.

unixODBC configuration files

Now, you are enabled to connect to most of the common databases. To check the connection, you can test it using `isql`, as follows:

1. If you didn't specify the username and password inside the `odbc.ini` file, it can be passed to the DSN with the following syntax:

    ```
    $ isql <DSN> <user> <password>
    ```

2. Otherwise, if everything is specified, you can simply check the connection with the following command:

    ```
    $ isql mysql-test
    ```

3. If all goes well, you should see the following output:

    ```
    +---------------------------------------+
    | Connected!                            |
    ```

```
|                                    |
| sql-statement  .                   |
| help [tablename]                   |
| quit                               |
|                                    |
+-----------------------------------+
SQL>
```

 If you get an error from unixODBC, such as `Data source name not found and no default driver specified`, make sure that the `ODBCINI` and `ODBCSYSINI` environment variables are pointing to the right `odbc.ini` file. For example, if your `odbc.ini` file is in `/usr/local/etc`, the environments should be set as follows:

```
export ODBCINI=/usr/local/etc/odbc.ini
export ODBCSYSINI=/usr/local/etc
```

4. If a DSN is presenting issues, the following command can be useful:

   ```
   $ isql -v <DSN>
   ```

This enables the **verbose mode**, which is very useful to debug a connection.

A good thing to know is that `/etc/obcinst.ini` is a common file, hence you'll have all your unixODBC entries there.

Compiling Zabbix with ODBC

Now if you connect to the target database that is to be monitored, it is time to compile the Zabbix server with ODBC support by performing the following steps:

 If your Zabbix is already up and running, don't run the `make install` command during a normal installation as it will copy too many files, and it's possible that some of them will be overwritten. In this case, it is better to just copy the Zabbix server's executable file.

1. Now you can get the `configure` command line with all the options used as specified in *Chapter 1, Deploying Zabbix*, by adding the `--with-unixodbc` parameter as follows:

   ```
   $ ./configure --enable-server --with-postgresql --with-net-snmp
   --with-libcurl --enable-ipv6 --with-openipmi --enable-agent
   --with-unixodbc
   ```

2. You should see the following between the output lines:

```
checking for odbc_config... /usr/local/bin/odbc_config
checking for main in -lodbc... yes
checking whether unixodbc is usable... yes
```

3. This will confirm that all the needed ODBC binaries are found and are usable. Once the configuring phase is completed, you can run the following command:

```
$ make
```

4. Once this is completed, just take a backup of the previous `zabbix_server` file that was installed, and copy the new version.

5. On starting `zabbix_server`, take a look into the log file, and you should see the following output:

```
****** Enabled features ******
SNMP monitoring: YES
IPMI monitoring: YES
WEB monitoring: YES
Jabber notifications: YES
Ez Texting notifications: YES
ODBC: YES
SSH2 support: YES
IPv6 support: YES
*****************************
```

This means that all went fine.

Database monitor items

Now it is time to use the Zabbix ODBC functionality. In order to do so, you need to create an item of the **Database monitor** type, as shown in the following screenshot:

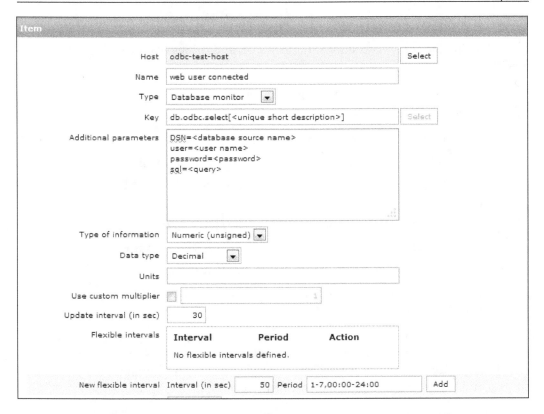

The item where the retrieved value will be stored is identified by the item key as follows:

```
db.odbc.select[<unique short description>]
```

`<unique short description>` is a string that must be unique and can be whatever you want. An example is as follows:

```
db.odbc.select[web_user_connected_on_myapp]
```

Inside the **Additional parameters** field, you need to specify the following:

```
DSN=<database source name>
user=<user name>
password=<password>
sql=<query>
```

Where the DSN should exist in /etc/odbc.ini and whether the username and password are stored in the DSN definition or not can be specified here. In the last line, you need to specify the SQL query.

Some considerations about the ODBC SQL query

The following are some restrictions to the use of, and things to consider about, a SQL query:

- The SQL must begin with a select clause
- The SQL can't contain any line breaks
- The query must return only one value
- If the query returns multiple columns, only the first one is read
- If the query returns multiple rows, only the first column of the first row is read
- Macros are not to be replaced (for example, {HOSTNAME})
- The SQL command must begin with lowercase, that is, `sql=`
- The query needs to terminate before the timeout
- The query must return exactly the value type specified; otherwise, the item will be unsupported

As you can see, there are only some limitations that you can accept. In particular, you can't call a function if that function returns only one value. You can't execute a stored procedure; you can only select the data. Also, the query can't contain any line breaks, so long and complex queries will not be easily readable.

The following are some other points to consider:

- If the database is particularly loaded, it can respond with a delay (the login can also suffer a delay caused by the workload)
- Every query executes a login
- If the database is listening on `127.0.0.1`, the connection can have issues
- If you use proxies, they too need to be compiled with the unixODBC support

If you consider a database that will be under heavy stress, don't have a pool introduced for an overhead that is not necessary. Also, in this case, it is possible that just to have a connection, you need to wait for more than 5 seconds.

The 5 seconds mentioned previously is not a random value; indeed, the timeout of a connection is defined when you open a connection. During the initialization of that, you need to define your expected timeout before considering the connection impossible.

Zabbix defines this timeout in the following command:

`src/libs/zbxdbhigh/odbc.c`

On line 130 of the file, we have the definition of the connection timeout for Zabbix as follows:

```
SQLSetConnectAttr(pdbh->hdbc, (SQLINTEGER)SQL_LOGIN_TIMEOUT,
   (SQLPOINTER)5, (SQLINTEGER)0);
```

This `(SQLPOINTER)5` sets `SQL_LOGIN_TIMEOUT` to 5 seconds. If your database doesn't respond in 5 seconds, you will get the following error inside the log file:

```
[ODBC 3.51 Driver]Can't connect to MySQL server on 'XXX.XXX.XXX.XXX' (4)]
(2003).
```

> In the case of `SQL_LOGIN_TIMEOUT`, you can consider increasing it to 15 seconds and recompile the server and proxy as follows:
>
> ```
> SQLSetConnectAttr(pdbh->hdbc,
>    (SQLINTEGER)SQL_LOGIN_TIMEOUT, (SQLPOINTER)15,
>    (SQLINTEGER)0);
> ```

Zabbix JMX monitoring

Version 2.0 of Zabbix has a native support to monitor applications using JMX. The actor that monitors the JMX application is a Java daemon called the **Zabbix Java gateway**. Basically, it works like a gateway. When Zabbix wishes to know the value of a JMX counter, it simply asks the Java gateway, and the gateway will do all the work for Zabbix. All the queries are done using the JMX management API from Oracle.

The Zabbix Java gateway is in the early stages of development, thus providing great functionality but still experiencing some challenges.

The distinguishing characteristic of this method is that the application only needs to be started with the JMX remote console enabled and doesn't need to implement or extend the class or write new code to handle the Zabbix request because the entire request is a standard JMX.

The default way to enable the JMX console is to start the Java application with the following parameters:

```
-Dcom.sun.management.jmxremote
-Dcom.sun.management.jmxremote.port=<put-your-port-number-here>
-Dcom.sun.management.jmxremote.authenticate=false
-Dcom.sun.management.jmxremote.ssl=false
```

With these parameters, you are going to configure the JMX interface on the application's side. As usual, you need to define a port, the authentication method, and the encryption.

This basic setup is the simplest and easiest way, but unfortunately, it is not the safest and most secure configuration.

Considering JMX security aspects

Now, as you are going to open a door in your application, you are basically exposing your application to a security attack. The JMX console, on most of the widely diffused application servers, is not only an entry point to get values from the counter, but also something that is a lot more sophisticated. Basically, with a JMX console open in an application server, you can deploy an application. Start it, stop it, and so on, as you can figure out what a hacker can deploy, and start an application, or cause an issue on the running one. The JMX console can be called from the application server looping itself, using the post and get methods. Adding malicious content in the HEAD section of a web page results in the server that has a JMX console that is not secured and is easily hackable, which is the weakest point of your infrastructure. Once an application server is compromised, your entire network is potentially exposed, and you need to prevent all this. This can be done through the following steps:

1. The first thing to do is enable the authentication as follows:

   `-Dcom.sun.management.jmxremote.authenticate=true`

2. Now you need to specify a file that will contain your password, as follows:

   `-Dcom.sun.management.jmxremote.password.file=/etc/java-6-`
   `penjdk/management/jmxremote.password`

> There are potential security issues with password authentication for JMX remote connectors. Once the client obtains the remote connector from an insecure RMI registry (the default), such as for all the man-in-the-middle attacks, an attacker can start a bogus RMI registry on the target server right before the valid original one is started and can then steal the client's passwords.

3. Another good thing to do is to profile the users, specifying the following parameter:

```
-Dcom.sun.management.jmxremote.access.file=/etc/java-6-
    penjdk/management/jmxremote.access
```

4. The `access` file, for instance, should contain something similar to the following:

```
monitorRole readonly
controlRole readwrite
```

5. The password file should be as follows:

```
monitorRole <monitor-password-here>
controlRole <control-password-here>
```

6. Now, to avoid password stealing, you should enable the SSL as follows:

```
-Dcom.sun.management.jmxremote.ssl=true
```

7. This parameter is consequently tied with the following ones:

```
-Djavax.net.ssl.keyStore=<Keystore-location-here>
-Djavax.net.ssl.keyStorePassword=<Default-keystore-
    password>
-Djavax.net.ssl.trustStore=<Trustore-location-here>
-Djavax.net.ssl.trustStorePassword=<Trustore-password-here>
-Dcom.sun.management.jmxremote.ssl.need.client.auth=true
```

 The `-D` parameter will be written in the startup file of your application or application server as, after this configuration, your startup file will contain sensitive data (your `keyStore` and `trustStore` passwords) that needs to be protected and not be readable from other accounts in the same group or by other users.

Installing a Zabbix Java gateway

To compile the Java gateway, perform the following steps:

1. First of all, you need to install the required packages:

```
$ yum install java-devel
```

2. Then, you need to run the following command:

```
$ ./configure --enable-java
```

3. You should get an output as follows:

```
Enable Java gateway:      yes
Java gateway details:
   Java compiler:         javac
   Java archiver:         jar
```

4. This shows that the Java gateway is going to be enabled and compiled after the following command is used:

```
$ make && make install
```

5. The Zabbix Java gateway will be installed at the following location:

```
$PREFIX/sbin/zabbix_java
```

6. Basically, the directory structure will contain the following file—the Java gateway:

```
bin/zabbix-java-gateway-2.0.5.jar
```

7. The libraries needed by the gateway are as follows:

```
lib/logback-classic-0.9.27.jar
lib/logback-core-0.9.27.jar
lib/android-json-4.3_r3.1.jar
lib/slf4j-api-1.6.1.jar
```

8. Here are two configuration files:

```
lib/logback-console.xml
lib/logback.xml
```

9. The scripts to start and stop the gateway are as follows:

```
shutdown.sh
startup.sh
```

10. This is a common script sourced from the start and stop scripts that contain the following configuration:

```
settings.sh
```

11. Now, if you have enabled the SSL communication, you need to enable the same security level on the Zabbix Java gateway. To do this, you need to add the following parameter in the startup script:

    ```
    -Djavax.net.ssl.*
    ```

12. Once all this is set, you need to specify the following inside the Zabbix server configuration:

    ```
    JavaGateway=<ip-address-here>
    JavaGatewayPort=10052
    ```

> If you would like to use the Java gateway from your proxy, you need to configure both `JavaGateway` and `JavaGatewayProperties` in the proxy configuration file.

13. Since, by default, Zabbix doesn't start any Java poller, you need to specify that too, as follows:

    ```
    StartJavaPollers=5
    ```

14. Restart the Zabbix server or proxy once that is done.

15. Now you can finally start the Zabbix Java gateway by running the `startup.sh` command.

The logs will be available at `/tmp/zabbix_java.log` with the verbosity `"info"`.

> As the Zabbix Java gateway uses the `logback` library, you can change the log level or the log file location by simply changing the `lib/logback.xml` file. In particular, the following XML tags need to be changed:
>
> ```
> <fileNamePattern>/tmp/zabbix_java.log.%i</
> fileNamePattern><root level="info">
> ```
>
> Here, you can change all the `logrotation` parameters as well.

If you need to debug a Zabbix Java Gateway issue, another useful thing to know is that you can start the Java gateway in console mode. To do that, you simply need to comment out the `PID_FILE` variable contained in `settings.sh`. If the `startup.sh` script doesn't find the `PID_FILE` parameter, it starts the Java gateway as a console application, and Logback uses the `lib/logback-console.xml` file instead. This configuration file, other than enabling the log on console, changes even the log level to debug. Anyway, if you're looking for more details about logging on the Zabbix Java gateway, you can refer directly to the SLF4J user manual available at `http://www.slf4j.org/manual.html`.

Configuring Zabbix JMX

Now it is time to create a JMX monitored host with its relatively monitored JMX items. To do that, inside the host configuration, you need to add a JMX interface and address, as shown in the following screenshot:

Once you have done that for each of the JMX counters you want to acquire, you need to define an item of the **JMX agent** type. Inside the definition of the JMX agent, you need to specify the username, password, and the JMX query string. The JMX key is composed of the following:

- Object name of MBean
- Attribute name, that is, the attribute name of MBean

The following screenshot shows the **Item** configuration window:

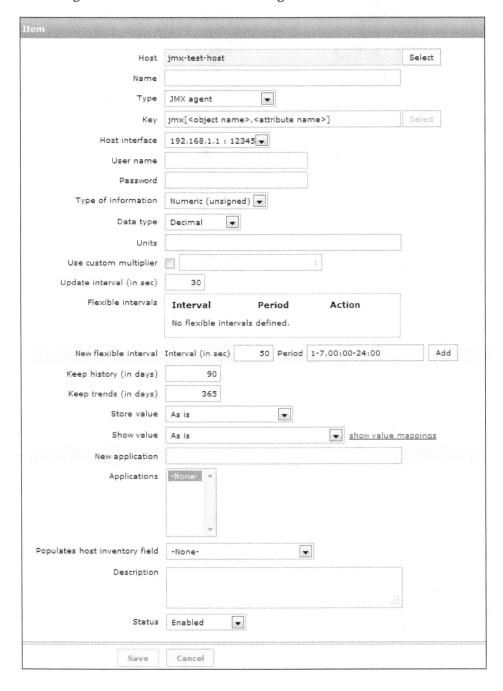

Data type in this configuration window permits us to store the unsigned integer values (such as 0 and 1) as numbers or as Boolean values (such as true or false).

JMX keys in detail

MBean is quite a simple string defined in your Java application. The other component is a bit more complex indeed; the attribute can return primitive data types or composite data.

The primitive data types are simple types, such as integers and strings. For instance, you can have a query such as the following:

```
jmx[com.example:Type=Test,weight]
```

This will return the weight expressed as a numerical floating point value.

If the attribute returns composite data, it is a bit more complicated but is handled since dots are supported. For instance, you can have a pen that can have two values that represent color and the remaining ink, usually dot separated, as shown in the following code:

```
jmx[com.example:Type=Test,pen.remainink]
jmx[com.example:Type=Test,pen.color]
```

Now, if you have an attribute name that includes a dot in its name, such as all.pen, you need to escape the dot, as shown in the following code:

```
jmx[com.example:Type=Test,all\.pen.color]
```

If your attribute name also contains a backslash (\), this needs to be escaped twice, as shown in the following code:

```
jmx[com.example:Type=Test,c:\\utility]
```

If the object name or attribute name contains spaces or commas, it needs to be double-quoted:

```
jmx[com.example:type=Hello,""c:\\documents and settings""]
```

Issues and considerations about JMX

Unfortunately, JMX support is not as flexible and customizable as it should be; at least at the time of writing this book, JMX still had some problems.

For instance, from my personal experience, I know that JBoss, which is one of the most widely used application servers, can't be successfully enquired. The JMX endpoint is currently hardcoded into `JMXItemChecker.java` as follows:

```
service:jmx:rmi:///jndi/rmi://" + conn + ":" + port + "/jmxrmi"
```

Some applications use different endpoints for their JMX management console. JBoss is one of them. The endpoint is not configurable as per the host or frontend, and you can't add a parameter to specify this endpoint on the host's configuration window.

Anyway, the development is really active and things are getting better and are improving every day. At the moment, the status is that the Zabbix Java gateway needs some improvement. Also, the current implementation of the Zabbix Java gateway suffers because of the workload; if you have more than 100 JMX items per host, the gateway needs to be restarted periodically. It is possible that you face some errors of the following kind:

```
failed: another network error, wait for 15 seconds
```

This is followed by:

```
connection restored
```

Also, there is another aspect to consider: in a real-word scenario, it might happen that you have multiple JVMs running on the same hosts. In this case, you need to configure each JMX port creating multiple items and host aliases, one for each network interface; well, this scenario can't be resolved with low-level discovery and requires a lot of manually redundant configuration work. It is fundamental that the implementer of the Zabbix monitoring infrastructure knows not only all the strong points of the product but also the cons and limitations. The implementer can then choose whether they want to develop something in-house, use an open source alternative, try to fix the possible issues, or ask the Zabbix team for a new functionality or fix.

Zabbix SNMP monitoring

Simple Network Monitoring Protocol (SNMP) may not be as simple as the name suggests; it's a de facto standard for many appliances and applications. It's not just ubiquitous—it's often the only sensible way in which one can extract the monitoring information from a network switch, disk array enclosure, UPS battery, and so on.

The basic architecture layout for SNMP monitoring is actually straightforward. Every monitored host or appliance runs an SNMP agent. This agent can be queried by any probe (whether it's just a command-line program to do manual queries or a monitoring server such as Zabbix) and will send back information on any metric it has made available or even change certain predefined settings on the host itself as a response to a set command from the probe. Furthermore, the agent is not just a passive entity that responds to the get and set commands but can also send warnings and alarms as SNMP traps to a predefined host when some specific conditions arise.

Things get a little more complicated when it comes to metric definitions. Unlike a regular Zabbix item, or any other monitoring system, an SNMP metric is part of a huge hierarchy, a tree of metrics that spans hardware vendors and software implementers across all of the IT landscape. This means that every metric has to be uniquely identified with some kind of code. This unique metric identifier is called **OID** and identifies both the object and its position in the SNMP hierarchy tree.

OIDs and their values are the actual content that is passed in the SNMP messages. While this is most efficient from a network traffic point of view, OIDs need to be translated into something usable and understandable by humans as well. This is done using a distributed database called **Management Information Base (MIB)**. MIBs are essentially text files that describe a specific branch of the OID tree, with a textual description of its OIDs, their data types, and a human-readable string identificator.

MIBs let us know, for example, that OID **1.3.6.1.2.1.1.3** refers to the system uptime of whatever machine the agent is running on. Its value is expressed as an integer, in hundredths of a second and can generally be referred to as **sysUpTime**. The following diagram shows this:

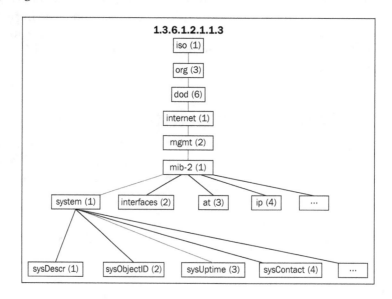

As you can see, this is quite different from the way Zabbix agent items work, both in terms of the connection protocol, item definition, and organization. Nevertheless, Zabbix provides facilities to translate from SNMP OIDs to Zabbix items—if you compiled the support for the server in SNMP, it will be able to create the SNMP queries natively, and with the help of a couple of supporting tools, it will also be able to process SNMP traps.

This is, of course, an essential feature if you need to monitor appliances that only support SNMP and have no way of installing a native agent on network appliances in general (switcher, routers, and so forth), disk array enclosures, and so on. But the following may be reasons for you to actually choose SNMP as the main monitoring protocol in your network and completely dispense with Zabbix agents:

- You may not need many complex or custom metrics apart from what is already provided by an operating system's SNMP OID branch. You, most probably, have already set up SNMP monitoring for your network equipment, and if you just need simple metrics, such as uptime, CPU load, free memory, and so on, from your average host, it might be simpler to rely on SNMP for it as well instead of the native Zabbix agent. This way, you will never have to worry about agent deployment and updates—you just let the Zabbix server contact the remote SNMP agents and get the information you need.

- The SNMP protocol and port numbers are well known by virtually all the products. If you need to send monitoring information across networks, it might be easier to rely on the SNMP protocol instead of the Zabbix one. This could be because traffic on the UDP ports 161 and 162 is already permitted or because it might be easier to ask a security administrator to allow access to a well-known protocol instead of a relatively more obscure one.

- SNMP Version 3 features built-in authentication and security. This means that, contrary to the Zabbix protocol, as you have already seen in *Chapter 2, Distributed Monitoring*, SNMPv3 messages will have integrity, confidentiality, and authentication. While Zabbix does support all three versions of SNMP, it's strongly advised that you use Version 3 wherever possible because it's the only one with real security features. In contrast, Version 1 and 2 only have a simple string sent inside a message as a very thin layer of security.

- While there may be good reasons to use SNMP monitoring as much as possible in your Zabbix installation, there are still a couple of strong reasons to stick with the Zabbix agent. The Zabbix agent has a few, very useful built-in metrics that would need custom extensions if implemented through an SNMP agent. For example, if you want to monitor a log file, with automatic log rotation support, and skip old data, you just need to specify the logrt[] key for a Zabbix active item. The same thing applies if you want to monitor the checksum, the size of a specific file, or the **Performance Monitor** facility of the Windows operating system, and so on. In all these cases, the Zabbix agent is the most immediate and simple choice.

- The Zabbix agent has the ability to discover many kinds of resources that are available on the host and report them back to the server, which will, in turn, automatically create items and triggers and destroy them when the said resources are not available anymore. This means that with the Zabbix agent, you will be able to let the server create the appropriate items for every host's CPU, mounted filesystem, number of network interfaces, and so on. While it's possible to define low-level discovery rules based on SNMP, it's often easier to rely on the Zabbix agent for this kind of functionality.

So, once again, you have to balance the different features of each solution in order to find the best match for your environment. But generally speaking, you could make the following broad assessments: if you have simple metrics but need strong security, go with SNMP v3; if you have complex monitoring or automated discovery needs and can dispense with strong security (or are willing to work harder to get it, as explained in *Chapter 2, Distributed Monitoring*), go with the Zabbix agent and protocol.

That said, there are a couple of aspects worth exploring when it comes to Zabbix SNMP monitoring. We'll first talk about simple SNMP queries and then about SNMP traps.

SNMP queries

An SNMP monitoring item is quite simple to configure. The main point of interest is that while the server will use the **SNMP OID** that you provided to get the measurement, you'll still need to define a unique name for the item and, most importantly, a unique item key. Keep in mind that an item key is used in all of Zabbix's expressions that define triggers, calculated items, actions, and so on. So, try to keep it short and simple, while easily recognizable. As an example, let's suppose that you want to define a metric for the incoming traffic on network port number 3 of an appliance, the OID would be 1.3.6.1.2.1.2.2.1.10.3, while you could call the key something similar to port3.ifInOctects, as shown in the following screenshot:

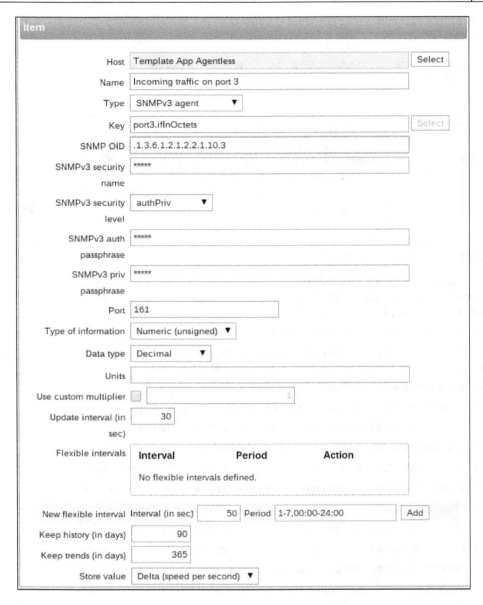

If you don't already have your SNMP items defined in a template, an easy way to get them is using the `snmpwalk` tool to directly query the host that you need to monitor and get information about the available OIDs and their data types.

For example, the following command is used to get the whole object tree from the appliance at `10.10.15.19`:

```
$ snmpwalk -v 3 -l AuthPriv -u user -a MD5 -A auth -x DES -X priv -m ALL
10.10.15.19
```

> You need to substitute the `user` string with the username for the SNMP agent, `auth` with the authentication password for the user, `priv` with the privacy password, `MD5` with the appropriate authentication protocol, and `DES` with the privacy protocol that you defined for the agent. Please remember that the authentication password and the privacy password must be longer than eight characters.

The SNMP agent on the host will respond with a list of all its OIDs. The following is a fragment of what you could get:

```
HOST-RESOURCES-MIB::hrSystemUptime.0 = Timeticks: (8609925)
23:54:59.25HOST-RESOURCES-MIB::hrSystemDate.0 = STRING: 2013-7-
28,9:38:51.0,+2:0

HOST-RESOURCES-MIB::hrSystemInitialLoadDevice.0 = INTEGER: 393216

HOST-RESOURCES-MIB::hrSystemInitialLoadParameters.0 = STRING: "root=/dev/
sda8 ro"

HOST-RESOURCES-MIB::hrSystemNumUsers.0 = Gauge32: 2

HOST-RESOURCES-MIB::hrSystemProcesses.0 = Gauge32: 172

HOST-RESOURCES-MIB::hrSystemMaxProcesses.0 = INTEGER: 0

HOST-RESOURCES-MIB::hrMemorySize.0 = INTEGER: 8058172 KBytes

HOST-RESOURCES-MIB::hrStorageDescr.1 = STRING: Physical memory

HOST-RESOURCES-MIB::hrStorageDescr.3 = STRING: Virtual memory

HOST-RESOURCES-MIB::hrStorageDescr.6 = STRING: Memory buffers

HOST-RESOURCES-MIB::hrStorageDescr.7 = STRING: Cached memory

HOST-RESOURCES-MIB::hrStorageDescr.8 = STRING: Shared memory

HOST-RESOURCES-MIB::hrStorageDescr.10 = STRING: Swap space

HOST-RESOURCES-MIB::hrStorageDescr.35 = STRING: /run

HOST-RESOURCES-MIB::hrStorageDescr.37 = STRING: /dev/shm

HOST-RESOURCES-MIB::hrStorageDescr.39 = STRING: /sys/fs/cgroup

HOST-RESOURCES-MIB::hrStorageDescr.53 = STRING: /tmp

HOST-RESOURCES-MIB::hrStorageDescr.56 = STRING: /boot
```

Let's say that we are interested in the system's memory size. To get the full OID for it, we will reissue the `snmpwalk` command using the `fn` option for the `-O` switch. These will tell `snmpwalk` to display the full OIDs in a numeric format. We will also limit the query to the OID we need, as taken from the previous output:

```
$ snmpwalk -v 3 -l AuthPriv -u user -a MD5 -A auth -x DES -X priv -m ALL
-O fn 10.10.15.19 HOST-RESOURCES-MIB::hrMemorySize.0

.1.3.6.1.2.1.25.2.2.0 = INTEGER: 8058172 KBytes
```

And there we have it. The OID we need to put in our item definition is `1.3.6.1.2.1.25.2.2.0`.

SNMP traps

SNMP traps are a bit of an oddball if compared to all the other Zabbix item types. Unlike other items, SNMP traps do not report a simple measurement but an event of some type. In other words, they are the result of a kind of check or computation made by the SNMP agent and sent over to the monitoring server as a status report. An SNMP trap can be issued every time a host is rebooted, an interface is down, a disk is damaged, or a UPS has lost power and is keeping the servers up using its battery.

This kind of information contrasts with Zabbix's basic assumption, that is, an item is a simple metric not directly related to a specific event. On the other hand, there may be no other way to be aware of certain situations if not through an SNMP trap either because there are no related metrics (consider, for example, the event *the server is being shut down*) or because the appliance's only way to convey its status is through a bunch of SNMP objects and traps.

So, traps are of relatively limited use to Zabbix as you can't do much more than build a simple trigger out of every trap and then notify about the event (not much point in graphing a trap or building calculated items on it). Nevertheless, they may prove essential for a complete monitoring solution.

To manage SNMP traps effectively, Zabbix needs a couple of helper tools: the **snmptrapd** daemon, to actually handle connections from the SNMP agents, and a kind of script to correctly format every trap and pass it to the Zabbix server for further processing.

The snmptrapd process

If you have compiled an SNMP support into the Zabbix server, you should already have the complete SNMP suite installed, which contains the SNMP daemon, the SNMP trap daemon, and a bunch of utilities, such as `snmpwalk` and `snmptrap`.

If it turns out that you don't actually have the SNMP suite installed, the following command should take care of the matter:

```
# yum install net-snmp net-snmp-utils
```

Just as the Zabbix server has a bunch of daemon processes that listen on the TCP port `10051` for incoming connections (from agents, proxies, and nodes), `snmptrapd` is the daemon process that listens on the UDP port `162` for incoming traps coming from remote SNMP agents.

Once installed, `snmptrapd` reads its configuration options from an `snmptrapd.conf` file, which can be usually found in the `/etc/snmp/` directory. The bare minimum configuration for `snmptrapd` requires only the definition of a community string in the case of versions 1 and 2 of SNMP, which is as follows:

```
authCommunity log public
```

Alternatively, the definition of a user and a privacy level in the case of SNMP Version 3 is as follows:

```
createUser -e ENGINEID user MD5 auth DES priv
```

> You need to create a separate `createUser` line for every remote Version 3 agent that will send traps. You also need to substitute all the `user`, `auth`, `priv`, `MD5`, and `DES` strings with what you have already configured on the agent, as explained in the previous note. Most importantly, you need to set the correct `ENGINEID` for every agent. You can get it from the agent's configuration itself.

With this minimal configuration, `snmptrapd` will limit itself to log the trap to syslog. While it could be possible to extract this information and send it to Zabbix, it's easier to tell `snmptrapd` how it should handle the traps. While the daemon has no processing capabilities of its own, it can execute any command or application by either using the `trapHandle` directive or leveraging its embedded `perl` functionality. The latter is more efficient as the daemon won't have to fork a new process and wait for its execution to finish, so it's the recommended one if you plan to receive a significant number of traps. Just add the following line to `snmptrapd.conf`:

```
perl do "/usr/local/bin/zabbix_trap_receiver.pl";
```

> You can get the `zabbix_trap_receiver` script from the Zabbix sources. It's located in `misc/snmptrap/zabbix_trap_receiver.pl`.

Once it is restarted, the snmptrapd daemon will execute the perl script of your choice to process every trap received. As you can probably imagine, your job doesn't end here—you still need to define how to handle the traps in your script and find a way to send the resulting work over to your Zabbix server. We'll discuss both of these aspects in the following section.

The perl trap handler

The perl script included in the Zabbix distribution works as a translator from an SNMP trap format to a Zabbix item measurement. For every trap received, it will format it according to the rules defined in the script and will output the result in a log file. The Zabbix server will, in turn, monitor the said log file and process every new line as an SNMP trap item, basically matching the content of the line to any trap item defined for the relevant host. Let's see how it all works by looking at the perl script itself and illustrating its logic:

```
#!/usr/bin/perl

#
# Zabbix
# Copyright (C) 2001-2013 Zabbix SIA
#
#########################################
#### ABOUT ZABBIX SNMP TRAP RECEIVER ####
#########################################


# This is an embedded perl SNMP trapper receiver designed for
# sending data to the server.
# The receiver will pass the received SNMP traps to Zabbix server
# or proxy running on the
# same machine. Please configure the server/proxy accordingly.
#
# Read more about using embedded perl with Net-SNMP:
#        http://net-snmp.sourceforge.net/wiki/index.php/Tut:Extending_
snmpd_using_perl
```

This first section contains just the licensing information and a brief description of the script. Nothing that's worth mentioning, except a simple reminder—check that your perl executable is correctly referenced in the first line, or change it accordingly. The following section is more interesting, and if you are happy with the script's default formatting of SNMP traps, it may also be the only section that you will ever need to customize:

```
##################################################
#### ZABBIX SNMP TRAP RECEIVER CONFIGURATION ####
```

```
#################################################

$SNMPTrapperFile = '/tmp/zabbix_traps.tmp';
$DateTimeFormat = '%H:%M:%S %Y/%m/%d';
```

Just set `$SNMPTrapperFile` to the path of the file that you wish the script to log its trap to, and set the `SNMPTrapperFile` option in your `zabbix_server.conf` file to the same value. While you are at it, also set `StartSNMPTrapper` to 1 in `zabbix_server.conf` so that the server will start monitoring the said file.

`$DateTimeFormat`, on the other hand, should match the format of the actual SNMP traps you receive from the remote agents. Most of the time, the default value is correct, but take the time to check it and change it as needed.

The following section contains the actual logic of the script. Notice how the bulk of the logic is contained in a subroutine called `zabbix_receiver`. This subroutine will be called and executed towards the end of the script but is worth examining in detail:

```
####################################
#### ZABBIX SNMP TRAP RECEIVER ####
####################################
use Fcntl qw(O_WRONLY O_APPEND O_CREAT);
use POSIX qw(strftime);
sub zabbix_receiver
{
        my (%pdu_info) = %{$_[0]};
        my (@varbinds) = @{$_[1]};
```

The `snmptrapd` daemon will execute the script and pass the trap that it just received. The script will, in turn, call its subroutine, which will immediately distribute the trap information into two lists—the first argument is assigned to the `%pdu_info` hash and the second one to the `@varbinds` array:

```
# open the output file
unless (sysopen(OUTPUT_FILE, $SNMPTrapperFile,
  O_WRONLY|O_APPEND|O_CREAT, 0666))
  {
    print STDERR "Cannot open [$SNMPTrapperFile]:
    $!\n";
    return NETSNMPTRAPD_HANDLER_FAIL;
  }
```

Here, the script will open the output file or fail graciously if it somehow cannot. The next step consists of extracting the hostname (or IP address) of the agent that sent the trap. This information is stored in the %pdu_info hash we defined previously:

```
# get the host name
my $hostname = $pdu_info{'receivedfrom'} || 'unknown';
if ($hostname ne 'unknown') {
   $hostname =~ /\[(.*?)\].*/;
   $hostname = $1 || 'unknown';
}
```

Now, we are ready to build the actual SNMP trap notification message. The first part of the output will be used by Zabbix to recognize the presence of a new trap (by looking for the ZBXTRAP string and knowing which of the monitored hosts the trap refers to). Keep in mind that the IP address or hostname set here must match the SNMP address value in the host configuration as set using the Zabbix frontend. This value must be set even if it's identical to the main IP/hostname for a given host. Once the Zabbix server has identified the correct host, it will discard this part of the trap notification:

```
# print trap header
#         timestamp must be placed at the beginning of the first line
(can be omitted)
#         the first line must include the header "ZBXTRAP [IP/DNS
address] "
#         * IP/DNS address is the used to find the corresponding SNMP
trap items
#         * this header will be cut during processing (will not appear
in the item value)
printf OUTPUT_FILE "%s ZBXTRAP %s\n",
strftime($DateTimeFormat, localtime), $hostname;
```

After the notification header, the script will output the rest of the trap as received by the SNMP agent:

```
# print the PDU info
print OUTPUT_FILE "PDU INFO:\n";
foreach my $key(keys(%pdu_info))
{
   printf OUTPUT_FILE "  %-30s %s\n", $key,
   $pdu_info{$key};
}
```

The `printf` statement in the previous code will circle over the `%pdu_info` hash and output every key-value pair:

```
# print the variable bindings:
print OUTPUT_FILE "VARBINDS:\n";
foreach my $x (@varbinds)
{

    printf OUTPUT_FILE "  %-30s type=%-2d value=%s\n",
       $x->[0], $x->[2], $x->[1];
}
close (OUTPUT_FILE);
return NETSNMPTRAPD_HANDLER_OK;
}
```

The second `printf` statement, `printf OUTPUT_FILE "  %-30s type=%-2d value=%s\n", $x->[0], $x->[2], $x->[1];`, will output the contents of the @ varbinds array one by one. This array is the one that contains the actual values reported by the trap. Once done, the log file is closed and the execution of the subroutine ends with an exit message:

```
NetSNMP::TrapReceiver::register("all", \&zabbix_receiver) or
        die "failed to register Zabbix SNMP trap receiver\n";
print STDOUT "Loaded Zabbix SNMP trap receiver\n";
```

The last few lines of the script set the `zabbix_receiver` subroutine as the actual trap handler and give feedback about its correct setup. Once the trap handler starts populating the `zabbix_traps.log` log file, you need to define the corresponding Zabbix items.

As you've already seen, the first part of the log line is used by the Zabbix trap receiver to match a trap with its corresponding host. The second part is matched to the aforesaid host's SNMP trap item's RegExp definitions, and its contents are added to every matching item's history of values. This means that if you wish to have a startup trap item for a given host, you'll need to configure an SNMP trap item with an `snmptrap["coldStart"]` key, as shown in the following screenshot:

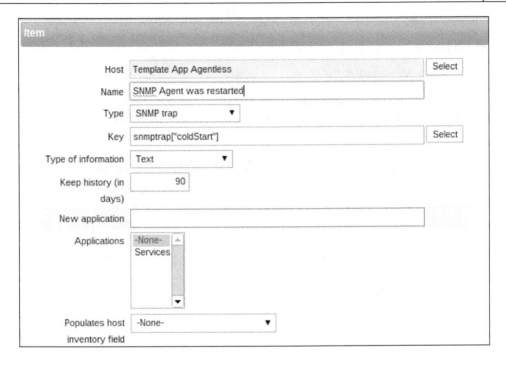

From now on, you'll be able to see the contents of the trap in the item's data history.

Monitoring Zabbix SSH

The SSH monitoring functionality provided by Zabbix, since it's server-triggered and even agentless, is quite useful. This specific functionality is precious as it allows us to run remote commands on a device that doesn't support the Zabbix agent. This functionality is tailor-made for all the cases where, for support reasons, we can't install a Zabbix agent. Some practical cases are given as follows:

- A third-party, vendor-specific appliance where you can't install software
- A device that has a custom-made operating system or a closed operating system

 To be able to run SSH checks, Zabbix needs to be configured with SSH2 support; here, the minimum supported libssh2 is Version 1.0.0.

SSH checks support for two different kinds of authentication:

- SSH with username and password
- Key file based authentication

To use the username/password pair authentication, we don't need to do any special configuration; it is enough to have compiled Zabbix with the SSH2 support.

Configuring the SSH key authentication

To use the key authentication, the first thing to do is configure `zabbix_server.conf`; in particular, we need to change the following entry:

```
# SSHKeyLocation=
```

Uncomment this line and specify the directory that contains the public and private keys for instance:

```
# SSHKeyLocation=/home/zabbixsvr/.ssh
```

Once this is done, you need to restart the Zabbix server from root with the following command:

```
$ service zabbix-server restart
```

Now, we can finally create a new pair of SSH keys running the following command from root:

```
$ sudo -u zabbix ssh-keygen -t rsa -b 2048
Generating public/private rsa key pair.
Enter file in which to save the key (/home/zabbix/.ssh/id_rsa):
Created directory '/home/zabbix/.ssh'.
Enter passphrase (empty for no passphrase):
Enter same passphrase again:
Your identification has been saved in /home/zabbix/.ssh/id_rsa.
Your public key has been saved in /home/zabbix/.ssh/id_rsa.pub.
The key fingerprint is:
a9:30:a9:ce:c6:22:82:1d:df:33:41:aa:df:f3:e4:de zabbix@localhost.
localdomain
The key's randomart image is:
+--[ RSA 2048]----+
|                 |
|                 |
```

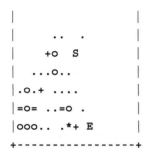

```
|                 |
|    ..   .       |
|    +o   S       |
|   ...o..        |
|.o.+ ....        |
|=o= ..=o .       |
|ooo.. .*+ E      |
+-----------------+
```

Now, on the remote host, we need to create a dedicated restricted account as we don't want to expose the system but only monitor it, and then we can finally copy our keys. In the following example, we are supposed to have created the account zabbix_mon on the remote host:

```
$ sudo -u zabbix ssh-copy-id zabbix_mon@<remote-host-ip>
```

Now you can check whether everything went fine by simply triggering a remote connection with:

```
$ sudo -u zabbix ssh zabbix_mon@<remote-host-ip>
```

Now, if all has been properly configured, we will have a session on the remote host.

Finally, we can define a custom item to retrieve the output of uname -a and then have the kernel version retrieved as an item. This is shown in the following screenshot:

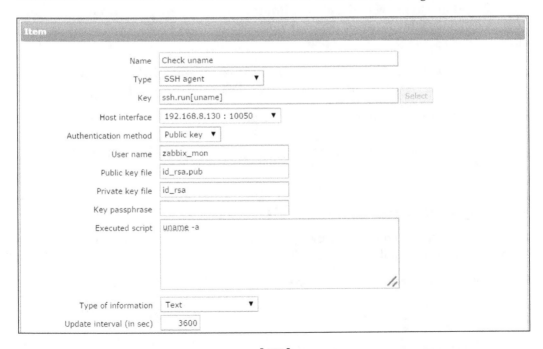

This requires some consideration; first of all, it is possible that libssh2 truncates the output to 32 K, in which case it is better to be aware. Also, it is better to always use the fully qualified path for all the command specified. Here too, it is worth considering that the SSH can introduce a delay and can slow down the whole process. All those considerations are valid even for the Telnet agent checks. The negative side is that, of course, Telnet is not encrypted and is not a secure protocol. Also, as you know, it supports only username and password authentication. Especially if you're going to use Telnet, it is fundamental, if not critical, to have a read-only account made for Telnet checks.

Monitoring Zabbix IPMI

Nowadays, you can quickly monitor the health and availability of you devices using IPMI. Definitely, the main requirement here is that your device supports **Intelligent Platform Management Interface (IPMI)**. IPMI is a hardware level specification that is *software neutral*, meaning it is not tied in any way with BIOS and operating systems. One interesting feature is that the IPMI interface can be available even when the system is in the powered-down state. This is possible because inside each IPMI-enabled device, there is a separate device that consumes less power, independent of any other board or software. Nowadays, IPMI is fully supported by most server vendors, and talking about servers, it is usually exposed by the management cards: HP ILO, IBM RSA, Sun SSP, DELL RDAC, and so on.

If you would like to know in detail how IMPI works, since is a standard designed by Intel, you can find the documentation at `http://www.intel.com/content/www/us/en/servers/ipmi/ipmi-specifications.html`.

Obviously, to perform an IPMI check, you need to have compiled Zabbix with IPMI `--with-openipmi` support, please refer to *Chapter 1, Deploying Zabbix*.

IPMI uses a request-response protocol over a message-based interface to dialogue with all the device components, but more interesting is that other than retrieving components metrics or accessing the non-volatile system event log, you even can retrieve data from all the sensors installed in your hardware.

The first steps with IPMI

First of all, you need to make sure that you've installed all the required packages; otherwise, you can install them with this command executed from root:

```
$ yum install ipmitool OpenIPMI OpenIPMI-libs
```

Now, we can already retrieve temperature metrics using IPMI, for instance, using the following command:

```
$ ipmitool sdr list | grep Temp
Ambient Temp | 23 degrees C | ok
CPU 1 Temp   | 45 degrees C | ok
CPU 2 Temp   | disabled     | ns
CPU 3 Temp   | disabled     | ns
CPU 4 Temp   | disabled     | ns
```

Note that in the previous example, we've got three `disabled` lines as those CPU sockets are empty. As you can see, we can quickly retrieve all the internal parameters via the IPMI interface. Now, it is interesting to see all the possible states that can apply to our IPMI ID, which is `CPU 1 Temp`, please note that since the IPMI ID contains spaces, we need to use the double quote notation:

```
$ ipmitool event "CPU 1 Temp" list
Finding sensor CPU 1 Temp... ok
Sensor States:
   lnr : Lower Non-Recoverable
   lcr : Lower Critical
   lnc : Lower Non-Critical
   unc : Upper Non-Critical
   ucr : Upper Critical
   unr : Upper Non-Recoverable
```

Those are all the possible `CPU 1 Temp` states. Now, IPMI is a simple, read-only protocol, but you can even simulate errors or configure parameters. We are now going to simulate a low-temperature threshold, just to see how this works. Running the following command, you can simulate a `-128` degrees Celsius reading:

```
$ ipmitool event "CPU 1 Temp" "lnc : Lower Non-Critical"
Finding sensor CPU 1 Temp... ok
0 | Pre-Init Time-stamp | Temperature CPU 1 Temp | Lower Non-critica l |
going low | Reading -128 < Threshold -128 degrees C
```

Now, we can quickly verify that this has been logged in the system event log with:

```
$ ipmitool sel list | tail -1
1c0 | 11/19/2008 | 21:38:22 | Temperature #0x98 | Lower Non-critical
going low
```

This is one is the best nondisruptive tests that we can do to make you aware that it's required to profile read-only IPMI accounts. Using the admin IPMI account, you can reset your management controller, trigger a shutdown, trigger a power-reset, change the boot list, and so on.

Configuring IPMI accounts

To configure an IPMI account, you have essentially two ways:

- Use the management interface itself (RDAC, ILO, RS, and so on)
- Using OS tools and then OpenIPMI

First of all, it is better to change the default root password; you can do it with:

```
$ ipmitool user set password 2 <new_password>
```

Here, we are resetting the default password for the root account that has the user ID 2.

Now, it is important to create a Zabbix user account that can query the signor's data and has no rights to restart a server or change any configuration.

In the next line, we are creating the Zabbix user with the user ID 3; please check whether you already have the user ID 3 in your system. First of all, define the user login with this command from root:

```
$ ipmitool user set name 3 zabbix
```

Then, set the relative password:

```
$ ipmitool user set password 3
Password for user 3:
Password for user 3:
```

Now, we need to grant our Zabbix the required privileges:

```
$ ipmitool channel setaccess 1 3 link=on ipmi=on callin=on privilege=2
```

Activate the account:

```
$ ipmitool user enable 3
```

Verify that all is fine:

```
$ ipmitool channel getaccess 1 3
Maximum User IDs    : 15
```

```
Enabled User IDs      : 2


User ID               : 3
User Name             : zabbix
Fixed Name            : No
Access Available      : call-in / callback
Link Authentication   : enabled
IPMI Messaging        : enabled
Privilege Level       : USER
```

The use we've just created is named `zabbix`, and it has the USER privilege level. Anyway, the account is not enabled to access from the network; to enable this account, we need to activate the MD5 authentication for LAN access for this user group:

```
$ ipmitool lan set 1 auth USER MD5
```

We can verify this with:

```
$ ipmitool lan print 1
Set in Progress         : Set Complete
Auth Type Support       : NONE MD5 PASSWORD
Auth Type Enable        : Callback :
                        : User     : MD5
                        : Operator :
                        : Admin    : MD5
                        : OEM      :
```

Now we can finally run the queries remotely from our Zabbix server directly with this command:

```
$ ipmitool -U Zabbix -H <ip-of-IPMI-host-here> -I lanplus sdr list | grep
Temp
Ambient Temp | 23 degrees C  | ok
CPU 1 Temp   | 45 degrees C  | ok
CPU 2 Temp   | disabled      | ns
CPU 3 Temp   | disabled      | ns
CPU 4 Temp   | disabled      | ns
```

Now we are ready to use our Zabbix server to retrieve IPMI items.

Configuring Zabbix IPMI items

When you're looking for IPMI metrics, the most difficult part is the setup that we've just done. In Zabbix, the setup is quite easy. First of all, we need to uncomment the following line in `zabbix_server.conf`:

```
# StartIPMIPollers=0
```

Change the value to something reasonable for the amount of IPMI interface you're going to monitor. Anyway, this is not critical; the most important part is to enable the IPMI Zabbix poller that is disabled by default. In this example, we will use:

```
StartIPMIPollers=5
```

Now, we need to restart Zabbix from root by running:

```
$ service zabbix-server restart
```

Now, we can finally switch on the web interface and start adding IPMI items.

The first step is configure the IPMI parameters at the host level and then go to **Configuration | Host**. There, we need to add **IPMI interface**, the relative port, as shown in the following screenshot:

Then, we need to switch on the **IPMI** tab, which is where the other configuration parameters are.

In the **IPMI** tab for **Authentication algorithm**, select **MD5**, and as per our example configuration done previously, for the **Privilege** level, select **User**. In the **Username** field, you can write Zabbix, and in **Password**, you can write the password you've specified during the configuration, as shown in the following screenshot:

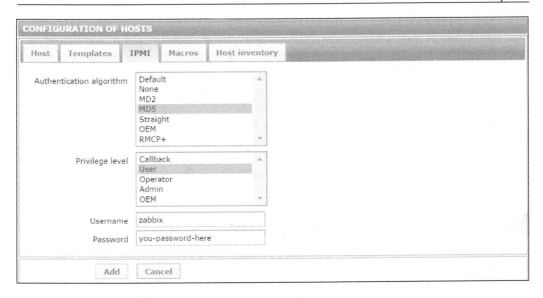

Now, we can add our item of the type **IPMI agent**. As per the previous example, the item we're acquiring here is **CPU 1 Temp**, and the the **Type** is **Numeric (float)**. The following screenshot shows this:

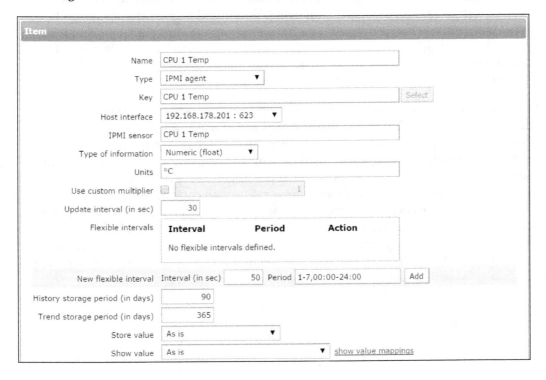

Configuring the Zabbix side of IPMI is a straightforward process; anyway, if you're using a different OpenIPMI version, please be aware that there are known issues with OpenIPMI Version 2.0.7, and that Zabbix is not working fine with this version. Then, the version 2.0.14 or later is required to make it work. In some devices, such as network temperature sensors that have only one interface card, logically, the same card will expose even the IPMI interface. If this is your case, please bear in mind to configure it on the same IP address as that of your device. Another important thing to know about IPMI is that the names of discrete sensors have been changed between OpenIPMI 2.0.16, 2.0.17, 2.0.18, and 2.0.19. Thus, it is better to check the correct name using the OpenIPMI version that you have deployed in the Zabbix server.

Monitoring the web page

In this day and age, web applications are virtually ubiquitous. Some kinds of websites or a collection of web pages is typically the final product or the service of a complex structure that comprises different databases, application servers, web servers, proxies, network balancers and appliances, and more. When it comes to monitoring duties, it makes sense to go just a step further and monitor a resulting site or web page in addition to all the backend assets that enable the said page. The advantages as far as warnings and notifications go, are fairly limited, as failure to reach a web page is certainly a critical event. But it hardly gives any insight into what may be the actual problem if you haven't set up the correct metrics and triggers on the backend side. On the other hand, it may be crucial to have a collection of data about a website's performance. In order to anticipate possible problems, substantiate SLA reporting, and plan for hardware or software upgrades.

One big advantage of Zabbix's web-monitoring facilities is the scenario concept. You can define a single web scenario that is composed of many simple steps, each one building on the previous and sharing a common set of data. Furthermore, every such definition includes the automatic creation of meaningful items and graphs, both at the scenario level (overall performance) and at the single-step level (local performance). This makes it possible to not only monitor a single web page but also simulate entire web sessions so that every component of a web application will contribute to the final results. A single scenario can be very complex and requires a great number of items that would end up being difficult to track and group together. This is the reason why web monitoring in Zabbix has its own web configuration tab and interface, separate from regular items, where you can configure monitoring on a higher level.

To perform web monitoring, the Zabbix server must be initially configured with cURL (libcurl) support. Please refer to *Chapter 1, Deploying Zabbix*.

Web scenarios support plain HTTP/HTTPS, BASIC, NTLM, form-based authentication, cookies, submission of form fields, and checking of page content in addition to the HTTP code responses.

For all their power, web scenarios also suffer from a few limitations when it comes to monitoring the modern Web.

First of all, JavaScript is not supported, so you can't simulate a complete AJAX session exactly as a human user would experience it. This also means that any kind of automated page reloads won't be executed in the scenario.

Furthermore, while you can submit forms, you have to know in advance both the name of the fields and their content. If either of them is generated dynamically from page to page (as many ASP.NET pages are to keep the session information), you won't be able to use it in subsequent steps.

These may seem to be negligible limitations, but they may prove to be quite important if you need to monitor any site that relies heavily on client-side elaborations (JavaScript and friends) or on dynamic tokens and form fields. The reality is that an increasing number of web applications or frameworks use one or both of these features.

Nevertheless, even with these limitations, Zabbix's web monitoring facilities prove to be a very useful and powerful tool that you may want to take full advantage of, especially if you produce a lot of web pages as the final result of an IT pipeline.

Authenticating web pages

To create a web scenario, you need to go through **Configuration | Host** and then click on **Create scenario**. You'll see a window, as shown in the following screenshot:

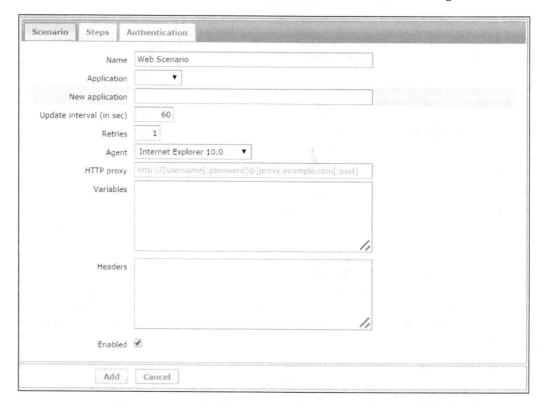

Within this form, you can define parameters other than the usual ones, such as **Name**, **Application**, and **Update interval**, which represents the frequency with which our scenario is executed. Even the user **Agent** and the number of **Retries** can be defined. Once you've defined the user **Agent** that you would like to use, Zabbix will act as the selected browser by presenting itself as the browser defined. Regarding **Retries**, it is important to know that Zabbix will not repeat a step due to a wrong response or a mismatch of the required string.

Another important and new section is **Headers**. Here, you can specify the HTTP headers that will be sent when Zabbix executes a request.

 The custom headers are supported starting from Zabbix 2.4. In this field, you can use the HOST.* macros and user macros.

There are three methods of authentication supported for web monitoring; you can see them in the relative **Authentication** tab, as shown in the following screenshot:

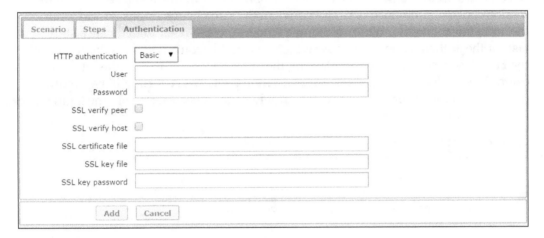

Those method are Basic, NTLM, and form-based. The first two are fairly straightforward and just need to be defined at the scenario level. The NTLM authentication will provide two additional fields to enter the username and password. Starting with Zabbix 2.2, we have now fully supported the use of user macros in the username and password fields. Again, on this tab, we can even enable the SSL verification. The **SSL verify peer** checkbox enables the web server certificate checking, and the **SSL verify host** checkbox is used to verify the **Common Name** field or the **Subject Alternate Name** field of the web server certificate. The **SSL certificate file** checkbox is used for client-side authentication; here, you need to specify a PEM certificate file. If the PEM certificate contains even the private key, you can avoid specifying the relative key on **SSL key file** and **SSL key password**.

The certificate location can be configured in the main configuration file, zabbix_server.conf. There are indeed three SSL configuration parameters: SSLCertLocation, SSLKeyLocation, and SSLCALocation.

Both fields, **SSL certificate files** and **SSL key file**, support HOST.* macros.

Coming back to authentication, we need to highlight form-based authentication, which relies on the ability of the client (a Zabbix server in this instance) to keep the session cookies, and which is triggered when the said client submits a form with the authentication data. While defining a scenario, you'll need to dedicate a step just for the authentication. To know which form fields you'll need to submit, look at the HTML source of the page containing the authentication form. In the following example, we'll look at the Zabbix authentication page. Every form will be slightly different, but the general structure will largely be the same (here, only the login form is shown in an abbreviated manner):

```
<form action="index.php" method="post">
  <input type="hidden" name="request" class="input hidden" value="" />
  <!-- Login Form -->
  <div>Username</div>
  <input type="text" id="name" name="name" />
  <div>Password</div>
  <input type="password" id="password" name="password" />
  <input type="checkbox" id="autologin" name="autologin" value="1"
checked="checked" />
  <input type="submit" class="input" name="enter" id="enter"
value="Sign in" />
</form>
```

You need to take note of the input tags and their name options because these are the form fields you are going to send to the server to authenticate. In this case, the username field is called name, the password field is called password, and finally, the submit field is called enter and has the value Sign in.

We are now ready to create a scenario; we will then define our scenario as shown in the following screenshot:

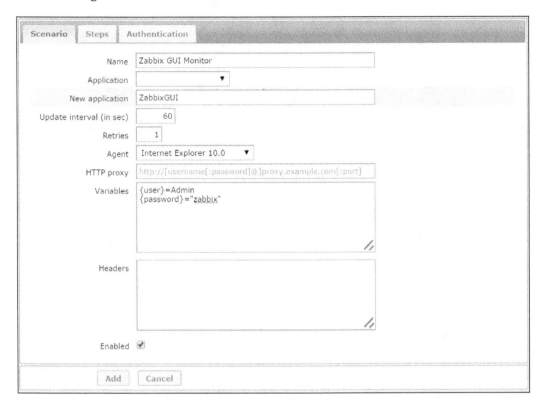

As you can see, in the **Variables** field, we have defined two variables that we're going to use in the next steps and then in the authentication step. This is a useful feature as it allows us to the variable defined across the scenario.

The next thing to do is the authentication, and then we need to add one step to our scenario, as shown in the following screenshot:

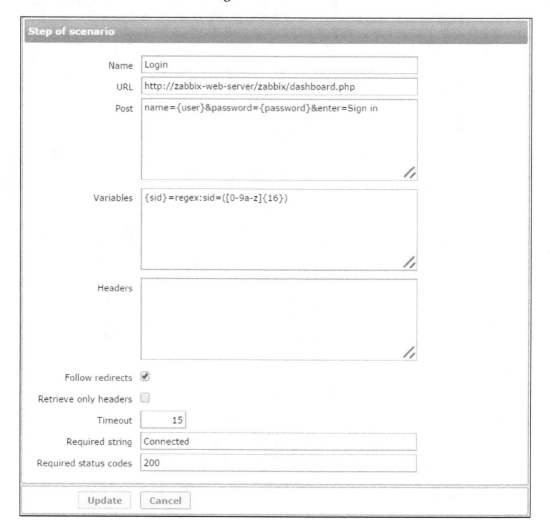

Please note the usage of the predefined variables {user} and {password}. As per the required string, we can use Connected, which appears right in the footer once you're connected, and, of course, **Required status codes** will be 200. In this example, we are defining a new variable that represents the authentication token. This variable will be used during the logout process and will be populated by the data received. From now on, every URL that you'll check or every form that you'll submit, will be in the context of an authenticated session, assuming the login process was successful, of course.

> Starting with Zabbix 2.4, each step defined supports web redirects. If the checkbox is flagged Zabbix, set the cURL option CURLOPT_FOLLOWLOCATION (http://curl.haxx.se/libcurl/c/CURLOPT_FOLLOWLOCATION.html). Also, it is possible to retrieve only the header for each page instead of setting the cURL option CURLOPT_NOBODY. More information is available at http://curl.haxx.se/libcurl/c/CURLOPT_NOBODY.html.

Logging out

One common mistake when it comes to web monitoring is that the authentication part is taken care of at the start of a scenario but rarely at the end during logout. If you don't log out of a website, depending on the system used to keep track of the logged-in users and active sessions, a number of problems may arise.

Active sessions usually range from a few minutes to a few days. If you are monitoring the number of logged-in users, and your session's timeouts are on the longer side of the spectrum, every login scenario would add to the number of active users reported by the monitoring items. If you don't immediately log out at the end of the scenario, you may, at the very least, end up with monitoring measurements that are not really reliable, and they would show a lot of active sessions that are really just monitoring checks.

In the worst-case scenario, your identity manager and authentication backend may not be equipped to handle a great number of non-expiring sessions and may suddenly stop working, bringing your whole infrastructure to a grinding halt. We can assure you that these are not hypothetical situations but real-life episodes that occurred in the authors' own experience.

At any rate, you certainly can't go wrong by adding a logout step to every web scenario that involves a log in. You'll make sure that your monitoring actions won't cause any unforeseen problem, and at the very least, you will also test the correct functioning of your session's tear-down procedures. Logout steps are also usually quite easy as they normally involve just a GET request to the correct URL. In the case of the Zabbix frontend, you would create the following final step (as shown in the following screenshot) before ending the scenario:

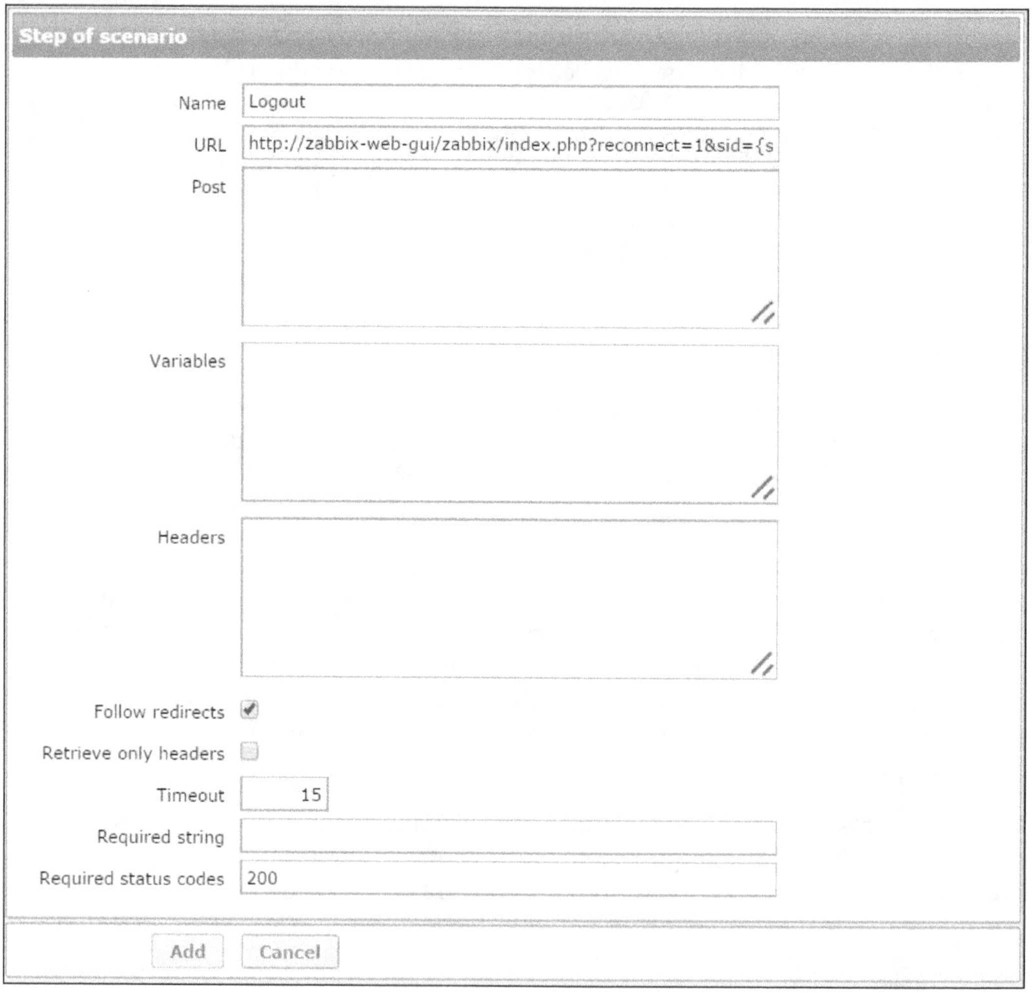

Step of scenario	
Name	Logout
URL	http://zabbix-web-gui/zabbix/index.php?reconnect=1&sid={s
Post	
Variables	
Headers	
Follow redirects	✔
Retrieve only headers	☐
Timeout	15
Required string	
Required status codes	200
Add	Cancel

Once you have defined this logout step, your scenario will look similar to the following screenshot:

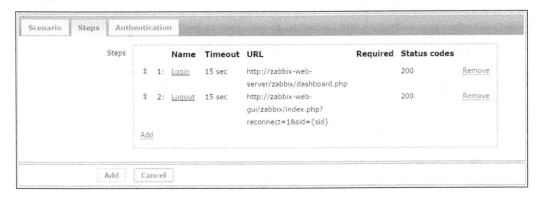

Please note the use of the {sid} variable in the logout string. Also, in this example, we have used `zabbix-web-gui`. This obviously needs to be replaced with your own web server.

Furthermore, please consider that every new session uses up a small amount of computing resources whether it's disk space or memory. If you create a large number of sessions in a short time, due to frequent checks, you could end up significantly degrading the website's performances. So, take care to:

- Include all the required steps within your scenario
- Avoid duplicating scenarios for simple checks
- Always define a logout step
- Bear in mind that the frequency needs to be a reasonable value and doesn't affect the monitored system

Also, it is important to know that you can't skip steps included in web scenarios. They are all executed in the defined order. Also, if you need a more verbose log, you can increase it at the real-time HTTP poller using the following command:

```
$ zabbix_server -R log_level_increase="http poller"
```

As a last tip, bear in mind that the history for which we are monitoring items is of 30 days and for 90 trends.

Aggregated and calculated items

Until now, every item type described in this chapter could be considered a way to get raw measurements as single data points. In fact, the focus of the chapter has been more on setting up Zabbix to retrieve different kinds of data than on what is actually collected. This is because on the one hand, a correct setup is crucial for effective data gathering and monitoring, while on the other hand, the usefulness of a given metric varies wildly across environments and installations, depending on the specific needs that you may have.

When it comes to aggregated and calculated items though, things start to become really interesting. Both types don't rely on probes and measurements at all; instead, they build on existing item values to provide a whole new level of insight and elaboration on the data collected in your environment.

This is one of the points where Zabbix's philosophy of decoupling measurements and triggering logic really pays off, because it would be quite cumbersome, otherwise, to come up with similar features, and it would certainly involve a significant amount of overhead.

The two types have the following features in common:

- Both of them don't make any kind of checks (agent-based, external, SNMP, JMX, or otherwise) but directly query the Zabbix database to process the existing information.

- While they have to be tied to a specific host because of how the Zabbix data is organized, this is a loose connection compared to a regular item. In fact, you could assign an aggregated item to any host regardless of the item's specifics, although it's usually clearer and easier if you define one or more simple dedicated hosts that will contain aggregated and calculated items so that they'll be easier to find and reference.

- Aggregated and calculated items only work with numeric data types—there's no point in asking for the sum or the average of a bunch of text snippets.

Aggregated items

The simpler of the two types discussed here, aggregated items can perform different kinds of calculations on a specific item that is defined for every host in a group. For every host in a given group, an aggregated item will get the specified item's data (based on a specified function) and then apply the group function on all of the values collected. The result will be the value of the aggregated item measurement at the time that it was calculated.

To build an aggregated item, you first need to identify the host group that you are interested in and then identify the item, shared by all the group's hosts, which will form the basis of your calculations. For example, let's say that you are focusing on your web application servers, and you want to know something about the active sessions of your Tomcat installations. In this case, the group would be something similar to `Tomcat Servers`, and the item key would be `jmx["Catalina:type=Manag er,path=/,host=localhost",activeSessions]`.

Next, you need to decide how you want to retrieve every host's item data. This is because you are not limited to just the last value but can perform different kinds of preliminary calculations. Except for the `last` function, which indeed just retrieves the last value from the item's history, all the other functions take a period of time as a further argument.

Function	Description
avg	This is the average value in a specified time period
sum	This is the sum of all values in a specified time period
min	This is the minimum value recorded in a specified time period
max	This is the maximum value recorded in a specified time period
last	This is the latest value recorded
count	This is the number of values recorded in a specified time period

What you now have is a bunch of values that still need to be brought together. The following table explains the job of the group function:

Function	Description
grpavg	This is the average of all the values collected
grpsum	This is the sum of all values collected
grpmin	This is the minimum value in a collection
grpmax	This is the maximum value in a collection

Now that you know all the components of an aggregated item, you can build the key; the appropriate syntax is as follows:

```
groupfunc["Host group","Item key",itemfunc,timeperiod]
```

The Host group part can be defined locally to the aggregated item definition. If you want to bring together data from different hosts that is not part of the same group and you don't want to create a host group just for this, you can substitute the host group name with a list of the hosts— ["HostA, HostB, HostC"].

Continuing with our example, let's say that you are interested in collecting the average number of active sessions on your Tomcat application server every hour. In this case, the item key would look as follows:

```
grpavg["Tomcat servers",
  "jmx["Catalina:type=Manager,path=/,
  host=localhost",activeSessions]", avg, 3600]
```

You could also use 1h or 60m as a time period if you don't want to stick to the default of using seconds.

Using the same group and a similar item, you would also want to know the peak number of concurrent sessions across all servers, this time every 5 minutes, which can be done as follows:

```
grpsum["Tomcat servers",
  "jmx["Catalina:type=Manager,path=/,host=localhost",maxActive]",
  last, 0]
```

Simple as they are, aggregated items already provide useful functionality, which would be harder to match without a collection of measurements as simple data that is easily accessible through a database.

Calculated items

This item type builds on the concept of item functions expressed in the previous paragraphs and takes it to a new level. Unlike aggregated items, with calculated ones, you are not restricted to a specific host group, and more importantly, you are not restricted to a single item key. With calculated items, you can apply any of the functions available for the trigger definitions to any item in your database and combine different item calculations using arithmetic operations. As with other item types that deal with specialized pieces of data, the item key of a calculated item is not used to actually define the data source but still needs to be unique so that you can refer to the item in triggers, graphs, and actions. The actual item definition is contained in the formula field, and as you can imagine, it can be as simple or as complex as you need.

In keeping with our Tomcat server's example, you could have a calculated item that gives you a total application throughput for a given server as follows:

```
last(jmx["Catalina:type=GlobalRequestProcessor,name=http-
    8080",bytesReceived]) +
    last(jmx["Catalina:type=GlobalRequestProcessor,name=http-
    8080",bytesSent]) +
    last(jmx["Catalina:type=GlobalRequestProcessor,name=http-
    8443",bytesReceived]) +
    last(jmx["Catalina:type=GlobalRequestProcessor,name=http-8443",
    bytesSent]) +
    last(jmx["Catalina:type=GlobalRequestProcessor,name=jk-8009",
    bytesReceived]) +
    last(jmx["Catalina:type=GlobalRequestProcessor,name=jk-
    8009",bytesSent])
```

Alternatively, you could be interested in the ratio between the active sessions and the maximum number of allowed sessions so that, later, you could define a trigger based on a percentage value instead of an absolute one, as follows:

```
100*last(jmx["Catalina:type=Manager,path=/,
    host=localhost",activeSessions]) /
    last(jmx["Catalina:type=Manager,path=/,host=localhost",
    maxActiveSessions])
```

As previously stated, you don't need to stick to a single host either in your calculations.

The following is how you could estimate the average number of queries on the database per single session, on an application server, every 3 minutes:

```
avg(DBServer:mysql.status[Questions], 180) /
    avg(Tomcatserver:Catalina:type=Manager,path=/,host=localhost",
    activeSessions], 180)
```

The only limitation with calculated items is that there are no easy group functions such as those available to aggregated items. So, while calculated items are essentially a more powerful and flexible version of aggregated items, you still can't dispense with aggregated items, as you'll need them for all group-related functions.

Despite this limitation, as you can easily imagine, the sky is the limit when it comes to calculated items. Together with aggregated items, these are ideal tools to monitor the host's group performances, such as clusters and grids, or to correlate different metrics on different hosts that contribute to the performance of a single service.

Whether you use them for performance analysis and capacity planning or as the basis of complex and intelligent triggers, or both, the judicious use of aggregated and calculated items will help you to make the most out of your Zabbix installation.

Summary

In this chapter, we delved into various aspects of item definitions in Zabbix. At this point, you should know the main difference between a Zabbix item and a monitoring object of other products and why Zabbix's approach of collecting simple, raw data instead of monitoring events is a very powerful one. You should also know the ins and outs of monitoring the data flow traffic and how to affect it based on your needs and environment. You should be comfortable to move beyond the standard Zabbix agent when it comes to gathering data and be able to configure your server to collect data from different sources—database queries, SNMP agents, IPMI agents, web pages, JMX consoles, and so on.

Finally, you have, most probably, grasped the vast possibilities implied by the two powerful item types—aggregated and calculated.

In the next chapter, you'll learn how to present and visualize all the wealth of data you are collecting using graphs, maps, and screens.

5
Visualizing Data

Zabbix is a flexible monitoring system. Once implemented on an installation, it is ready to support a heavy workload and will help you acquire a huge amount of every kind of data. The next step is to graph your data, interpolate, and correlate the metrics between them. The strong point is that you can relate different type of metrics on the same axis of time, analyzing patterns of heavy and light utilization, identifying services and equipment that fail most frequently in your infrastructure, and capturing relationships between the metrics of connected services.

Beyond the standard graphs facility, Zabbix offers you a way to create your custom graphs and to add them on your own template, thus creating an easy method to propagate your graphs across all the servers. Those custom graphs (and also the standard and simple graphs) can be collected into screens. Inside Zabbix, a screen can contain different kinds of information—simple graphs, custom graphs, other screens, plain text information, trigger overviews, and so on.

In this chapter, we will cover the following topics:

- Generating custom graphs
- Creating and using maps with shortcuts and nested maps
- Creating a dynamic screen
- Creating and setting up slides for a large monitor display
- Generating an SLA report

As a practical example, you can think of a big data center, where there are different layers or levels of support; usually, the first level of support needs to have a general overview of what is happening on your data center, the second level can be the first level of support divided for typology of service, for example, DBA, application servers, and so on. Now, your DBA (second level of support) will need the entire database-related metrics, whereas an application server specialist most probably will need all the Java metrics, plus some other standard metrics, such as CPU memory usage. Zabbix's responses to this requirement are maps, screens, and slides.

Once you create all your graphs and have retrieved all the metrics and messages you need, you can easily create screens that collect, for instance, all the DBA-related graphs plus some other standard metrics; it will be easy to create a rotation of those screens. The screen will be collected on slides, and each level of support will see its groups of screens in a slide show, which has an immediate qualitative and quantitative vision of what is going on.

Data center support is most probably the most complex slide show to implement, but in this chapter, you will see how easy it is to create it. Once you have all the pieces (simple graphs, custom graphs, triggers, and so on), you can use them and also reuse them on different visualization types. On most of the slides, for instance, all the vital parameters, such as CPU, memory, swap usage, and network I/O, need to be graphed. Once done, your custom graphs can be reused in a wide number of dynamic elements. Zabbix provides another great functionality, that is, the ability to create dynamics **maps**. A map is a graphical representation of a network infrastructure. All those features will be discussed in this chapter.

When you are finally ready to implement your own custom visualization screen, it is fundamental to bear in mind the audience, their skills or background, and their needs. Basically, be aware of what message you will deliver with your graphs.

Graphs are powerful tools to transmit your message; they are a flexible instrument that can be used to give more strength to your speech as well as give a qualitative overview of your service or infrastructure. This chapter is pleasant and will enable you to communicate using all the Zabbix graphical elements.

Graphs

Inside Zabbix, you can divide the graphs into two categories—simple graphs and custom graphs. Both of these are analyzed in the next section.

Analyzing simple graphs

Simple graphs in Zabbix are something really immediate since you don't need to put in a lot of effort to configure this feature. You only need to go to **Monitoring | Latest data**, eventually filter by the item name, and click on the graph. Zabbix will show you the historical graph, as shown in the following screenshot:

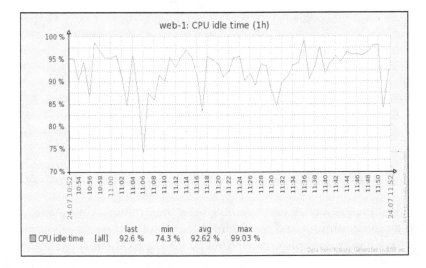

Clearly, you can graph only numeric items, and all the other kinds of data, such as text, can't be shown on a graph. On the latest data item, you will see the graph link instead—a link that will show the history.

 No configuration is needed, but you can't customize this graph.

At the top of the graphs, there is the time period selector. If you enlarge this period, you will see the aggregated data. As long as the period is little and you would like to see very recent data, you will see a single line. If the period is going to enquire the database for old data, you will see three lines. This fact is tied to history and trends; since the values are contained in the history table, the graph will only show one line. Once you're going to retrieve data from the trends, there will be three lines, as shown in the following screenshot:

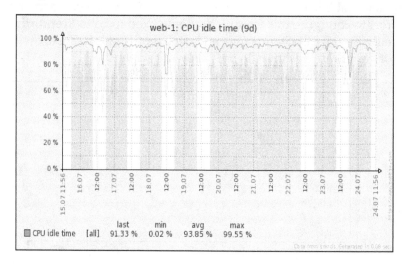

In the previous screenshot, we can see three lines that define a yellow area. This area is designed by the minimum and maximum values, and the green line represents the mean value. For a quite complete discussion about trends/history tables, see *Chapter 1, Deploying Zabbix*. Here, it is important to have all those three values graphed.

> The longevity of an item in history is defined in the item itself in the field Keep history (in days) and persistence on the trends table is defined in the Keep trends (in days) field.

In the following screenshot, you can see how the mean values may vary with respect to the minimum and maximum values. In particular, it is interesting to see how the mean value remains almost the same at **12:00** too. You can see quite an important drop in the **CPU idle time** (the light-green line) that didn't influence the mean value (green line) too much since, most likely, it was only a small and quick drop, so it is basically lost on the mean value but not on our graph since Zabbix preserves the minimum and maximum values.

Graphs show the working hours with a white background, and the non-working hours in gray (using the original template); the working time is not displayed if the graph needs to show more than 3 months. This is shown in the following screenshot:

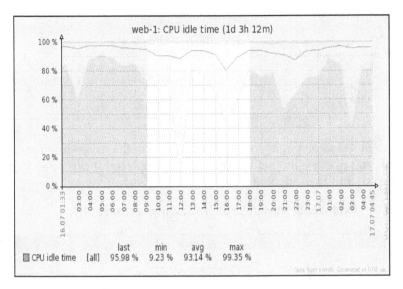

Simple graphs are intended just to graph some on-the-spot metrics and check a particular item. Of course, it is important to interpolate the data; for instance, on the CPU, you have different metrics and it is important to have all of them.

Analyzing ad hoc graphs

This is a brand-new feature available, starting with Zabbix 2.4. It's actually a very nice feature as it enable you to create on the fly an ad hoc graph.

Now Zabbix can graph and represent, on the same graph, multiple metrics related to the same timescale.

 Thanks to this new functionality, everyone without administrative privileges can produce graphs on the fly with a few clicks.

To have an ad hoc graph generated for your metrics, you simply need to go to **Monitoring | Latest data** and, from there, mark the checkbox relative to the item you would like to graph, as shown in the following screenshot:

At the bottom of the same page, you need to choose in the drop-down menu the kind of graph you prefer—the default graph is stacked, but it can be switched to the standard graph—and then, click on Go.

The result of our example is shown in the following screenshot:

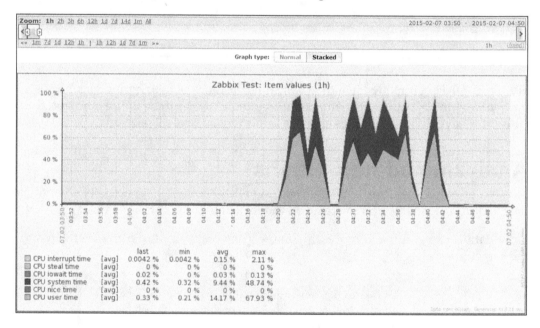

Note that on this screen, you can quickly switch between Stacked and Normal.

 This feature doesn't keep you tied with a host-specific graph. This means that everyone is now enabled to generate a graph with data coming from many different hosts; for example, you can relate the CPU of your DB server with the one coming from the application server.

Now we can dig a little into those ad hoc graphs and see some nice features.

Hacking ad hoc graphs

Now let's see something that can be quickly reused later on your screens.

Zabbix generates URLs for custom ad hoc graphs, such as `http://<YOUR-ZABBIX-GUI>/zabbix/history.php?sid=<SID >&form_refresh=2&action=batchgraph&itemids[23701]=23701&itemids[23709]=23709&itemids[23705]=23705&itemids[23707]=23707&itemids[23704]=23704&itemids[23702]=23702&graphtype=1&period=3600`.

This URL is composed of many components:

- `sid`: This represents your session ID and is not strictly required
- `form_refresh`: This is a kind of refresh option — not strictly required
- `itemids[id]=value`: This is the actual item that Zabbix will show you on the graph
- `action=[batchgraph|showgraph]`: This specifies the kind of graph we want

It is quite interesting to see how we can quickly switch from the default `batchgraph` action in the URL by just replacing it with `showgraph`. The main difference here is that `batchgraph` will show you only average values in the graph. Instead, it can be a lot more useful to use `showgraph`, which includes the triggers — the maximum and minimum values for each item.

An example of the same graph seen before with `showgraph` is as follows:

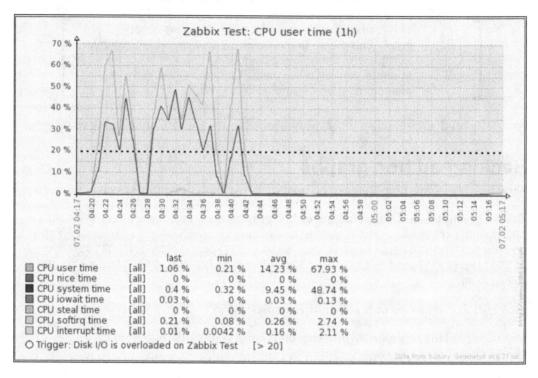

Here, you can clearly see that you now have the trigger included. Since you can find it very useful to use this kind of approach, especially when you're an application-specific engineer and you're looking for standard graphs that are not strictly required on your standard template, let's see another hidden functionality.

Now if you want to retrieve the graph directly to reuse it somewhere else, the only thing you need to do is call with the same parameter, but instead of using the `history.php` page, you need to use `chart.php`. The output will be the following screenshot:

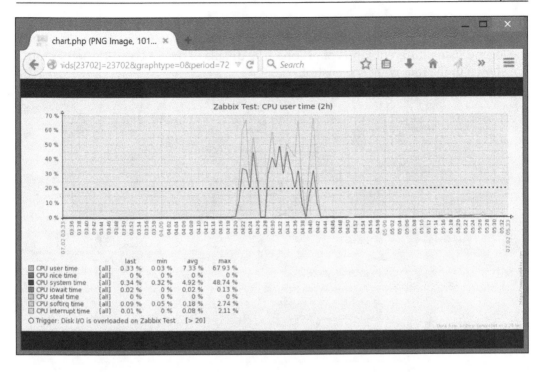

The web page will display only the pure graph. Then, you can quickly save the most used graphs among your favorites and retrieve them with a single click!

Analyzing custom graphs

We have only discussed the graph components here rather than the full interaction functionality and their importance in seeing historical trends or delving into a specific time period on a particular date. Zabbix offers the custom graphs functionality — these graphs need to be created and customized by hand. For instance, there are certain predefined graphs on the standard **Template OS Linux**. To create a custom graph, you need to go to **Configuration** | **Hosts** (or **Templates**), click on **Graphs**, and then on **Create graph**.

General graphs should be created in templates so that they can be easily applied to a group of servers. An example is the graph of CPU utilization on Template OS Linux. This one is quite general; it is composed of several metrics aggregated and is nice to have across all your Linux servers.

Graphs on Zabbix are really a strong point of the monitoring infrastructure. Inside this custom graph, you can choose whether you want to show the working time and the legend using different kinds of graphs. The details of the CPU Utilization graph are shown in the following screenshot:

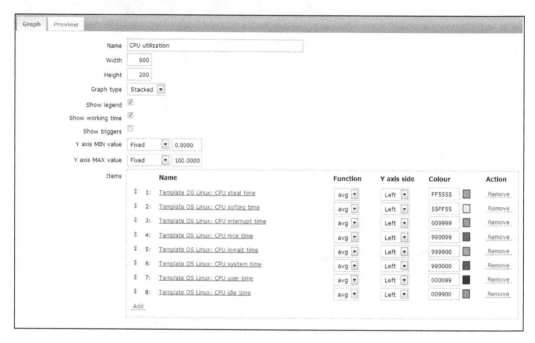

As you can see, the following graph is stacked and shows the legend of the x axis defined with a fixed y axis scale. In this particular case, it doesn't make any sense to use a variable for the minimum or maximum values of the y axis since the sum of all the components represents the whole CPU and each component is a percentage. Since a stacked graph represents the sum of all the stacked components, this one will always be 100 percent, as shown in the following screenshot:

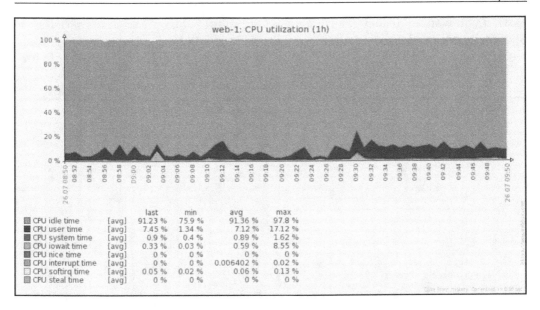

There are a few considerations when it comes to triggers and working hours. These are only two checks, but they change the flavor of the graph. In the previous graph, the working hours are displayed on the graph but not the triggers, which is mostly because there aren't triggers defined for those metrics. The working hours, as mentioned earlier, are displayed in white. Displaying working hours is really useful in all the cases where your server has two different life cycles or serves two different tasks. As a practical example, you can think about a server placed in New York that monitors and acquires all the market transactions of the U.S. market. If the working hours — as in this case — coincide with the market's opening hours, the server will, most probably, acquire data most of the time. Think about what will happen if the same trading company works in the Asian market; most probably, they will enquire the server in New York to see what happened while the market was open. Now, in this example, the server will provide a service in two different scenarios and have the working hours displayed in a graph, which can be really useful.

[Displaying the working time in graphs is useful. See whether your trigger goes on fire in this period.]

Now, if you want to display the triggers in your graph, you only need to mark the **Show triggers** checkbox, and all the triggers defined will be displayed on the graph. Now, it can happen that you don't see any lines about the triggers in your graph; for instance, look at the following screenshot:

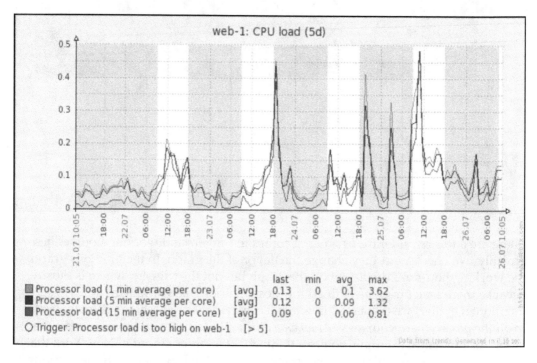

Now where is your expected trigger line? Well, it is simple. Since the trigger is defined for a processor load greater than five, to display this line you need to make a few changes in this graph, in particular the **Y axis MIN value** and **Y axis MAX value** fields. In the default, predefined CPU load graph, the minimum value is defined as zero and the maximum value is calculated. Both need to be changed as follows:

Now refresh your graph. Finally, you will see the trigger line, which wasn't visible in the previous chart because the CPU was almost idle, and the trigger threshold was too high and not displayed due to the auto-scaling on the *y* axis. This is shown in the following screenshot:

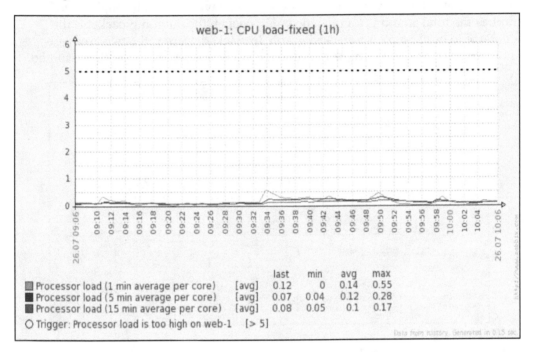

As you probably already noticed, Zabbix doesn't display periods shorter than an hour. The minimum graph period is about 1 hour.

Zabbix supports the following kinds of custom graph:

- Normal
- Stacked
- Pie
- Exploded

Zabbix also supports different kinds of drawing styles. Graphs that display the network I/O, for instance, can be made using gradient lines; this will draw an area with a marked line for the border, so you can see the incoming and outgoing network traffic on the same scale. An example of this kind is shown in the following screenshot, which is easy to read. Since you don't have the total throughput to have graphed the total amount from the incoming packet, the outgoing packet is the better one to be chosen for a stacked graph. In stacked graphs, the two areas are summarized and stacked, so the graph will display the total bandwidth consumed.

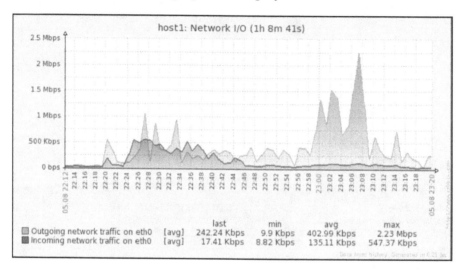

To highlight the difference between a normal graph and a stacked one, the following screenshot displays the same graph during the same time period, so it will be easier to compare them:

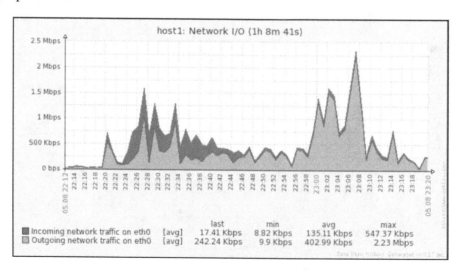

As you can see, the peaks and the top line are made by aggregating the network input and output of your network card. The preceding graph represents the whole network traffic handled by your network card.

Reviewing all the combinations of graph properties

Zabbix is quite a flexible system and the graphs are really customizable to better explore all the possible combinations of attributes and parameters that can be customized. All the possible combinations of graph attributes are reviewed in the following table:

Parameter	Description
Name	This is the graph name (note that this needs to be unique)
Width	This is the graph width in pixels
Height	This is the graph height in pixels
Graph type	Normal (values displayed as lines, filled region, bold lines, dots, dashed lines, and gradient lines) • Stacked values are displayed as stacked areas • Pie values are displayed as a pie • Exploded values are displayed as a pie but exploded
Show legend	If checked, the graph will display the legend.
Show working time	If checked, the non-working hours will be in gray and working hours in a white background.
Show triggers	If checked, a single trigger line is displayed (note that this is not available for pie and exploded).
Percentile line (left/ right)	Note that this is only available on normal graphs. If checked, it displays a line where the value falls under the percentage (for example, for 90, it will display a line where 90 percent of the values fall under).
Y axis MIN/MAX value	This sets the minimum and maximum value for the y axis, which can be any of the following: • **Calculated**: The minimum and maximum values will be calculated on the basis of the displayed area • **Fixed**: The fixed value will be used as per maximum or minimum • **Item**: The last value of the selected item will be used as minimum/maximum
3D View	This displays the graphs in 3D (note that this is only available for pie and exploded pie graphs).

This second table describes the item configuration:

Parameter	Description
Sort order	This represents the priority for a particular item over an other and is useful to give priority to the region displayed, for example, in front of or behind the other items. Here, you can drag and drop items in the right order. Note that zero is the first processed item; Zabbix supports up to 100 items.
Name	The name of the item is displayed here. The metric name is composed in the form of `<source>` : `<metric_name>`. This means that if you are inside the host configuration, you will see `<hostname>`:`<metric_name>`. If you are creating the graphs inside a template, you will see `<template_name>`:`<metric_name>`.
Type	Note that this is available only for the pie and exploded pie graphs: • Simple • Graph sum
Function	This determines the value to display if more than one is present; it can be one of the following: • **All**: This shows minimum, average, and maximum values • **Min**: This only shows minimum values • **Avg**: This only shows average values • **Max**: This only shows maximum values
Draw style	This is only available for normal graphs: • Line • Filled region • Bold line • Dot • Dashed line
Y axis side	Note: This is available only on stacked and normal graphs and defines the y axis side for each element.
Colour	Other than the standard displayed on the palette, you can set all the colors that you want in the RGB hex format.

You can easily play with all those functionalities and attributes. In version 2.0 of Zabbix, you have a **Preview** tab that is really useful when you're configuring a graph inside a host. If you're defining your graph at a template level, this tab is useless because it doesn't display the data. When you are working with templates, it is better to use two windows to see in real time by refreshing (the *F5* key) the changes directly against the host that inherits the graphs from the template.

All the options previously described are really useful to customize your graphs as you have understood that graphs are really customizable and flexible elements.

You can display only three trigger lines, and if the graph is less than 120 pixels, triggers are not displayed; so, take care to properly set up your graphs and check all the changes.

Visualizing the data through maps

Zabbix provides a powerful element to visualize data and a topological view in Zabbix, which will help you to create maps. Maps are a graphical representation of your physical infrastructure, where you can display your server, network components, and the interconnection between them.

The great thing is that maps on Zabbix are completely dynamic, which means that you will see your active warnings, issues, and triggers represented on the map, with different icons, colors, and labels. This is a powerful representation of your data center or of the service that you're representing. The elements that you can put in a map are as follows:

- Host
- Host groups
- Triggers
- Images
- Maps

All those elements are dynamically updated by triggers or using macros, thus providing a complete status of the maps and their elements.

 To enable a user to create, configure, or customize maps, the user needs to be of the *Zabbix administrator* type. This means that there isn't a role dedicated to map creation. Also, the user needs to have a read/write permission on all the hosts that he needs to put into a map. This means that there isn't a way to restrict the privileges to map creation only, but you can limit the administration to a certain number of hosts included in a group.

An example of a map that you can easily produce with Zabbix is shown in the following screenshot:

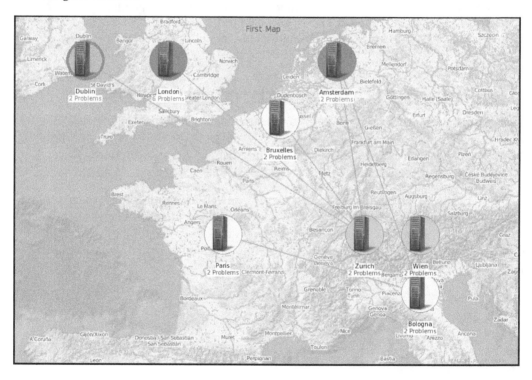

In the preceding screenshot, you can see that there are a lot of graphical combinations of icons, round backgrounds, and information. To better understand what this map represents, it is important to see how Zabbix treats hosts and triggers in a map. In the following screenshot, you can see all the possible combinations of trigger severity and status change:

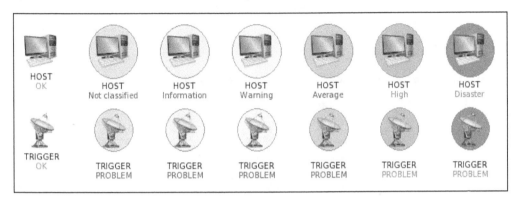

The preceding screenshot illustrates, from left to right, the following:

- A host that doesn't have a trigger on fire
- A host with the trigger severity that is shown as **Not classified** in the alarm
- A host with the trigger severity **Information** in the alarm
- A host with the trigger severity **Warning** in the alarm
- A host with the trigger severity **Average** in the alarm
- A host with the trigger severity **High** in the alarm
- A host with the trigger severity **Disaster** in the alarm

The trigger line follows the same classification.

> The trigger severity is expressed with the background color and not with the name that you see under the **HOST** label. The label in red color is the name of the trigger. In the preceding screenshot, triggers are callers, just as their classification says, to simply make the picture more verbose. Please notice that in the case of **TRIGGER** representation, right after the **TRIGGER** label is displayed, the trigger status is displayed and not the trigger name that is on fire, as in the case of **HOST**.

Now if a trigger changed recently, its status will be displayed as shown in the following diagram:

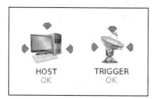

Now if a host has issues and a trigger is on fire, this will be represented with the following icons:

Please note that, in this case, the icon is shown with arrows because it just changed the status. The following screenshot shows that there are six problems:

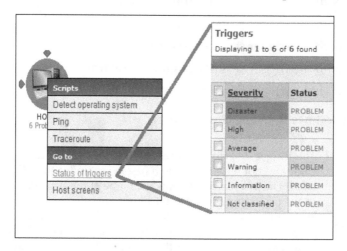

As you can see, there are different triggers with problems. The one that has the most critical severity is the one that gives the color to the circle around the icon. Once all the triggers are acknowledged, the icon will show a green circle around it, as shown in the following screenshot:

The second icon displays details of all the problems that your host is facing and the number of unacknowledged ones, so you have an immediate status of how many issues are under control and how many are new.

The third icon with the square background is a host that has been disabled, represented in gray; it will be in red once it becomes unreachable.

Creating your first Zabbix map

Map configuration can be easily reached by navigating to **Configuration | Maps | Create map**. The resulting window that you will see is shown in the following screenshot:

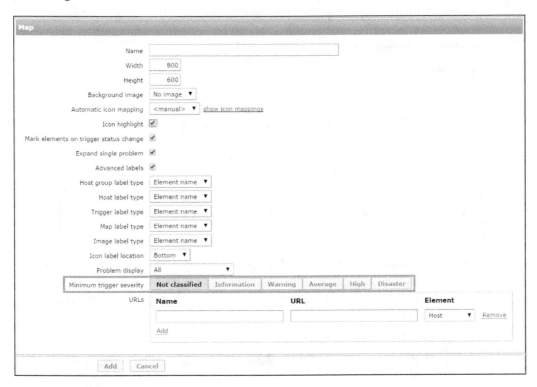

Most of the properties are quite intuitive; the **Name** field needs to be a unique name, and **Width** and **Height** are expressed in pixels.

> If you define a large size, and the second time, you want to reduce it, it is possible that some of your hosts will fall outside the map and are no more visible. Don't be scared; nothing is lost. They are still inside the map, only not displayed. You can restore them to their original size, and they will appear again.

Now we will take a look at all the other parameters:

- **Background image**: In the background image field, you can define your map's background, choosing between loaded backgrounds.

> Zabbix, by default, doesn't have any backgrounds defined. To add your own background, you need to go to go to **Administration | General**, and select **Images** from the listbox. Please check to add your image as **Background** and not **Icon**. A good source for royalty-free maps is `www.openstreetmap.org`.

- **Automatic icon mapping**: This flag enables user-defined icon mapping for a certain host inventory field. This can be defined by navigating to **Administration | General | Icon mapping**.

- **Icon highlight**: This is the flag responsible for generating the round background around the icon with the same color as that of the most critical severity trigger.

- **Mark elements on trigger status change**: This flag is responsible for highlighting a trigger status change (with the red triangle shown earlier in the screenshot displaying the status change).

> Markers are displayed only for 30 minutes, after which they will be removed, and the changed trigger status will become the new normal status.

- **Advanced labels**: This check enables you to customize the label's type for all the elements that you can put in a map. So, for each one of those items — host, host group, trigger, map, and image — you can customize the label type. The possible label types are as follows:
    ○ **Label**: This is the icon label
    ○ **IP Address**: This is the IP address (available only on the host)

- ○ **Element name**: This is the element name, such as `hostname`
- ○ **Status only**: This is only for the status, so it will be `OK`/`PROBLEM`
- ○ **Nothing**: This means that there is no label at all
- ○ **Custom label**: A free test area (macros are allowed)

- **Icon label location**: This field defines where you will see all the labels by default. This can be selected among the following values: **Bottom**, **Left**, **Right**, and **Top**.

- **Problem display**: This listbox permits you to choose between the following:
  - ○ **All**: A complete problem count will be displayed
  - ○ **Separated**: This displays the unacknowledged problem count separated as a number of the total problem count
  - ○ **Unacknowledged only**: With this selected, only the unacknowledged problem count will be displayed

- **URLs**: Here, a URL for each kind of element can be used with a label. This label is a link, and here you can use macros, for example, `{MAP.ID}`, `{HOSTGROUP.ID}`, `{HOST.ID}`, and `{TRIGGER.ID}`.

Starting with Zabbix 2.2, a new feature has been introduced. The map configuration feature provides you with the option of defining the lowest trigger severity.

With this configuration, only the triggers at the defined level or more will still be displayed in the map; this will reduce the number of triggers displayed, and all the triggers with a severity below the defined one will not be displayed. This section is highlighted in the previous screenshot within a green rectangle.

The level that you have selected within the map configuration can be overwritten when viewing maps in **Monitoring | Maps** by selecting the desired **Minimum severity**, as shown in the following screenshot:

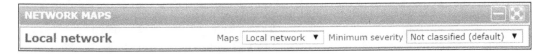

Important considerations about macros and URLs

The URL section is powerful, but here an example is needed because the usage is not intuitive and simple.

Now, if you see a trigger on fire or an alarm that is escalating, most probably the next action that you will take is to check the latest data of your host or jump to a screen that will group the graphs, triggers, and data that you need to check to have an idea of what is happening and do a first-level analysis. In a practical case of first-level support, once a server is highlighted and shows triggers with problems, it can be useful to have a link that will go straight ahead to the latest data of that host and also the screen. To automate this and reduce the number of clicks, you can simply copy the link of the desired page; for instance, the link to the latest data would be something similar to `http://<YOUR-ZABBIX-SERVER>/zabbix/latest.php?sid=eec82e6bdf51145f&form_refresh=1&groupid=2&hostid=10095`.

Now, looking into the URL to automate the jump to the latest data, you need to replace the variant part of the URL with the macros wherever available.

The `sid` value in the URL represents the session ID; it is passed to avoid the one-click attack, also known as **session riding**. This field can be removed. The `groupid` value in the specific latest data example can be omitted, so the URL can be reduced to `http://<YOUR-ZABBIX-SERVER>/zabbix/latest.php?form_refresh=1&hostid=10095`.

Now, the link is easy to generate. You can simply replace the `hostid` value with the macro `{HOST.ID}` as `http://<YOUR-ZABBIX-SERVER>/zabbix/latest.php?form_refresh=1&hostid={HOST.ID}`.

And configure the URL as shown in the following screenshot:

In the preceding screenshot, you can see that there is a link configured to **General Screen** that collects the most important graphs. The `http://<ZABBIX-SERVER>/zabbix/screens.php?sid=eec82e6bdf51145f&form_refresh=1&fullscreen=0&elementid=17&groupid=2&hostid=10094&period=3600&stime=20140807161304` URL is generated from the screen page of a particular host.

This time again, you can omit the `sid` value in the preceding URL since it specifies a period. If this parameter is absent, you will be taken to a screen that displays the last hour of data. You can also remove the `stime`, `groupid`, and `elementid` values. The reduced URL will be `http://<ZABBIX-SERVER>/zabbix/screens.php?form_refresh=1&fullscreen=0&hostid=10094& groupid=2`.

Now, to make it dynamic, you need to replace the values of `hostid` and `groupid` with the macros, such as `http://<ZABBIX-SERVER>/zabbix/screens.php?form_re fresh=1&fullscreen=0&hostid={HOST.ID}&groupid={HOSTGROUP.ID}`.

The result of this customization is shown in the following screenshot:

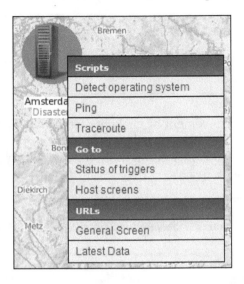

As you can see, by clicking on the host that has issues you have two new shortcuts other than **Latest Data** and **General Screen**, with a link that is dynamically created for each host.

This kind of behavior allows you to create a master-detail view. In this case, the master is your map, and the detail can be, for instance, the screen or the latest data window. You can create custom menus that can run a script or bring you directly to the trigger status or the **Host screens**.

> Here, you can add more scripts to run against the host. To add another script (and see it in the **Scripts** section), you need to go to **Administration | Scripts**. This will take you to the script's administration panel.

Finally, inside the map

Once you have completed this setup, you can begin the nice part of the configuration. Once inside the map, the options that you will find is quite simple and user friendly, as shown in the following screenshot:

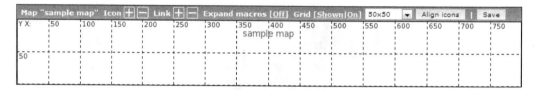

In the map, you can add an element by clicking on the **+** sign and remove it by clicking on the **-** sign. The element will appear in the upper-left corner of the map. By clicking on that icon, a configuration panel will appear, as shown in the following screenshot:

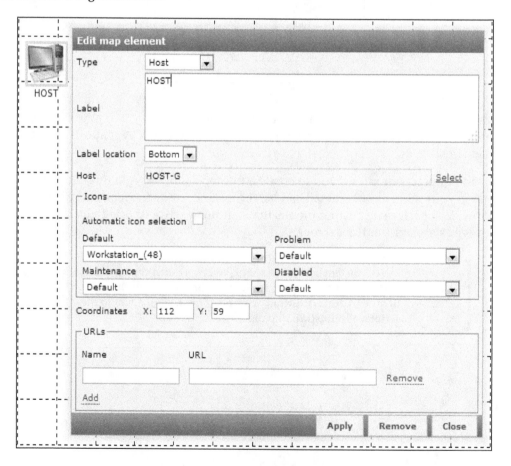

The element type, by default, is **Icon**. In the preceding screenshot, it is marked as **Host**, but it can be any one of the following:

- **Host**: This icon will represent the status of all the triggers of the selected host
- **Map**: This icon will represent the status of all the elements of the map
- **Trigger**: This icon will represent the status of the single trigger selected
- **Host group**: This icon will represent the status of all the triggers of all the hosts that belong to the selected group
- **Image**: This icon will just be an image not linked to any source (trigger host and so on)

The **Label** section is another strong point of the element. Here, you can freely write normal text or use macros.

The next field may vary depending on what you choose as the element type and can be one of the following:

- Host: This selects the host
- Map: This selects the map
- Trigger: This selects the trigger
- Host group: This selects the host group
- Icon (default): This selects the icon to be used

> With Host group, you can group all your hosts as per the location, for example, city, nations, or continents. This will group all the trigger statuses per location in a nice representation. You can also add a custom URL.

Hosts and triggers have already been covered and are quite intuitive to understand. Probably, it is not immediately understood why we should insert a map inside a map. An efficient use of this scenario is that you can produce a nice drilldown with a general map view that gathers together all the submaps detailed per location or nation. This helps you to produce a drilldown until the final destination; for instance, try to think about a drilldown that comes from nations, down to the city, and deep into the data center, ending on the rack where your server is contained.

The **Icon** element inside a map is an image that can have a URL associated with. Their function is to add a graphic element to your map that contains the URL, and have the shortcuts directly on your own map.

Right after that, there is the **Icons** section. Here, if you checked the **Automatic icon selection** checkbox, icon mapping (defined in the map configuration) would be used to choose the icons to be used.

 Defining an icon mapping in the map configuration will save you a lot of clicks. Also, it is a repetitive task. So, for instance, you can define your standard icons for the hosts, and they will then be used here.

If you haven't defined an icon mapping or if you want to use an item different from the previous choice, you can specify the icons that will be used in those cases, which can be one of the following:

- **Default**
- **Problem**
- **Maintenance**
- **Disable**

The **Coordinates** section expresses the exact location of the element in pixels and, as the previous item, you can configure a dedicated URL for this kind of host too.

Imagine that you have produced different kinds of screens (the screens will be discussed later in this chapter): one that collects all the metric graphs and triggers used to monitor an application server and another one with all the metrics needed to monitor the status of your database. Well, here, if your host is a DBMS, you can create a URL to jump directly to the RDBMS screen. If it is an application server, you can create a custom URL that will take you directly to the application server screens, and so on.

As you can see, this is an interesting feature and will make your map useful to your support team.

Selecting elements

In the map configuration, you can select multiple elements by selecting the first one, and then, keeping the *Ctrl* (or *Shift*) key pressed, selecting the other elements. For a multiple selection, you can drag a rectangle area, which will then select all the elements in the drawn rectangle.

Once you have selected more than one element, the element form switches to the **Mass update elements** window, as shown in the following screenshot:

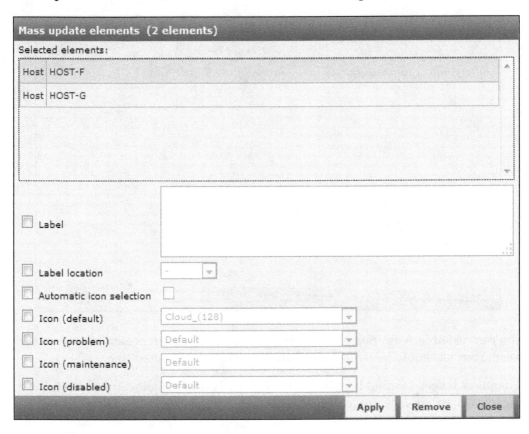

Here, you can update the icons, labels, and label locations for all the selected hosts in bulk.

To have an efficient update of all the labels, it is strongly advised that you use macros.

Now, it's time to inter link your servers in exactly the way that they are physically connected. To create a link between two hosts, you only need to select the hosts that need to be linked together and click on the + symbol in the **Link** section of the map.

The links section will appear right below the **Mass update elements** form, as shown
in the following screenshot:

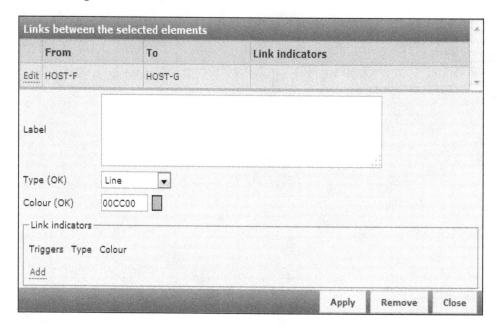

You can customize your link with labels and also change the representation type and
color. You can choose between **Line**, **Bold line**, **Dot**, and **Dashed line**.

An option to keep in mind here is the possibility of connecting the link indicator to a
trigger, so basically, the link will change its color once a trigger is on fire.

 Here, you can connect the link to multiple triggers and
associate a different color to each one of them so that you
can understand which trigger is changing your link.

Playing with macros inside maps

Previously, we discussed the **Label** section where you can customize the label in
your graphs. Here, I think an example can clarify a lot the power of this section and
how this can improve and introduce benefits in your maps. As an example, you
can play with macros inside the map. Now, you have certain requirements for this,
such as you need to show the hostname, IP address, the status of triggers events (the
number of acknowledged events and the number of unacknowledged ones), and the
network traffic of your network interfaces, directly in the map.

This seems challenging work and, in fact it, is, but if you have a bit of knowledge about macros, this becomes an easy task. The request can be satisfied with the following code:

```
{HOSTNAME}
{HOST.CONN}
trigger events ack: {TRIGGER.EVENTS.ACK}
trigger events unack: {TRIGGER.EVENTS.UNACK}
Incoming traffic: {{HOSTNAME}:net.if.in[eth0].last(0)}
Outgoing traffic: {{HOSTNAME}:net.if.out[eth0].last(0)}
```

The first macro, {HOSTNAME}, will display the hostname of your selected host. The second macro, {HOST.CONN}, will display the IP address. The information about the triggers events, whether acknowledged or unacknowledged, is expressed in the next two lines using the macros {TRIGGERS.EVENTS.ACK} and {TRIGGER.EVENTS. UNACK}. The last two lines are more interesting because they are a composition of two nested macros.

In particular, to display the incoming traffic of your first network interface, you can ask Zabbix to retrieve the last value of the net.if.in[eth0] item. This kind of expression needs the hostname to be evaluated, so you need to write your hostname, that is, HOST-A (in this example) or use macros.

The last piece of information that Zabbix needs to produce as the requested output is the hostname. As mentioned earlier, this can be replaced with the {HOSTNAME} macro. So, the complete expression will be as follows:

```
Incoming traffic: {{HOSTNAME}:net.if.in[eth0].last(0)}
```

Obviously, for outgoing traffic, the expression is more or less the same, except that you need to retrieve the net.if.out[eth0] item of the network card. The result is shown in the following image:

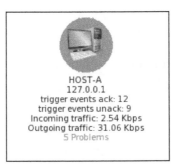

HOST-A
127.0.0.1
trigger events ack: 12
trigger events unack: 9
Incoming traffic: 2.54 Kbps
Outgoing traffic: 31.06 Kbps
5 Problems

Use {HOSTNAME} or {HOST.NAME} in all the labels and all the places where it is possible, so it will make things easy in the event of a mass update.

This is a comprehensive and charming output, wherein, without any clicks, you have your needed information directly in your map. In this example, you used the last() value of your item, but the other functions are also supported here such as last(), min(), max(), and avg().

Macros can be used in the same manner on links; an example is shown in the following screenshot:

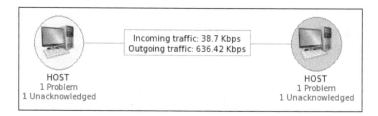

In the preceding screenshot, the traffic data on the link is generated using the same method that was previously explained. All those macro usages make your maps a lot more dynamic and appealing.

Visualizing through screens

In the previous section, we discussed adding custom URLs and introduced shortcuts to a screen section. Now it's time to go deep into **screens**. Screens are easy to generate and very intuitive to handle. Basically, a screen is a page that can display multiple Zabbix elements, such as graphs, maps, and text. One of the main differences between screens and maps is that in maps, you can place a lot of elements, but you can't, for instance, add a graph or the trigger status. They have two different targets. The screen can group all the elements that are common into a particular kind of server to have a complete picture of the situation.

Creating a screen

To create a screen, you need to navigate to **Configuration | Screen | Create**. A form will appear, asking for the screen name and the initial size in terms of columns and rows. After this step, you need to come back inside the screen that you just created.

In this part of the configuration, you will probably notice that there isn't a Save button. This is because screens are saved automatically every time that you complete an action, such as adding a graph. The screen appears similar to a table (basically, it is a table), as shown in the following screenshot:

CONFIGURATION OF SCREEN			
First screen			
	⊕	⊕	⊕
⊕	Change	Change	⊖
⊕	⊖	⊖	

Now, if you need more rows or columns, you only need to click on the **+** sign where you want to add fields as rows or as columns.

On a screen, you can add the following kinds of elements:

- **Action log**: This displays the history of recent actions
- **Clock**: This displays a digital or analog clock with the current server time or local time
- **Data overview**: This displays the latest data for a group of hosts
- **Graph**: This displays whether the graphs are single or custom
- **History of events**: This displays *n* lines (you can specify how many) of the latest events
- **Host group issues**: This displays the status of triggers filtered by `hostgroup`
- **Host issues**: This displays the status of triggers filtered by the host
- **Hosts info**: This displays high-level, host-related information
- **Map**: This displays a single map
- **Plain text**: This shows plain text data
- **Screen**: This displays another screen (one screen may contain other screens inside it)
- **Server info**: This displays the high-level server information
- **Simple graph**: This displays a single, simple graph
- **Simple graph prototype**: This displays a simple graph based on the item generated by low-level discovery
- **System status**: This displays the system status (it is close to **Dashboard**)
- **Triggers info**: This displays the high-level trigger-related information
- **Triggers overview**: This displays the status of triggers for a selected host group
- **URL**: Here, you can include content from an external source

All those sources have two common configuration parameters—the column span and the row span. With the column span, you can extend a cell to a certain number of columns. With the row span, you can extend a cell for a certain number of rows. For instance, in a table of two columns, if you indicate a column span of two, the cell will be centered in the table and will be widened with exactly two fields. This is useful to add a header to your screen.

Once you have inserted and configured your elements on the screen, you can move them using drag and drop, and all your settings will be preserved.

> You can freely drag and drop your configured elements; they will not lose their settings.

Most of the elements are not dynamic, which means that they will not be dynamically applied to all your hosts in a group.

Dynamic elements

Zabbix provides dynamic elements that are really useful:

- Graphs
- Graph prototype
- Simple graphs
- Simple graph prototype
- URL
- Plain text

The dynamic item Graph prototypes are based on custom graph prototypes created in low-level discovery (LLD) rules. Practically the Simple graph prototype is based on item prototypes in low-level discovery. While monitoring, the screen cell will display a graph created from an LLD-generated item. Please note that if the item is not generated, nothing will be displayed.

Also, starting with Zabbix 2.4, the URLs are now dynamic items. To properly support this new functionality, now we can use several macros in the URL field: {HOST.CONN}, {HOST.DNS}, {HOST.ID}, {HOST.IP}, {HOST.HOST}, {HOST.NAME}, and {$MACRO} user macro. These macros are quite useful, and we can do a lot with them, generating dynamic URLs to retrieve data from an external source.

> To properly see the dynamic URL elements displayed in **Monitoring | Screens**, you need to select a host. Without a selected host, you can only see the message No host selected.

Dynamic items can be identified by checking the following option:

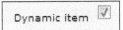

Now, for instance, you can add a map in your screen and some dynamic elements, such as graphs. When you add a dynamic element at the top of the screen, you will have a bar with some listboxes that will help you to change the target of your dynamic elements, as shown in the following screenshot:

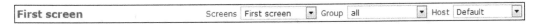

An example of a screen that mixes dynamic elements and standard elements is shown in the following screenshot:

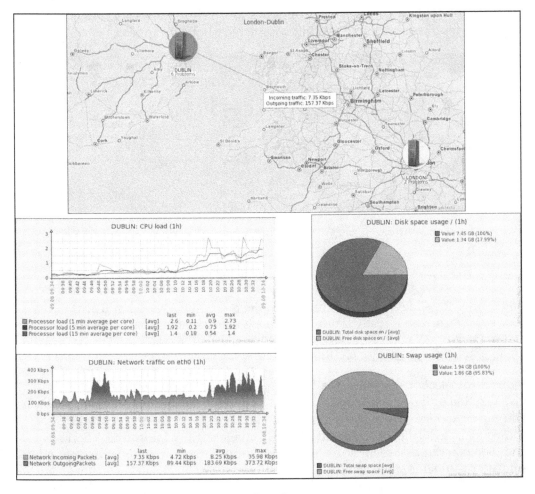

Obviously, when you choose and host this, it will affect only the dynamic graphs. You can switch between your two hosts and change the x axis. This will update all the dynamic elements on the same time base, making it easy to relate elements between them.

 Pie graphs and exploded pie graphs will display only the average value for your chosen period. To relate different groups of metrics between them, it is better to use a custom graph.

Visualizing the date through a slide show

Once you have created all your screens, you can provide a slide show to your helpdesk that implements a screen rotation.

Creating a slide show is easy; go to **Configuration | Slide shows | Create slide show**. A window, as shown in the following screenshot, will appear:

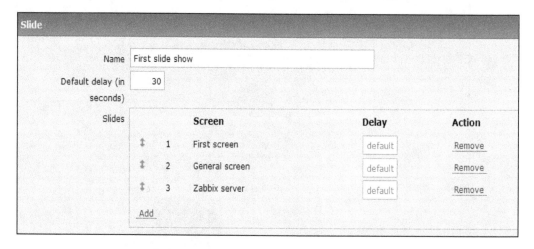

You can see the slide show configuration in the preceding screenshot. This configuration screen is really intuitive; **Name** identifies the name of your slide show, and in **Default delay (in seconds)**, you need to specify the default delay that will be applied to all the screens in the slide show.

In the **Slides** section—enumerated in the preceding screenshot to have a visualization order—you can specify a different delay for each one of them. Basically, you can customize how long each screen will be displayed. Once saved, your slide show will be available to be displayed upon navigating to **Monitoring | Screens**, and then you can choose in the `Slide shows` drop-down menu on the right-hand side after your slide show name.

In the slide show, you can only create a screen rotation. So, to add a single element, such as a graph or a map, on your rotation, you need to create a screen that contains your elements to be displayed. Using this method, you can basically add all that can be represented on a screen on the slide show.

If you want to speed up or slow down your slide show, you can change the refresh multiplier that will appear by clicking on the **Menu** icon (on the right-hand side of the listbox), which will return a window, as shown in the following screenshot:

Refresh time multiplier
x0.25
x0.5
x1
x1.5
x2
x3
x4
x5

Controlling center slides and the big display challenge

Displaying data on a big display is something challenging; first of all, you need to know who your target will be, their skills, and which role they exactly cover. After that, it is important to see where the screen is physically and its resolution.

You will most probably need to create an ad hoc screen for a big display to fit better on a widescreen. Screens for widescreen need to be developed horizontally. Most of the screens are usually developed with a web page in mind, so most probably they need to be scrolled down and up to read all the graphs. Such kinds of screens will not fit on your widescreen.

You need to bear in mind that the slide show doesn't scroll up and down automatically. You can add JavaScript to make it possible, but it is really complex to implement a screen that will rightly handle this scrolling up and down, and all this effort can be hardly justified. It is better and more productive to produce screens such that slide shows fit in the screen dimensions and resolution.

Considerations about slides on a big display

Once you have understood who your target is, their knowledge, and the typology of the work they do, you are already in a stable position. Now you can apply best practices that are generally useful when you need to show data on a big display. Basically, they need to be one of the following:

- Easy to read (comprehensible)
- Fit the big screen display
- Non-interactive
- Delay between the screens should be chosen as appropriate

First of all, keep things easy. This is a general rule: the easier the representations, the less the effort required by the helpdesk to read them. An easy and comprehensive screen will improve the helpdesk's reaction, which is our goal. You need to provide information in the best way. Never overload your screen with information; you need to choose the right amount of information to be displayed, and the fonts need to be comprehensive. Essentially, you need to choose which cut will have every screen, and the challenge is to choose how to display your monitored services.

If you need to monitor a large number of services, you need to choose the time to change the slide; don't spend too much time on the same screen. Keeping a screen for too much time on the monitor can become annoying, especially when the helpdesk is waiting to see the next slide. Unfortunately, there isn't a rule; you need to spend time with the first-level support and check with them as to what is the perfect timing.

One thing that simplifies the work is that you don't need to think about complex screens. A widescreen display doesn't need the drill-down feature implemented. People will just look at the screen, and the analysis will be done from their workstation.

Triggers are always welcome as they are easy to read, comprehensive, and immediate. But take care not to fill a page with them as it will then be unreadable.

Automated slide show

Once your slides are created and you are ready to run them, it is time to think about the user. Your widescreen and the relative workstation dedicated to this task need to have an account for sure.

In a real-world scenario, we do not want to see the login page on a big display. To avoid this, it is better to create a dedicated account with some customization.

The requirements are as follows:

- Avoid automatic disconnection
- Avoid the clicks needed to display the slide show

Both these features will be appreciated by your helpdesk.

To avoid automatic disconnection, there is a flag on the user configuration form that is designed just for that—the **Auto-login** flag. Once selected, you need to log in only the first time.

> The Auto-login flag will work only if your browser supports cookies; please ensure that plugins, antiviruses, and so on are not blocked.

Now since you have created a dedicated account, you need to customize the URL (after logging in) section; here, you need to link the URL to your screen.

To retrieve the appropriate URL, browse to your slide show and copy your link. For this example, the link would be `http://<your-zabbix-server> /zabbix/slides. php?sid=4258s278fa96eb&form_refresh=1&fullscreen=0&elementid=3`.

Basically, you need to know the `elementid` value of your slide show. In the following URL, you can remove the `sid` parameter. The definitive URL in our case will be `http://<your-zabbix-server> /zabbix/slides.php? form_refresh=1& fullscreen=0&elementid=3`.

> To jump directly to the full-screen mode, change the `fullscreen=0` parameter to `fullscreen=1`. This will further reduce human interaction.

Now this account has a first page. After login, the slide show starts in the fullscreen mode with really little human interaction.

> To properly present an automated slide show, it is very useful to run the browser in the fullscreen mode by pressing *F11*.

IT services

The last graphical element that will be discussed in this chapter is a high-level view of our monitored infrastructure. In a business-level view, there is no provision for low-level details, such as CPU usage, memory consumption, and free space. What the business would like to see is the availability of your services provided and the service-level agreements of your IT services.

Zabbix covers this point with **IT services**. A service is a hierarchical view of your service. Now imagine that you need to monitor your website (we discussed SLAs in *Chapter 1, Deploying Zabbix*). You need to identify your service components, for example, web server, application server, and DB server. For each one of them, you need to identify triggers that tell you whether the service is available or not. The hierarchical view is the one represented in the following screenshot:

Service	Status	Reason	Problem time		SLA / Acceptable SLA
root					
⊟ WEBSITE SLA Calculated	OK	-		0.0000	100.0000/ 99.9000
Web - Service on WEBSERVER is unavailable	OK	-		0.0000	100.0000/ 99.9000
RDBMS - Service on DATABASE SERVER is unavailable	OK	-		0.0000	100.0000/ 99.9000
Application - Service on DATABASE SERVER is unavailable	OK	-		0.0000	100.0000/ 99.9000

In this hierarchy, each node has a status; this status is calculated on the basis of triggers and propagated to the higher level with the selected algorithm. So, the lowest level of IT services is managed via triggers.

> Triggers are the core of IT service calculations; so, as you can imagine, they are of particular importance and really critical. You need to find out which your effective items are, to check for this trigger generation.

Triggers with the severities `Information` and `Not classified` are not considered and don't affect the SLA calculation.

Configuring an IT service

The way to configure an IT service is by navigating to **Configuration | IT services**; you can create your service here. The following screenshot displays a service previously configured:

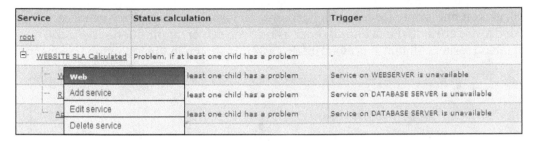

By clicking on a service, you can add a service, edit the current service, or delete it. The service configuration is composed of three forms: the first one describes the service, the second tab is dedicated to the dependencies, and the third is dedicated to the time.

On the service tab, you need to define your own service name. In this particular example, the website SLA is calculated; of course, a website is composed of different components, such as the web server, application server, and a DBMS. In a three-level environment, they are usually on a dedicated server. Now, since all the three components are vital for our merchant website, we need to calculate the SLA propagating the problems. This means that if the child of our website has a problem, the whole website has a problem, and this will reflect in the SLA calculation.

Zabbix provides the following three options in the status calculation algorithm:

- **Do not calculate**: This option ignores the status calculation completely.
- **Problem, if at least one child has a problem**: This means that if each one of our three components has an issue, the service will be considered unavailable. This is the case when each one of the servers doesn't have a failover node.
- **Problem, if all the children has a problem**: To propagate the problem, all the children need to be affected by the problem. This case is typical for a clustered or load-balanced service, where there are many nodes to provide a service, and all the nodes need to be down to propagate the issue to the parent node.

Once you define the algorithm, you need to define the SLA percentage of your service. This is used to display the SLA issue with different colors in the report.

The next step is the trigger definition that will enable Zabbix to know when your service has an issue. Since Zabbix provides a hierarchical view, you can have a service composed of many components, so the intermediate level can avoid a trigger definition that is needed on the lowest level.

The last option is **Sort order (0->999)**. This, of course, doesn't affect the SLA calculation but is only for cosmetic purposes. To visualize a report, for instance, your three levels are sorted in a logical order as the web server, application server, and database server. All that is previously discussed is shown in the following screenshot:

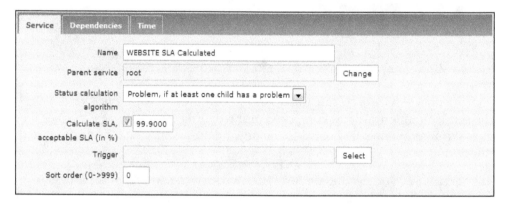

The following screenshot shows the dependencies; here, you don't need to define each one of them because they are defined automatically once you design your hierarchical view. Now, it is possible that one of your services is already defined for a reason in another layer of the service. If this is the case, you only need to mark the service as soft linked by checking the **Soft** checkbox:

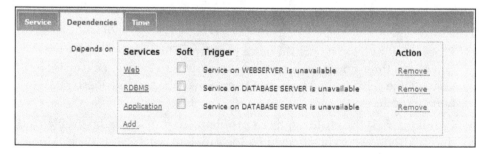

If a service has only soft-linked dependencies, it can be deleted. In this case, you don't need to delete all the child services first; this can be used to quickly delete the whole service.

The last tab is used to set the service time. By default, Zabbix considers that a service needs to be available 24 hours a day, for 7 days of the week, and the whole year (*24x7x365*). Fortunately, for system administrators, not all the services have this requirement. If this is true of you, you can define your **Uptime** and **Downtime** periods, as shown in the following screenshot:

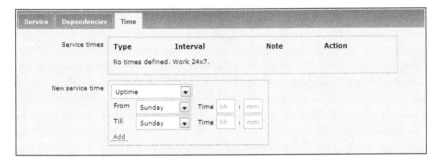

> The periods defined here are basically **Uptime** and **Downtime** windows. A problem that occurs during a **Downtime** window will not affect the SLA calculation. Here, it is possible to also add a one-time downtime, which is useful to define an agreed maintenance without an impact on the SLA.

Once you have completed the hierarchical definition of your service, the result is available by navigating to **Monitoring | IT services**.

Summary

In this chapter, we covered all the graphical elements that Zabbix provides and showed you how to use them in an efficient way. This chapter also enabled you to deliver efficient slide shows to your helpdesk, making you aware of the best practices in this difficult task. Now, you probably understood that this part of the Zabbix setup will require time to be well implemented. Also, it is easier to understand for a non-technical audience, and the information provided with the graphical elements has a big impact on your audience. This forces you to be precise and take a lot of care in this task, but this will be paid back to you by providing a lot of powerful elements to use and adding more strength to your argument. All those graphical elements are fundamentals if you need to argue with the business or the purchase manager to expand the business or buy hardware.

In the next chapter, you will see how to manage complex triggers and trigger conditions. The next chapter will also make you aware of the right amount of triggers and alarms that you should implement so as not to be overloaded by alarms, with the consequence of losing the critical ones.

6
Managing Alerts

Checking conditions and alarms is the most characteristic function of any monitoring system, and Zabbix is no exception. What really sets Zabbix apart is that every alarm condition or trigger (as it is known in this system) can be tied not only to a single measurement, but also to an arbitrary complex calculation based on all of the data available to the Zabbix server. Furthermore, just as triggers are independent from items, the actions that the server can take based on the trigger status are independent from the individual trigger, as you will see in the subsequent sections.

In this chapter, you will learn the following things about triggers and actions:

- Creating complex, intelligent triggers
- Minimizing the possibility of false positives
- Setting up Zabbix to take automatic actions based on the trigger status
- Relying on escalating actions

An efficient, correct, and comprehensive alerting configuration is a key to the success of a monitoring system. It's based on extensive data collection, as discussed in *Chapter 4, Collecting Data*, and eventually leads to managing messages, recipients, and delivery media, as we'll see later in the chapter. But all this revolves around the conditions defined for the checks, and this is the main business of triggers.

Understanding trigger expressions

Triggers are quite simple to create and configure—choose a name and a severity, define a simple expression using the expression form, and you are done. The expression form, accessible through the **Add** button, lets you choose an item, a function to perform on the item's data, and some additional parameters and gives an output as shown in the following screenshot:

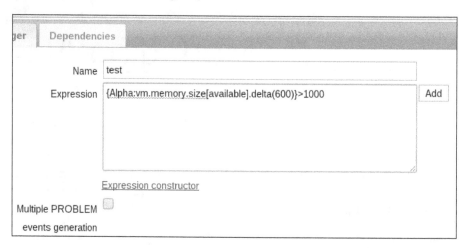

You can see how there's a complete item key specification, not just the name, to which a function is applied. The result is then compared to a constant using a *greater than* operator. The syntax for referencing item keys is very similar to that for a calculated item. In addition to this basic way of referring to item values, triggers also add a comparison operator that wraps all the calculations up to a Boolean expression. This is the one great unifier of all triggers; no matter how complex the expression, it must always return either a True value or a False value. This value is, of course, directly related to the state of a trigger, which can only be OK if the expression evaluates to False, or PROBLEM if the expression evaluates to True. There are no intermediate or soft states for triggers.

> A trigger can also be in an UNKNOWN state if it's impossible to evaluate the trigger expression (because one of the items has no data, for example).

A trigger expression has two main components:

- Functions applied to the item data
- Arithmetical and logical operations performed on the functions' results

From a syntactical point of view, the *item and function* component has to be enclosed in curly brackets, as illustrated in the preceding screenshot, while the arithmetical and logical operators stay outside the brackets:

Selecting items and functions

You can reference as many items as you want in a trigger expression as long as you apply a single function to every single item. This means that, if you want to use the same item twice, you'll need to specify it twice completely, as shown in the following code:

```
{Alpha:log[/tmp/operations.log,,,10,skip].nodata(600)}=1 or
{Alpha:log[/tmp/operations.log,,,10,skip].str(error)}=1
```

The previously discussed trigger will evaluate to PROBLEM if there are no new lines in the `operations.log` file for more than 10 minutes or if an error string is found in the lines appended to that same file.

> Zabbix doesn't apply short-circuit evaluation of the *and* and *or* (previously, until Zabbix 2.4, they were expressed with & and |) operators; every comparison will be evaluated regardless of the outcome of the preceding ones.

Of course, you don't have to reference items from the same host; you can reference different items from different hosts and on different proxies too (if you can access them), as shown in the following code:

```
{Proxy1:Alpha:agent.ping.last(0)}=0 and
{Proxy2:Beta:agent.ping.last(0)}=0
```

Here, the trigger will evaluate to PROBLEM if both the hosts `Alpha` and `Beta` are unreachable. It doesn't matter that the two hosts are monitored by two different proxies. Everything will work as expected as long as the proxy where the trigger is defined has access to the two monitored hosts' historical data. You can apply all the same functions available for calculated items to your items' data. The complete list and specification are available on the official Zabbix wiki (https://www.zabbix.com/documentation/2.4/manual/appendix/triggers/functions), so it would be redundant to repeat them here, but a few common aspects among them deserve a closer look.

Choosing between seconds and a number of measurements

Many trigger functions take a `sec` or `#num` argument. This means that you can either specify a time period in seconds or a number of measurements, and the trigger will take all of the item's data in the said period and apply the function to it. So, the following code will take the minimum value of Alpha's CPU idle time in the last 10 minutes:

```
{Alpha:system.cpu.util[,idle].min(600)}
```

The following code, unlike the previous one, will perform the same operation on the last ten measurements:

```
{Alpha:system.cpu.util[,idle].min(#10)}
```

> Instead of a value in seconds, you can also specify shortcuts such as `10m` for 10 minutes, `2d` for 2 days, and `6h` for 6 hours.

Which one should you use in your triggers? While it obviously depends on your specific needs and objectives, each one has its strengths that make it useful in the right context. For all kinds of passive checks initiated by the server, you'll often want to stick to a time period expressed as an absolute value. A `#5` parameter will vary quite dramatically as a time period if you vary the check interval of the relative item. It's not usually obvious that such a change will also affect related triggers. Moreover, a time period expressed in seconds may be closer to what you really mean to check and thus may be easier to understand when you'll visit the trigger definition at a later date. On the other hand, you'll often want to opt for the `#num` version of the parameter for many active checks, where there's no guarantee that you will have a constant, reliable interval between measurements. This is especially true for trapper items of any kind and for log files. With these kinds of items, referencing the number of measurements is often the best option.

The date and time functions

All the functions that return a time value, whether it's the current date, the current time, the day of the month, or the day of the week, still need a valid item as part of the expression. These can be useful to create triggers that may change their status only during certain times of the day or during certain specific days or, better yet, to define well-known exceptions to common triggers when we know that some otherwise unusual behavior is to be expected, for example, a case where there's a bug in one of your company's applications that causes a rogue process to quickly fill up a filesystem with huge log files. While the development team is working on it, they ask you to keep an eye on the said filesystem and kill the process if it's filling the disk up too quickly. As with many things in Zabbix, there's more than one way to approach this problem, but you decide to keep it simple and find that, after watching the trending data on the host's disk usage, a good indicator that the process is going rogue is that the filesystem has grown by more than 3 percent in 10 minutes:

```
{Alpha:vfs.fs.size[/var,pused].delta(600)}>3
```

The only problem with this expression is that there's a completely unrelated process that makes a couple of big file transfers to this same filesystem every night at 2 a.m. While this is a perfectly normal operation, it could still make the trigger switch to a PROBLEM state and send an alert. Adding a couple of time functions will take care of that, as shown in the following code:

```
{Alpha:vfs.fs.size[/var,pused].delta(600)}>3 and
({Alpha:vfs.fs.size[/var,pused].time(0)}<020000 or
  {Alpha:vfs.fs.size[/var,pused].time(0)}>030000 )
```

Just keep in mind that all the trigger functions return a numerical value, including the date and time ones, so it's not really practical to express fancy dates, such as *the first Tuesday of the month* or *last month* (instead of the last 30 days).

Trigger severity

Severity is little more than a simple label that you attach to a trigger. The web frontend will display different severity values with different colors, and you will be able to create different actions based on them, but they have no further meaning or function in the system. This means that the severity of a trigger will not change over time based on how long that trigger has been in a PROBLEM state, nor can you assign a different severity to different thresholds in the same trigger. If you really need a warning alert when a disk is over 90 percent full and a critical alert when it's 100 percent full, you will need to create two different triggers with two different thresholds and severities. This may not be the best course of action though, as it could lead to warnings that are ignored and not acted upon, critical warnings that will fire up when it's already too late and you have already lost service availability, just a redundant configuration with redundant messages and more possibilities of mistakes, or an increased signal-to-noise ratio.

A better approach would be to clearly assess the actual severity of the potential for the disk to fill up and create just one trigger with a sensible threshold and, possibly, an escalating action if you fear that the warning could get lost among the others.

Choosing between absolute values and percentages

If you look at many native agent items, you'll see that a lot of them can express measurements either as absolute values or as percentages. It often makes sense to do this while creating one's own custom items as both representations can be quite useful in and of themselves. When it comes to creating triggers on them, though, the two can differ quite a lot, especially if you have the task of keeping track of available disk space.

Filesystem sizes and disk usage patterns vary quite a lot between different servers, installations, application implementations, and user engagements. While a free space of 5 percent of a hypothetical disk A could be small enough that it would make sense to trigger a warning and act upon it, the same 5 percent could mean a lot more space for a large disk array, enough for you to not really need to act immediately but plan a possible expansion without any urgency. This may lead you to think that percentages are not really useful in these cases and even that you can't really put disk-space-related triggers in templates as it would be better to evaluate every single case and build triggers that are tailor-made for every particular disk with its particular usage pattern. While this can certainly be a sensible course of action for particularly sensible and critical filesystems, it can quickly become too much work in a large environment where you may need to monitor hundreds of different filesystems.

This is where the delta function can help you create triggers that are general enough that you can apply them to a wide variety of filesystems so that you can still get a sensible warning about each one of them. You will still need to create more specialized triggers for those special, critical disks, but you'd have to anyway.

While it's true that the same percentages may mean quite a different thing for disks with a great difference in size, a similar percentage variation of available space on a different disk could mean quite the same thing: the disk is filling up at a rate that can soon become a problem:

```
{Template_fs:vfs.fs.size[/,pfree].last(0)}<5 and
({Template_fs:vfs.fs.size[/,pfree].delta(1d)} or
{Template_fs:vfs.fs.size[/,pfree].last(0,1d) } > 0.5)
```

The previously discussed trigger would report a PROBLEM state not just if the available space is less than 5 percent on a particular disk, but also if the available space has been reduced by more than half in the last 24 hours (don't miss the time-shift parameter in the last function). This means that no matter how big the disk is, based on its usage pattern it could quickly fill up. Note also how the trigger would need progressively smaller and smaller percentages for it to assume a PROBLEM state, so you'd automatically get more frequent and urgent notifications as the disk is filling up.

For these kinds of checks, percentage values should prove more flexible and easy to understand than absolute ones, so that's what you probably want to use as a baseline for templates. On the other hand, absolute values may be your best option if you want to create a very specific trigger for a very specific filesystem.

Understanding operations as correlations

As you may have already realized, practically every interesting trigger expression is built as a logical operation between two or more simpler expressions. Naturally, it is not that this is the only way to create useful triggers. Many simple checks on the status of an agent.ping item can literally save the day when quickly acted upon, but Zabbix also makes it possible, and relatively easy, to define powerful checks that would require a lot of custom coding to implement in other systems. Let's see a few more examples of relatively complex triggers.

Going back to the date and time functions, let's say that you have a trigger that monitors the number of active sessions in an application and fires up an alert if that number drops too low during certain hours because you know that there should always be a few automated processes creating and using sessions in that window of time (from 10:30 to 12:30 in this example). During the rest of the day, the number of sessions is neither predictable, nor that significant, so you keep sampling it but don't want to receive any alert. A first, simple version of your trigger could look like the following code:

```
{Appserver:sessions.active[myapp].min(300)}<5 and
{Appserver:sessions.active[myapp].time(0)} > 103000 and
{Appserver:sessions.active[myapp].time(0) } < 123000
```

 The session.active item could be a custom script, calculated item, or anything else. It's used here as a label to make the example easier to read and not as an instance of an actual ready-to-use native item.

The only problem with this trigger is that if the number of sessions drops below five in that window of time but it doesn't come up again until after 12:30, the trigger will stay in the PROBLEM state until the next day. This may be a great nuisance if you have set up multiple actions and escalations on that trigger as they would go on for a whole day no matter what you do to address the actual session's problems. But even if you don't have escalating actions, you may have to give accurate reports on these event durations, and an event that looks as if it's going on for almost 24 hours would be both incorrect in itself and for any SLA reporting. Even if you don't have reporting concerns, displaying a PROBLEM state when it's not there anymore is a kind of false positive that will not let your monitoring team focus on the real problems and, over time, may reduce their attention on that particular trigger.

A possible solution is to make the trigger return to the OK state outside the target hours if it was in a PROBLEM state, as shown in the following code:

```
({Appserver:sessions.active[myapp].min(300)}<5 and
{Appserver:sessions.active[myapp].time(0)} > 103000 and
{Appserver:sessions.active[myapp].time(0) } < 123000)) or
({TRIGGER.VALUE}=1 and
{Appserver:sessions.active[myapp].min(300)}<0 and
({Appserver:sessions.active[myapp].time(0)} < 103000 or
{Appserver:sessions.active[myapp].time(0) } > 123000))
```

The first three lines are identical to the trigger defined before. This time, there is one more complex condition, as follows:

- The trigger is in a PROBLEM state (see the note about the TRIGGER.VALUE macro)

- The number of sessions is less than zero (this can never be true)

- We are outside the target hours (the last two lines are the opposite of those defining the time frame preceding it)

> The TRIGGER.VALUE macro represents the current value of the trigger expressed as a number. A value of 0 means OK, 1 means PROBLEM, and 2 means UNKNOWN. The macro can be used anywhere you can use an item.function pair, so you'll typically enclose it in curly brackets. As you've seen in the preceding example, it can be quite useful when you need to define different thresholds and conditions depending on the trigger's status itself.

The condition about the number of sessions being less than zero makes sure that outside the target hours, if the trigger was in a PROBLEM state, the whole expression will evaluate to false anyway. False means that the trigger is switching to the OK state.

Here, you have not only made a correlation between an item value and a window of time to generate an event, but you have also made sure that the event will always spin down gracefully instead of potentially going out of control.

Another interesting way to build a trigger is to combine different items from the same hosts or even different items from different hosts. This is often used to spot incongruities in your system state that would otherwise be very difficult to identify.

An obvious case could be that of a server that serves content over the network. Its overall performance parameters may vary a lot depending on a great number of factors, so it would be very difficult to identify sensible trigger thresholds that wouldn't generate a lot of false positives or, even worse, missed events. What may be certain though is that if you see a high CPU load while network traffic is low, then you may have a problem, as shown in the following code:

```
{Alpha:system.cpu.load[all,avg5].last(0)} > 5 and
{Alpha:net.if.total[eth0].avg(300)} < 1000000
```

An even better example would be about the necessity to check for hanging or frozen sessions in an application. The actual way to do this would depend a lot on the specific implementation of the said application, but for illustrative purposes, let's say that a frontend component keeps a number of temporary session files in a specific directory, while the database component populates a table with the session data. Even if you have created items on two different hosts to keep track of these two sources of data, each number taken alone will certainly be useful for trending analysis and capacity planning, but they need to be compared to check whether something's wrong in the application's workflow. Assuming that we have previously defined a local command on the frontend's Zabbix agent that will return the number of files in a specific directory, and that we have defined an odbc item on the database host that will query the DB for the number of active sessions, we could then build a trigger that compares the two values and reports a PROBLEM state if they don't match:

```
{Frontend:dir.count[/var/sessions].last(0)} <>
{Database:sessions.count.last(0)}
```

 The <> term in the expression is the *not equal* operator that was previously expressed as # is now expressed with <> starting with Zabbix 2.4.

Aggregated and calculated items can also be very useful in building effective triggers. The following one will make sure that the ratio between active workers and the available servers doesn't drop too low in a grid or cluster:

```
{ZbxMain:grpsum["grid", "proc.num[listener]", last, 0].last(0)} /
{ZbxMain:grpsum["grid", "agent.ping", last, 0].last(0)} < 0.5
```

All these examples should help drive home the fact that once you move beyond checking for simple thresholds with single-item values and start correlating different data sources together in order to have more sophisticated and meaningful triggers, there is virtually no end to all the possible variations of trigger expressions that you can come up with.

By identifying the right metrics, as explained in *Chapter 4, Collecting Data*, and combining them in various ways, you can pinpoint very specific aspects of your system behavior; you can check log files together with the login events and network activity to track down possible security breaches, compare a single server's performance with the average server performance in the same group to identify possible problems in service delivery, and do much more.

This is, in fact, one of Zabbix's best-kept secrets that really deserve more publicity; its triggering system is actually a sophisticated correlation engine that draws its power from a clear and concise method to construct expressions as well as from the availability of a vast collection of both current and historical data. Spending a bit of your time studying it in detail and coming up with interesting and useful triggers that are tailor-made for your needs will certainly pay you back tenfold as you will end up not only with a perfectly efficient and intelligent monitoring system, but also with a much deeper understanding of your environment.

Managing trigger dependencies

It's quite common that the availability of a service or a host doesn't depend only on the said host by itself, but also on the availability of any other machine that may provide connectivity to it. For example, if a router goes down, whereby an entire subnet is isolated, you would still get alerts about all the hosts in the said network that will suddenly be seen as unavailable from Zabbix's point of view even if it's really the router's fault. A dependency relationship between the router and the hosts behind it would help alleviate the problem because it would make the server skip any trigger check for the hosts in the subnet in case the router becomes unavailable. While Zabbix doesn't support the kind of host-to-host dependencies that other systems do, it does have a trigger-to-trigger dependency feature that can largely perform the same function. For every trigger definition, you can specify a different trigger upon which your new trigger is dependent. If the parent trigger is in a PROBLEM state, the trigger you are defining won't be checked until the parent returns to the OK state. This approach is certainly quite flexible and powerful, but it also has a couple of downsides. The first one is that one single host can have a significant number of triggers, so if you want to define a host-to-host dependency, you'll need to update every single trigger, which may prove to be quite a cumbersome task. In this kind of situation, probably you can simplify the problem by adding your triggers within a custom template. Anyway, if you have only specific cases, this will not help as it would end up creating a template for each host, which is not ideal and will move the problem to the template. You can, of course, rely on the mass update feature of the web frontend as a partial workaround. A second problem is that you won't be able to look at a host definition and see that there is a dependency relationship with another host. Short of looking at a host's trigger configuration, there's simply no easy way to display or visualize this kind of relationship in Zabbix.

A distinct advantage of having a trigger-level dependency feature is that you can define dependencies between single services on different hosts. As an example, you could have a database that serves a bunch of web applications on different web servers. If the database is unavailable, none of the related websites will work, so you may want to set up a dependency between the web monitoring triggers and the availability of the database. On the same servers, you may also have some other service that relies on a separate license server or an identity and authentication server. You could then set up the appropriate dependencies so that you could end up having some triggers depend on the availability of one server and other triggers depend on the availability of another one, all in the same host. While this kind of configuration can easily become quite complex and difficult to maintain efficiently, a select few, well-placed dependencies can help cut down the amount of redundant alerts in a large environment. This, in turn, would help you to focus immediately on the real problems where they arise instead of having to hunt them down in a long list of trigger alerts.

Taking an action

Just as items only provide raw data and triggers are independent from them as they can access virtually any item's historical data, triggers, in turn, only provide a status change. This change is recorded as an event just as measurements are recorded as item data. This means that triggers don't provide any reporting functionality; they just check their conditions and change the status accordingly. Once again, what may seem to be a limitation and lack of power turns out to be the exact opposite as the Zabbix component in charge of actually sending out alerts or trying to automatically resolve some problems is completely independent from triggers. This means that just as triggers can access any item's data, actions can access any trigger's name, severity, or status so that, once again, you can create the perfect mix of very general and very specific actions without being stuck in a one-action-per-trigger scheme.

Unlike triggers, actions are also completely independent from hosts and templates. Every action is always globally defined and its conditions checked against every single Zabbix event. As you'll see in the following paragraphs, this may force you to create certain explicit conditions instead of implicit conditions, but that's balanced out by the fact that you won't have to create similar but different actions for similar events just because they are related to different hosts.

An action is composed of the following three different parts that work together to provide all the functionality needed:

- Action definition
- Action conditions
- Action operations

The fact that every action has a global scope is reflected in every one of its components, but it assumes critical importance when it comes to action conditions as it's the place where you decide which action should be executed based on which events. But let's not get ahead of ourselves, and let's see a couple of interesting things about each component.

Defining an action

This is where you decide a name for the action and can define a default message that can be sent as a part of the action itself. In the message, you can reference specific data about the event, such as the host, item, and trigger names, item and trigger values, and URLs. Here, you can leverage the fact that actions are global by using macros so that a single action definition could be used for every single event in Zabbix and yet provide useful information in its message.

You can see a few interesting macros already present in the default message when you create a new action, as shown in the following screenshot:

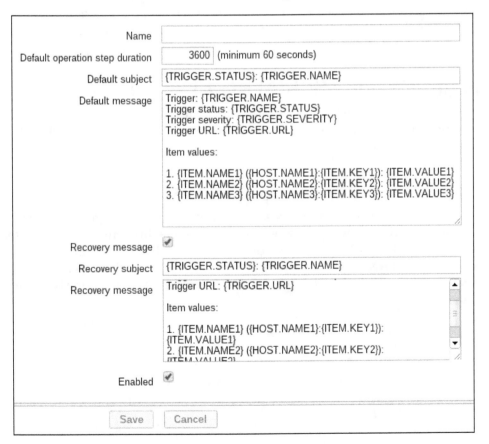

Most of them are pretty self-explanatory, but it's interesting to see how you can, of course, reference a single trigger—the one that generated the event. On the other hand, as a trigger can check multiple items from multiple hosts, you can reference all the hosts and items involved (up to nine different hosts and/or items) so that you can get a picture of what's happening by just reading the message.

Other interesting macros can make the message even more useful and expressive. Just remember that the default message can be sent not only via e-mail, but also via chat or SMS; you'll probably want to create different default actions with different messages for different media types so that you can calibrate the amount of information provided based on the media available.

You can see the complete list of supported macros in the official documentation wiki at `https://www.zabbix.com/documentation/2.4/manual/appendix/macros/supported_by_location`, so we'll look at just a couple of the most interesting ones.

The {EVENT.DATE} and {EVENT.TIME} macros

These two macros can help you to differentiate between the time a message is sent and the time of the event itself. It's particularly useful not only for repeated or escalated actions, but also for all media where a timestamp is not immediately apparent.

The {INVENTORY.SERIALNO.A} and friends macros

When it comes to hardware failure, information about a machine's location, admin contact, serial number, and so on, can prove quite useful to track it down quickly or to pass it on to external support groups.

Defining the action conditions

This part lets you define conditions based on the event's hosts, trigger, and trigger values. Just as with trigger expressions, you can combine different simple conditions with a series of **AND/OR** logical operators, as shown in the next screenshot. You can either have all **AND**, all **OR**, or a combination of the two, where conditions of different types are combined with **AND**, while conditions of the same type are combined with **OR**:

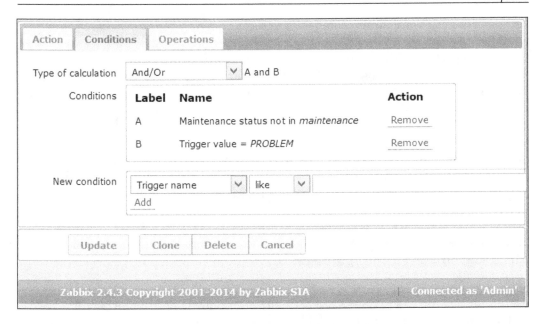

Observe how one of the conditions is **Trigger value = PROBLEM**. Since actions are evaluated for every event and since a trigger switching from PROBLEM to OK is an event in itself, if you don't specify this condition the action will be executed both when the trigger switches to PROBLEM and when the trigger switches back to OK. Depending on how you have constructed your default message and what operations you intend to do with your actions, this may very well be what you intended, and Zabbix will behave exactly as expected.

Anyway, if you created a different recovery message in the **Action** definition form and you forget the condition, you'll get two messages when a trigger switches back to OK — one will be the standard message, and one will be the recovery message. This can certainly be a nuisance as any recovery message would be effectively duplicated, but things can get ugly if you rely on external commands as part of the action's operations. If you forget to specify the condition **Trigger value = PROBLEM**, the external, remote command would also be executed twice — once when the trigger switches to PROBLEM (this is what you intended) and once when it switches back to OK (this is quite probably not what you intended). Just to be on the safe side, and if you don't have very specific needs for the action you are configuring, it's probably better if you get into the habit of putting **Trigger value = PROBLEM** for every new action you create or at least checking whether it's present in the actions you modify.

The most typical application to create different actions with different conditions is to send alert and recovery messages to different recipients. This is the part where you should remember that actions are global.

Let's say that you want all the database problems sent over to the database administrators group and not the default Zabbix administrators group. If you just create a new action with the condition that the host group must be DB Instances and, as message recipients, choose your DB admins, they will certainly receive a message for any DB-related event, but so will your Zabbix admins if the default action has no conditions configured. The reason is that since actions are global, they are always executed whenever their conditions evaluate to `True`. In this case, both the specific action and the default one would evaluate to `True`, so both groups would receive a message. What you could do is add an opposite condition in the default action so that it would be valid for every event, except for those related to the DB Instances host group. The problem is that this approach can quickly get out of control, and you may find yourself with a default action full of the *not in group* conditions. Truth is, once you start creating actions specific to message recipients, you either disable the default action or take advantage of it to populate a message archive for administration and reporting purposes.

Starting with Zabbix 2.4, there is another supported way of calculating action conditions. As you can easily imagine, the **And/Or** type of calculation clearly suffers from many limitations. Taking a practical example with two groups of the same condition type, you can't use the **AND** condition within a group and the **OR** condition within the other group. Starting with Zabbix 2.4, this limitation has been bypassed. If you take a look at the possible options to calculating the action condition, you can see that now we can choose even the **Custom expression** option, as shown in the following screenshot:

This new way allows us to use calculated formulas, such as:

- *(A and B) and (C or D)*
- *(A and B) or (C and D)*

But you can even mix the logical operators, as with this example:

- *((A or B) and C) or D*

This opens quite a few interesting scenarios of usage, bypassing the previous limitations.

Choosing the action operations

If the first two parts were just preparation, this is where you tell the action what it should actually do. The following are the two main aspects to this:

- Operation steps
- The actual operations available for each step

As with almost everything in Zabbix, the simplest cases that are very straightforward are most often self-explanatory; you just have a single step, and this step consists of sending the default message to a group of defined recipients. Also, this simple scenario can become increasingly complex and sophisticated but still manageable, depending on your specific needs. Let's see a few interesting details about each part.

Steps and escalations

Even if an action is tied to a single event, it does not mean that it can perform a single operation. In fact, it can perform an arbitrary number of operations called steps, which can even go on for an indefinite amount of time or until the conditions for performing the action are not valid anymore.

You can use multiple steps to both send messages as well as perform automated operations. Alternatively, you can use the steps to send alert messages to different groups or even multiple times to the same group with the time intervals that you want as long as the event is unacknowledged or even not yet resolved. The following screenshot shows a combination of different steps:

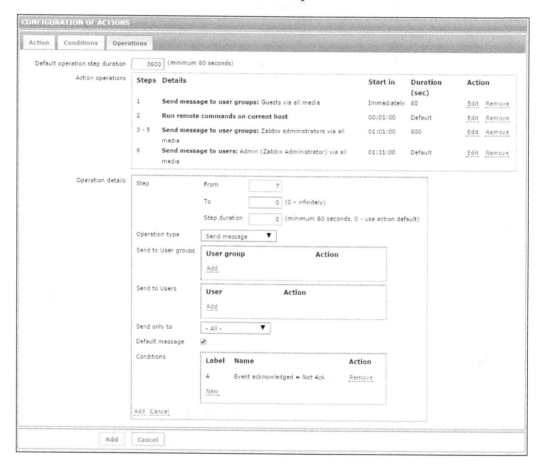

As you can see, step 1 starts immediately, is set to send a message to a user group, and then delays the subsequent step by just 1 minute. After 1 minute, step 2 starts and is configured to perform a remote command on the host. As step 2 has a default duration (which is defined in the main **Action** definition tab), step 3 will start after about an hour. Steps 3, 4, and 5 are all identical and have been configured together — they will send a message to a different user group every 10 minutes. You can't see it in the preceding screenshot, but step 6 will only be executed if the event is not yet acknowledged, just as step 7, which is still being configured. The other interesting bit of step 7 is that it's actually set to configure steps 7 to 0. It may seem counterintuitive, but in this case, step 0 simply means forever. You can't really have further steps if you create a step N to 0, because the latter will repeat itself with the time interval set in the step's **Duration(sec)** field. Be very careful in using step 0 because it will really go on until the trigger's status changes. Even then, if you didn't add a **Trigger status="PROBLEM"** condition to your action, step 0 can be executed even if the trigger switched back to OK. In fact, it's probably best never to use step 0 at all unless you really know what you are doing.

Messages and media

For every message step, you can choose to send the default message that you configured in the first tab of the **Action** creation form or send a custom message that you can craft in exactly the same way as the default one. You might want to add more details about the event if you are sending the message via e-mail to a technical group. On the other hand, you might want to reduce the amount of details or the words in the message if you are sending it to a manager or supervisor or if you are limiting the message to an SMS.

Remember that in the **Action** operation form, you can only choose recipients as Zabbix users and groups, while you still have to specify any media address for every user they are reachable to. This is done in the **Administration** tab of the Zabbix frontend by adding media instances for every single user. You also need to keep in mind that every media channel can be enabled or disabled for a user; it may be active only during certain hours of the day or just for one or more specific trigger severity, as shown in the following screenshot:

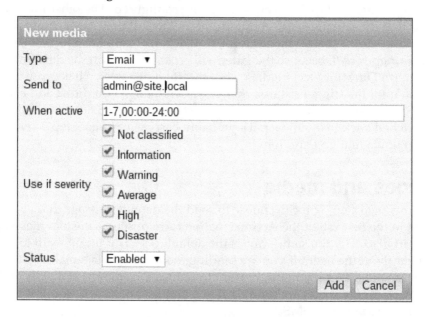

This means that even if you configure an action to send a message, some recipients may still not receive it based on their own media configuration.

While **Email, Jabber,** and **SMS** are the default options to send messages, you still need to specify how Zabbix is supposed to send them. Again, this is done in the **Media types** section of the **Administration** tab of the frontend. You can also create new media types there that will be made available both in the media section of user configuration and as targets to send messages to in the **Action** operations form.

If you have more than one server and you need to use them for different purposes or with different sender identifications, a new media type can be a different e-mail, jabber, or SMS server. It can also be a script, and this is where things can become interesting if not potentially misleading.

A custom media script has to reside on the Zabbix server in the directory that is indicated by the `AlertScriptPath` variable of `zabbix_server.conf`. When called upon, it will be executed with the following three parameters passed by the server:

- `$1`: The recipient of the message
- `$2`: The subject of the message
- `$3`: The body of the main message

The recipient will be taken from the appropriate user-media property that you defined for your users while creating the new media type. The subject and the message body will be the default ones configured for the action or some step-specific ones, as explained before. Then, from Zabbix's point of view, whether it's an old UUCP link, a modern mail server that requires strong authentication, or a post to an internal microblogging server, the script should send the message to the recipient by whatever custom methods you intend to use. The fact is that you can actually do what you want with the message; you can simply log it to a directory, send it to a remote file server, morph it to a syslog entry and send it over to a log server, run a speech synthesis program on it and read it aloud on some speakers, or record a message on an answering machine (as with every custom solution); the sky's the limit with custom media types. This is why you should not confuse custom media with the execution of a remote command—while you could potentially obtain roughly the same results with one or the other, custom media scripts and remote commands are really two different things.

Remote commands

These are normally used to try to perform corrective actions in order to resolve a problem without human intervention. After you've chosen the target host that should execute the command, the Zabbix server will connect to it and ask it to perform it. If you are using the Zabbix agent as a communication channel, you'll need to set `EnableRemoteCommands` to `1`, or the agent will refuse to execute any command. Other possibilities include SSH, Telnet, and IPMI (if you have compiled the relative options during server installation).

Remote commands can be used to do almost anything—kill or restart a process, make space on a filesystem by zipping or deleting old files, reboot a machine, and so on. They tend to seem powerful and exciting to new implementers, but in the authors' experience, they tend to be fragile solutions that tend to break things almost as often as they fix them. It's harder than it looks to make them run safely without accidentally deleting files or rebooting servers when there's no need to. The real problem with remote commands is that they tend to hide problems instead of revealing them, which should really be the job of a monitoring system. Yes, they can prove useful as a quick patch to ensure the smooth operation of your services, but use them too liberally and you'll quickly forget that there actually are recurring problems that need to be addressed because some fragile command somewhere is trying to fix things in the background for you. It's usually better to really try to solve a problem than to just hide it behind an automated temporary fix. This is not just from a philosophical point of view as, when these patches fail, they tend to fail spectacularly and with disastrous consequences.

So, our advice is that you use remote commands very sparingly and only if you know what you are doing.

Summary

This chapter focused on what is usually considered the core business of a monitoring system—its triggering and alerting features. By concentrating separately and alternately on the two parts that contribute to this function—triggers and actions—it should be clear to you how, once again, Zabbix's philosophy of separating all the different functions can give great rewards to the astute user. You learned how to create complex and sophisticated trigger conditions that will help you have a better understanding of your environment and have more control over what alerts you should receive. The various triggering functions and options as well as some of the finer aspects of item selection, along with the many aspects of action creation, are not a secret to you now.

In the next chapter, you will explore the final part of Zabbix's core monitoring components: templates and discovery functions.

7

Managing Templates

For all the monitoring power of Zabbix's items, graphs, maps, and triggers, it would be incredibly cumbersome to manually create every single one of these objects for every monitored host. In the case of a large environment, with hundreds or thousands of monitored objects, it would be practically impossible to manually configure all the items, graphs, and triggers needed for each host.

Using the templates facility, you'll define different collections of items, triggers, and, graphs in order to apply common configurations to any number of hosts, while still being able to manage any single aspect you may need to tweak for any single host.

The perfect complement to the template facility is Zabbix's discovery feature. Using it, you'll define a set of rules to let Zabbix know of new hosts without having to manually create them. You can also take advantage of the low-level discovery powers of the Zabbix agent so that you can automatically assign the correct items even for those highly variable parts of a system, such as the number and nature of disks, filesystems, and network interfaces.

In this chapter, you will learn the following things:

- Creating and leveraging the power of nested templates
- Combining different templates for the same hosts
- Using host discovery and actions to add templates to new hosts
- Configuring a low-level discovery to make templates even more general

Let's start from the beginning and see how a template is different from a regular host even if they look almost the same.

Creating templates

A host template is very similar to a regular host. Both are collections of items, triggers, graphs, screens, and low-level discovery rules. Both need a unique name just as any other entity in Zabbix. Both can belong to one or more groups. The crucial difference is that a host has one or more means to be contacted so that the Zabbix server can actually take item measurements on it, as illustrated in *Chapter 4, Collecting Data*. These can be one or more IP addresses, or host names, that represent agent interfaces, or SNMP, JMX, and IPMI ones. So, a host is an object that the Zabbix server will ask for information to or wait for data from. A template, on the other hand, doesn't have any access interface, so the Zabbix server will never try to check whether a template is alive or ask it for the latest item measurements.

The creation of a template is very straightforward, and there is not much to say about it. You navigate to the **Configuration | Templates** tab and click on the **Create template** button. The template creation form that will appear is composed of three different tabs. We'll look at the **Linked templates** tab and the **Macros** tab later in the chapter as these are not essential to create a basic template. In fact, the only essential element for a basic template is its name, but it can be useful to assign it to one or more groups in order to find it more easily in the other section of the web interface. If you have configured hosts already, you can also assign the template to the hosts you're interested in directly from the template creation tab. Otherwise, you'll need to go to the **Hosts** configuration tab and assign templates there. Once you're done, the template is created and available in the template list, but it's still an empty object. Your next job is to create the template's items, trigger, graphs, screens, and discovery rules, if any.

Adding entities to a template

Adding an item or any other entity to a template is virtually identical to the same operation performed on a regular host. This is especially true for items. As you already know, item keys are the basic building blocks of the Zabbix monitoring pipeline, and you don't have to specify any kind of address or interface when you create them as Zabbix will take this kind of information from the host the item is assigned to. This means that when you create items for a template, you are effectively creating items for an ideal host that will be later applied to real ones once you have linked the template to the hosts you want to monitor.

Templates, just like hosts, are essentially collections of items, triggers, and graphs. Since many of the concepts that we will explore apply equally to items, triggers, and graphs, for the rest of the chapter we'll use the term *entity* to refer to any of the three types of objects. In other words, you can understand an item, trigger, or graph every time you read *entity*, and items, triggers, and graphs when you read *entities* as a collective term.

This applies to other types of entities as well, but as they always reference one or more existing items, you need to make sure that you select the items belonging to the right template and not to a regular host:

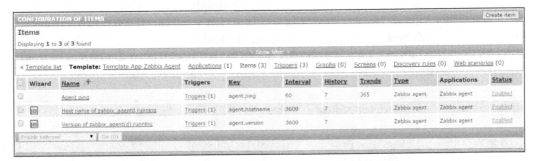

This may seem obvious, but it is far too easy to select the **Items**, **Graphs**, or **Screens** contained in the template using the links at the top of the window.

The main difference between template entities and host entities, especially when it comes to triggers, is that with template entities, macros are quite useful to make trigger and graph names or parameters more expressive and adaptable.

We can summarize the entities that can be grouped in a template as:

- Items
- Triggers
- Graphs
- Applications
- Screens
- Low-level discovery rules
- Web scenarios (since Zabbix 2.2)

It's important to also bear in mind that to be able to link a template to a host, the host itself needs to have items with unique names. Then, if the host already contains the template's items or a subset of them, we need to sort out the duplicates issue.

Using macros

As you've already seen in *Chapter 6, Managing Alerts,* macros are very useful to make a message general enough for it to be applied to a wide range of events. It will be the Zabbix server's job to substitute all the macros in a message with the actual content based on the specific event it's handling. Since an action message is effectively a template that has to be applied to a particular event, it's easy to see how the same concept is essential for the effectiveness of host templates. What changes is the context; while an event has a context that is quite rich since it can reference a trigger and one or more different items and hosts, the context of a simple, regular host is admittedly more limited. This is reflected in the number of macros available, as they are just a handful:

Macro name	Macro translates to	Notes
{HOST.CONN}	Hostname or IP address of the host	This will be identical to either {HOST.IP} or {HOST.DNS} depending on the **Connect to** option in the host's configuration form.
{HOST.DNS}	The host's hostname	This must correspond to the host's fully qualified domain name as defined in the domain's DNS server.
{HOST.HOST}	The host's name as defined in Zabbix	This is the main host identifier. It must be unique for the specific Zabbix server. If using an agent, the same name must be present in the agent's configuration on the host.
{HOST.IP}	The host's IP address	A host can have more than one IP address. You can reference them using {HOST.IP1}, {HOST.IP2}, and so on, up to {HOST.IP9}.
{HOST.NAME}	The host's visible name as defined in Zabbix	This will be the name visible in lists, maps, screens, and so on.

To better clarify the differences between the various {HOST.*} macros, let's see an example host configuration:

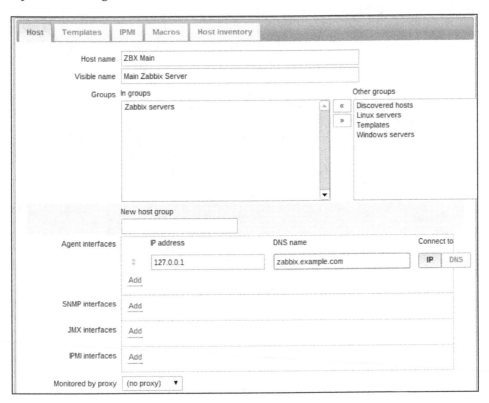

In this case, {HOST.HOST} will resolve to ZBX Main, {HOST.NAME} to Main Zabbix Server, {HOST.IP} to 127.0.0.1, and {HOST.DNS} to zabbix.example.com. Finally, since the **Connect to** option is set to **IP**, {HOST.CONN} will resolve to 127.0.0.1 as well.

The most obvious use of these macros is to make trigger and graph names more dynamic and adaptable to the actual hosts they will be used into. Since a graph's name is displayed as a header when viewing the graph, it's vital to distinguish between different graphs of the same type belonging to different hosts, especially when they are displayed together in a screen, as explained in *Chapter 5, Visualizing Data*.

A less obvious use of these macros is inside an item's key definition. We touched briefly on external scripts in *Chapter 4, Collecting Data*, and you'll meet them again in the next chapter, so we won't get into too much detail about them here. It would suffice to say that from an item creation point of view, all you need to know about an external script is its name and any parameters you may need to pass in order to execute it correctly.

Since external scripts, as is their nature, don't share any information with the rest of Zabbix other than the arguments they are passed and their return value, it's often essential to include the host's IP address or hostname as one of the arguments. This ensures that the script will connect to the right host and collect the right data. A single, well-configured script can perform the same operation on many different hosts thanks to the template systems and macros, such as {HOST.CONN}, {HOST.IP}, and so on.

Take, for example, a script that checks whether a particular application is alive using a custom protocol. You could have an external script, say app_check.sh, which takes a host name or IP address as an argument, connects to it using the application's protocol, and returns 1 if it's alive and well and 0 if the check fails. Your template item's key would look similar to the following screenshot:

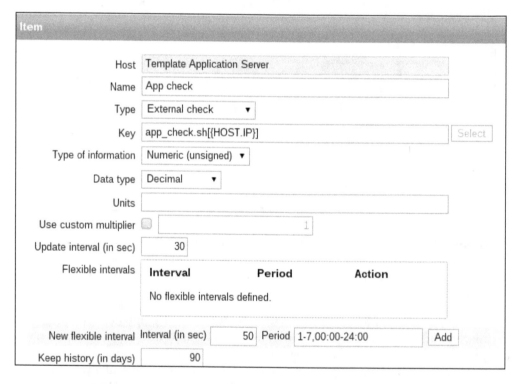

In these cases, using a macro as the argument to the item's key is the only way to make an external check for a part of a template and is useful for any regular host.

Another example would be that of a bunch of Zabbix hosts that don't represent regular operating system machines, physical or virtual, but single applications or single database instances. In a scenario like this, all the application hosts would share the same connections and interfaces—those of the actual server hosting the applications—and they would be linked to a template holding only items relevant to application-level (or database-level) measurements. To keep things simple, let's say that you have an application server (Alpha) hosting three different applications:

- A document archival facility (doku)
- A customer survey form manager (polls)
- A custom, internal microblogging site (ublog)

For each of these applications you are interested in, by and large, take the same measurements:

- The number of active sessions
- The amount of memory consumed
- The number of threads
- The network I/O
- The number of connections to the database

Again, for simplicity's sake, let's say that you have a bunch of external scripts that, given an IP address and an application name, can measure exactly the preceding metrics. External script keys tend to be easy to read and self-explanatory, but all of this can be equally applied to JMX console values, Windows performance counters, database queries, and any other kind of items.

One way to monitor this setup is to create only one host, Alpha and, in addition to all the regular OS- and hardware-monitoring items, a number of items dedicated to application measurements, which are repeated for each one of them. This can certainly work, but if you have to add a new application, you'll need to create all the items, triggers, and graphs related to it even if they differ from the rest by just the application's name.

As that is the only difference in an otherwise identical collection of entities, a more flexible solution would be to split the monitoring of every application to a different host and apply a common template.

> A host, from Zabbix's point of view, is just a collection of entities with one or more connection interfaces. It doesn't have to be an actual, physical (or virtual!) machine with a regular operating system. Any abstract but coherent collection of metrics and a means to retrieve them can be configured as a host in Zabbix. Typical examples are applications, database instances, and so on.

Instead of creating many similar items, triggers, and so on for the host, Alpha, you would create a custom application template and fill it with items that would look similar to the following screenshot:

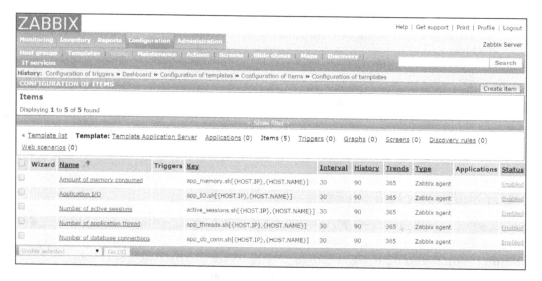

You can then create one host for each application, with Alpha's IP address as the connection interface, and with the application's name as the hostname. Linking the template you just created to the hosts would give you the same basic results as before but with much more flexibility; adding an application to be monitored now is a simple matter of creating a host and linking it to the correct template. If you move an application from one server to another, you just need to update its IP address. If you put all these application hosts in a separate group, you can even grant access to their monitoring data to a specific group of users without necessarily giving them access to the application server's monitoring data. And, it goes without saying that adding, deleting, or modifying an entity in the template apply immediately to all the monitored applications.

User-defined macros

A special class of macros is user-defined, template- and host-level macros. You can configure them in the **Macros** tab of every host or template creation and administration form. They are quite simple as they only provide a translation facility from a custom label to a predefined, fixed value. The following screenshot shows this:

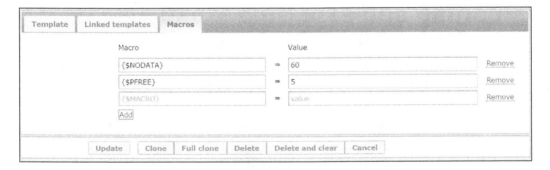

When used in a template, they prove quite useful in defining common thresholds for triggers, so if you need to modify a bunch of time-out triggers, you can just modify the {$NODATA} macro instead of changing every single trigger that uses it. User-defined macros can be used everywhere built-in macros can be used.

> If a user macro is used in items or triggers in a template, it is better to add that macro to the template in any case even if is defined on a global level. Doing so once you've exported your template to XML, you can freely import it into another system without taking the care to have all the user macros properly configured.

The usefulness is even greater when used in connection with nested templates, as we'll see in a short while.

The most common use cases of global and host macros are:

- Using all the advantages of a template with host-specific attributes: port numbers, filenames, accounts, and so on
- Using global macros for one-click configuration changes and fine-tuning

A practical example of macro usage can be the use of host-level macros in the item keys, such as *Status of SSH daemon*:

```
net.tcp.service[ssh,,{$SSH_PORT}]
```

This item can be assigned to multiple hosts once you've defined at the host level the value of {$SSH_PORT}. By doing so, you're generalizing a custom item where $SSH_PORT may change across servers; this can be done for HTTP services too, among others.

Importing and exporting templates

Zabbix provides a good and useful import/export functionality. The objects that can be exported and imported are the following:

- **Templates**: This includes all directly attached items, triggers, graphs, screens, discovery rules, and template linkage
- **Hosts**: This includes all directly attached items, triggers, graphs, discovery rules, and template linkage
- **Network maps**: This includes all related images; map export/import is supported since Zabbix 1.8.2
- Images
- Screens

 Using the Zabbix API, it is possible to export and import even the host groups.

The export functionality is quite easy to understand; anyway, the import function has been extended. The following screenshot captures this discussion:

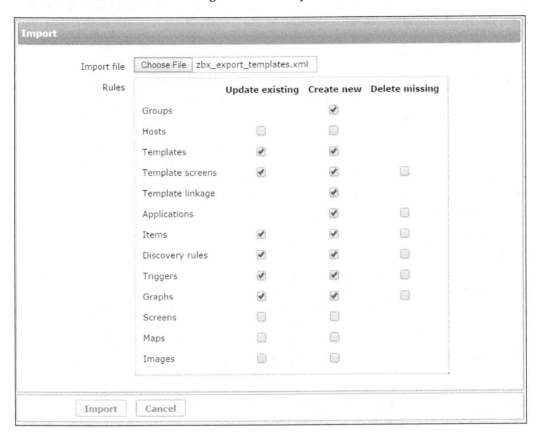

The import section is divided into three columns; the first one, **Update existing**, will force the update if an element is already defined. This function is fundamental if you want to update an element or simply add the missing objects. The second column, **Create new**, is quite simple to understand as it will enable the new element. The third and last column has been added with Zabbix 2.4. **Delete missing**, if selected, will delete all the elements that have not been exported if they are present in our setup.

As you can see, the Template objects are well defined as we can decide to export only **Template screens**, **Template linkage** and/or **Templates**.

Linking templates to hosts

To link a template to a host, you can either select the hosts you want to link from the template's configuration form, as we saw in the *Creating templates* section, or you can choose the template you need for a host in that host's configuration form by going into the **Template** tab.

Once linked, a host will inherit all of the template's entities. *Previously existing entities with the same name will be overwritten*, but entities not included in the template will remain as they are and will not be touched in any way by the linking operation.

All entities will maintain their original template's name when displayed in the configuration section of the web interface even when viewed from a host configuration page. However, this doesn't mean that modifying them from a template's configuration tab is the same as modifying them from a linked host's configuration tab.

If you modify an entity (item, trigger, graph, and so on) from a template's configuration tab, the modifications will apply immediately to all linked hosts. On the other hand, if you modify a template entity from a particular host's configuration tab, the changes will only apply to that host and not on a template level. While this can be useful to address any special circumstances for an otherwise regular host, it can also generate some confusion if you make many local changes that can become hard to keep track of. Moreover, not every aspect of a template entity can be modified at the host level. You can change the frequency of an item, for example, but not its key.

Unlinking a template from a host doesn't eliminate its entities unless you unlink and clear it. Be careful with this operation as all the items' historical data and trends would become unavailable. If you have collected any actual data, it's probably better to just unlink a template from a host and then disable any unused items and triggers, while retaining all of their historical data.

Nesting templates

Just as you can link a template to a host, you can also link a template to another template. The operation is identical to linking a template to a host; you navigate to the **Linked templates** tab in a template's configuration form and choose the templates you want to link.

While this may seem an awkward operation, it can prove quite useful in two cases.

The first application of nested templates is to make user macros even more general. Since a template inherits all of its linked templates' entities and properties, any custom macro will also be inherited and, thus, made available to the actual monitored hosts.

To take a concrete example, let's say you have a Template Macros template containing a {$PFREE} user macro with the value 5, among many others. You could use this macro to represent the amount of free disk space in percentages to check against, free available memory, or any other such threshold. This template could be linked to both the Template OS Linux and Template OS Windows templates, and the {$PFREE} macro used in these templates' triggers. From now on, if you ever need to modify the default value of the free disk space percentage to check against, you'll just need to change the original Template Macros template, and the updated value will propagate through the linked templates down to the monitoring hosts.

A second, somewhat more limited but still useful, way to use nested templates is to extend the inheritance beyond macros to all the other entities. This may become an advantage when you have a common set of features on a given technological layer but different uses on other layers. Let's take, for instance, the case where you have a large number of virtually identical physical servers that host just a couple of versions of operating systems (Linux and Windows, for simplicity's sake) but that in turn perform many different specialized functions: database, file server, web server, and so on.

You can certainly create a few monolithic templates with all the items you need for any given server, including hardware checks, OS checks, and application-specific ones. Alternatively, you can create a sort of hierarchy of templates. A common, hardware-level template that enables IPMI checks will be inherited by a couple of OS-specific templates. These, in turn, will be inherited by application-specific templates that will have names such as Linux Apache Template or Win Exchange Template. These templates will have all the items, triggers, and graphs specific to the applications that they are meant to monitor in addition to all the OS-specific checks they have inherited from the OS-level templates and the hardware-specific ones they have inherited from the HW-level templates. This means that, when creating a host, you will still just need to link it to a single template, but you'll also have a lot of flexibility in creating new templates and nesting them or modifying existing ones in only one place and watching the changes propagate along the template-linking chain. This also means maximum generality, while still maintaining the ability to make host-specific customizations if you need to.

Combining templates

Another way to make templates modular is to create specific templates for any given technological layer and product but not link them in a hierarchy at the template level.

You can instead link them — as many as you want — directly to the host you need to monitor as long as they don't have any conflicting or overlapping item names or keys. As in the preceding scenario, Host A could have an IPMI checks template, an OS Linux one, and an Apache server one linked, while Host B could have an IPMI checks template and an OS Linux one but then also have a PostgreSQL database template.

The end result is practically the same as the nested templates solution described previously, so which one should you choose? This is largely a matter of preference, but a possible criterion could be that if you have a relatively low number of low-level templates and good consistency in your hardware, OS, and technological configuration, the nested solution might be easier to manage. You'll only have to connect the templates once and then use them on a large number of hosts. This approach also works well with the host discovery facility as it keeps things simple when linking templates to hosts. If, on the other hand, you have a great number of low-level templates and great variability in your technological configuration and landscape, you may just as well pick and choose the templates you need when you create your hosts. Any pre-configuration, in fact, would only prove too rigid to be really useful. This approach works well if you want to always ponder how you are creating and configuring your hosts and also need a great deal of local customization that would make any aggressive inheritance feature a moot point.

Discovering hosts

A third way to link templates to hosts is to let the server do it automatically by combining Zabbix's host-discovery facility with discovery actions.

Zabbix's discovery facilities consist of a set of rules that periodically scan the network to look for new hosts or disappearing ones according to predetermined conditions.

The three methods that Zabbix can use to check for new or disappeared hosts, given an IP range, are:

- The availability of a Zabbix agent
- The availability of an SNMP agent
- Response to simple external checks (FTP, SSH, and so on)
- These checks can also be combined, as illustrated in the following example:

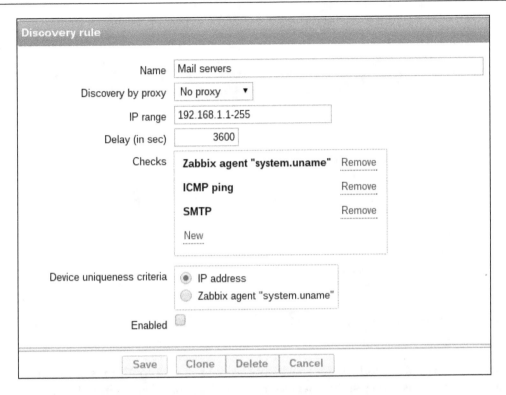

As you can see, when enabled, this rule will check every hour in the IP range
192.168.1.1-255 for any server that:

- Responds to an **ICMP ping** probe
- Has a correctly configured Zabbix agent that will return a value when asked for the system.uname item
- Has an **SMTP** listening port, which is usually associated with a mail server

As usual, with all things Zabbix, a discovery rule will not do anything by itself, except generate a discovery event. It will then be the job of Zabbix's actions facility to detect the said event and decide whether and how to act on it. Discovery event actions are virtually identical to trigger event actions. As you saw trigger event actions in *Chapter 6, Managing Alerts*, the following are the only differences when it comes to discovery events.

First, action conditions are a bit different, as can be expected, as shown in this following screenshot:

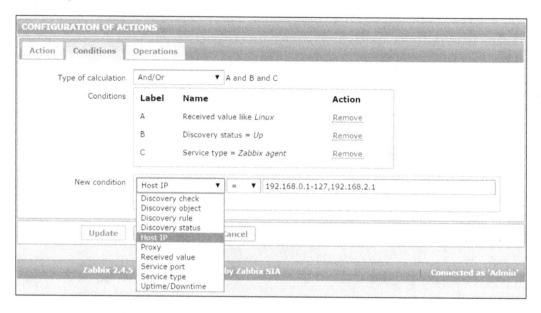

Instead of hostnames and trigger specifications, you can set conditions based on things such as **Discovery status**, **Service type**, and **Uptime/Downtime**. The **Received value** condition is of particular interest as it allows things such as differentiating between operating systems, application versions, and any other information you can get from a Zabbix or SNMP agent query.

This kind of information will be critical when it comes to configuring the action's operations. The following screenshot shows this:

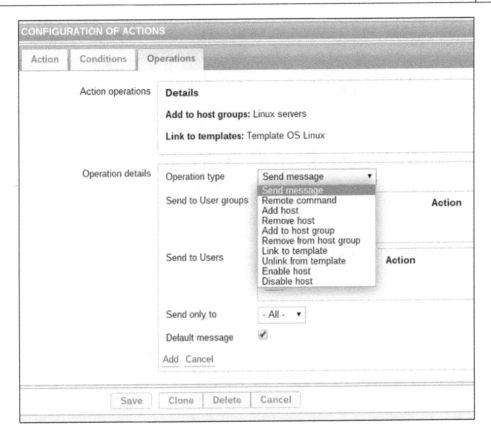

Sending a message and executing a remote command are the exact equivalents of the same operations available to trigger event actions. On the other hand, if adding (or removing) a host is quite a self-explanatory action when it comes to adding to a host group or linking to a template, it becomes clear that a good set of actions with specific received value conditions and template-linking operations can give a high level of automation to your Zabbix installation.

This high level of automation is probably more useful in rapidly changing environments that still display a good level of predictability depending on the kind of hosts you can find, such as fast-growing grids or clusters. In these kinds of environments, you can have new hosts appearing on a daily basis and perhaps old hosts disappearing at almost the same rate, but the kind of host is more or less always the same. This is the ideal premise for a small set of well-configured discovery rules and actions, so you don't have to constantly and manually add or remove the same types of hosts. On the other hand, if your environment is quite stable or you have very high host-type variability, you may want to look more closely at what and how many hosts you are monitoring as any error can be much more critical in such environments.

On the other hand, limiting discovery actions to sending messages about discovered hosts can prove quite useful in such chaotic environments or where you don't directly control your systems' inventory and deployment. In such a case, getting simple alerts about new hosts, or disappearing ones, can help the monitoring team keep Zabbix updated despite any communication failure between IT departments—accidental or otherwise.

The active agent auto-registration

Starting with Zabbix 2.0, it is possible to instruct the active Zabbix agent for auto-registration. This way, new hosts can be added for monitoring without configuring them manually on the server. The auto-registration of an unknown host can be triggered when an active agent asks for checks. This feature can be precious to implement an automatic monitoring of new cloud nodes. When a new node in the cloud comes up, Zabbix will automatically start collecting performance metrics and checking the availability of the host.

The active agent auto-registration can also monitor hosts that have passive checks. When the active agent asks for checks, provide them to the Zabbix server's `ListenIP` and `ListenPort` configuration parameters defined in the agent configuration file.

 Please note that if you have multiple IP addresses specified, only the first one will be sent to the server.

On the server side, Zabbix uses the IP and port that has been received by the agent.

 Here, in the event that the IP address has been delivered, Zabbix will use the IP address seen during the incoming connection. Also, if the port value is not delivered, Zabbix uses port `10050`.

Configuring the auto-registration

Let's see how we can configure this feature; we will look first at the agent side. On the agent side, you need to have the `Server` parameter specified within the agent configuration file. Then, if you've specified even the `Hostname` parameter in `zabbix_agentd.conf`, the server will use it to register the new monitored host; otherwise, Zabbix will use the physical hostname.

On the server side, we need to configure an action, select **Configuration | Actions**, select **Auto registration** as the event source, and then click on **Create action**. In the screenshot that follows, we've created an action named `Active auto-registration`:

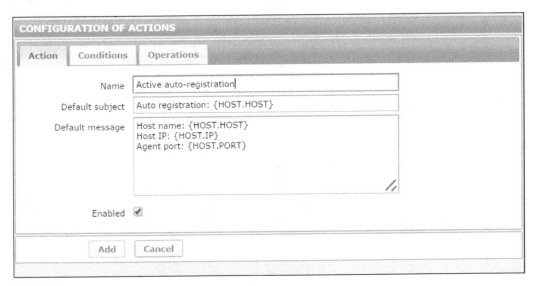

The real-case scenario

Here, you can play as much as you want with automation. If the hosts that will be auto-registering are supposed to be only supported for active monitoring (for instance, hosts that are behind a firewall), then it is worth creating a specific template and linking it to the new hosts. Let's see how we can play with auto-registration.

Here, to customize properly and automate the host configuration, we can define `HostMetadata` and `HostMetadataItem` on the agent side. A good example to understand this automation can be the following scenario—we would like to link Template OS Linux to all the auto-registered Linux hosts.

To do this, we need to add the following value to the `/etc/zabbix/zabbix_agentd.conf` agent configuration file:

```
HostMetadataItem=system.uname
```

Then, in our real-world scenario, `HostMetadataItem` will contain:

```
Linux servername.example.com 2.6.32-504.16.2.el6.x86_64 #1 SMP Wed Apr
22 06:48:29 UTC 2015 x86_64 x86_64 x86_64 GNU/Linux
```

Then, on the frontend, our action will be configured as follows:

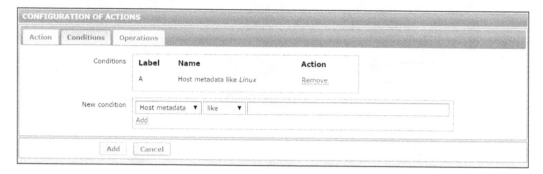

With **Conditions** such as **Host metadata like Linux**, the **Operations** tab will contain the elements shown in the following screenshot:

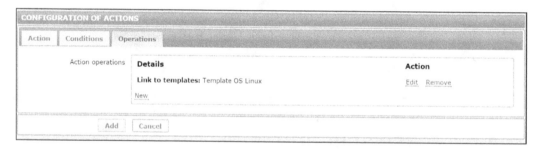

As you can see, once all the **Conditions** of the relative tab are satisfied, the **Operation** tab will link the host to **Template OS Linux**.

Now, as you can see, if we package the agent with the configuration file premade, we can heavily reduce the startup time of new hosts.

Low-level discovery

An even more useful and important feature of Zabbix templates is their ability to support special kinds of items, which are called low-level discovery rules. Once applied to actual hosts, these rules will query the host for whatever kind of resources they are configured to look for: filesystems, network interfaces, SNMP OIDs, and more. For every resource found, the server will then dynamically create items, triggers, and graphs according to special entity prototypes connected to the discovery rules.

The great advantage of low-level discovery rules is that they take care of the more variable parts of a monitored host, such as the type and number of network interfaces, in a dynamic and general way. This means that, instead of manually creating specific items and triggers of every host's network interfaces or filesystems or creating huge templates with any possible kind of item for a particular operating system and keeping most of these items disabled, you can have a reasonable number of general templates that will adapt themselves to the specifics of any given host by creating on the fly any entity needed based on discovered resources and previously configured prototypes.

Out of the box, Zabbix supports four discovery rules:

- Network interfaces
- Filesystem types
- SNMP OIDs
- CPUs and CPU cores

As discovery rules are effectively a special kind of item, you can create your own rules, provided you understand their peculiarity compared to regular items.

If we don't consider the fact that you need to create and manage low-level discovery rules in the **Discovery rules** section of the template configuration and not in the usual **Items** section, the main difference between the two kinds of items is that while a regular item usually returns a single value, as explained in *Chapter 4, Collecting Data*, a discovery item always returns a list of macro/value pairs expressed in JSON. This list represents all the resources found by the discovery items together with the means to reference them.

The following table shows Zabbix's supported discovery items and their return values together with a generalization that should give you an idea on how to create your own rules:

Discovery item key	Item type	Return values

`vfs.fs.discovery`	Zabbix agent	`{"data": [`
		`{"{#FSNAME}":"<path>",`
		`"{#FSTYPE}":"<fstype>"},`
		`{"{#FSNAME}":"<path>",`
		`"{#FSTYPE}":"<fstype>"},`
		`{"{#FSNAME}":"<path>",`
		`"{#FSTYPE}":"<fstype>"},`
		`...`
		`] }`

Discovery item key	Item type	Return values

`net.if.discovery`	Zabbix agent	`{"data":[`
		`{"{#IFNAME}":"<name>"},`
		`{"{#IFNAME}":"<name>"},`
		`{"{#IFNAME}":"<name>"},`
		`...`
		`]}`

`system.cpu.discovery`	Zabbix agent	`{"data": [`
		`{"{#CPU.NUMBER}":"<idx>",    "{#CPU.`
		`STATUS}":"<value>"},`
		`{"{#CPU.NUMBER}":"<idx>",    "{#CPU.`
		`STATUS}":"<value>"},`
		`{"{#CPU.NUMBER}":"<idx>",    "{#CPU.`
		`STATUS}":"<value>"},`
		`...`
		`] }`

`snmp.discovery`	SNMP (v1, v2, or v3) agent	`{"data":[`
		`{"{#SNMPINDEX}":"<idx>",`
		`"{#SNMPVALUE}":"<value>},`
		`{"{#SNMPINDEX}":"<idx>",`
		`"{#SNMPVALUE}":"<value>},`
		`{"{#SNMPINDEX}":"<idx>",`
		`"{#SNMPVALUE}":"<value>},`
		`...`
		`]}`

`custom.discovery`	Any	`{"data":[`
		`{"{#CUSTOM1}":"<value>","{#CUSTOM2}":"`
		`<value>"},`
		`{"{#CUSTOM1}":"<value>","{#CUSTOM2}":"`
		`<value>"},`
		`{"{#CUSTOM1}":"<value>","{#CUSTOM2}":"`
		`<value>"},`
		`...`
		`]}`

As with all SNMP items, an item key is not really important as long as it is unique. It's the SNMP OID value that you ask an agent for that makes the difference; you can create different SNMP discovery rules that look for different kinds of resources by changing the item key and looking for different OID values. The custom discovery example is even more abstract as it will depend on the actual item type.

As you can see, a discovery item always returns a list of values, but the actual contents of the list change depending on what resources you are looking for. In the case of a filesystem, the returned list will contain values such as {#FSNAME}:/usr, {#FSTYPE}:btrfs, and so on, for every discovered filesystem. On the other hand, a network discovery rule will return a list of the names of the discovered network interfaces.

When configuring a template's discovery rules, you don't need to care about the actual values returned in such lists, nor the lists' length. The only thing you have to know is the name of the macros that you can reference in your prototypes. These are the second half of the mechanisms of low-level discovery. You create them as regular template entities, thus making sure that you use the discovery item macros where needed, as exemplified in the following screenshot:

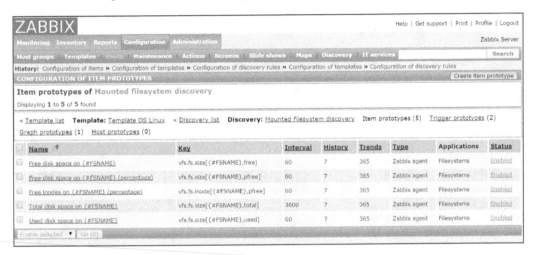

When you apply the template to a host, it will create items, triggers, and graphs based on the resources discovered by the discovery items and configured according to the discovery prototypes.

Custom discovery rules, from this point of view, work exactly in the same way as custom items whether you decide to use agent-side scripts (thereby using a custom zabbix.agent item key), external scripts, database queries, or anything else. The only things you have to make sure of is that your custom items' return values must respect the JSON syntax as shown in the preceding table and that you reference your custom macros in the entities' prototypes that you will create.

Now, let's see how you can create a custom script to implement simple, low-level discovery.

In this example, we're going to use low-level discovery to find all the hard disks connected to a physical server. First of all, here we require a script, and this script needs to be deployed to the agent side and, of course, needs to produce JSON-formatted output.

The shell script used in this example is the following:

```
#!/bin/bash
disks=`ls -l /dev/sd* | awk '{print $NF}' | sed 's/[0-9]//g' | uniq`
elementn=`echo $disks| wc -w`
echo "{"
echo "\"data\":["
i=1
for disk in $disks
do
if [ $i == $elementn ]
then
     echo "     {\"{#DISKNAME}\":\"$disk\",\"{#SHORTDISKNAME}\":\"${di
sk:5}\"}"
else
     echo "     {\"{#DISKNAME}\":\"$disk\",\"{#SHORTDISKNAME}\":\"${di
sk:5}\"},"
fi
i=$((i+1))
done
echo "]"
echo "}"
```

This script will produce the following JSON-formatted output:

```
{
"data":[
    {"{#DISKNAME}":"/dev/sda","{#SHORTDISKNAME}":"sda"},
    {"{#DISKNAME}":"/dev/sdb","{#SHORTDISKNAME}":"sdb"},
    {"{#DISKNAME}":"/dev/sdc","{#SHORTDISKNAME}":"sdc"},
    ...
]
}
```

Practically, the script lists all the sd<X> devices after taking care to remove the duplicates, if present, and even the partition.

To enable the script on the agent side, we need to change the `zabbix_agentd.conf` configuration file and add the following lines:

```
EnableRemoteCommands=1
UnsafeUserParameters=1
UserParameter=discovery.hard_disk,/<location-of-our-script>/discover_
hdd.sh
```

Of course, once done, we need to restart the Zabbix agent on the remote machine. Now it's time to define the discovery rule, as shown in the next screenshot:

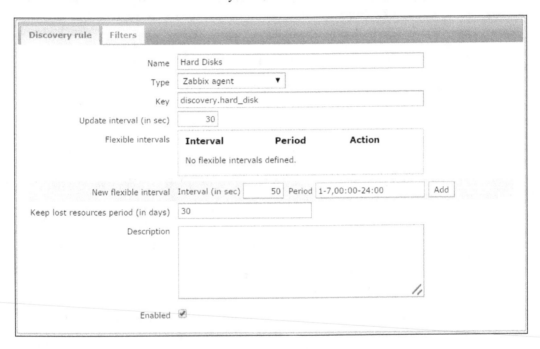

Then, we need to define the item and trigger prototype based on `#DISKNAME` or `#SHORTDISKNAME` we've just found. A good example of an item prototype is the I/O currently in progress on our discovered hard disk. To acquire this metric, we can simply check `/proc/diskstats`:

```
$ grep sda /proc/diskstats |head -1 | awk '{print $12}'
19
```

And, as you can see, we get back the number of I/Os done at the moment.

 For greater detail about /proc/diskstats, refer to the official kernel documentation available at https://www.kernel.org/doc/Documentation/ABI/testing/procfs-diskstats.

You can see that there are quite a few interesting metrics that we can acquire and historicize for capacity planning and management. Then, we can register UserParameter in our Zabbix agent to retrieve those metrics. A good set of them can be:

```
UserParameter=custom.vfs.dev.read.ops[*],grep $1 /proc/diskstats |
head -1 | awk '{print $$4}'
UserParameter=custom.vfs.dev.read.ms[*],grep $1 /proc/diskstats | head
-1 | awk '{print $$7}'
UserParameter=custom.vfs.dev.write.ops[*],grep $1 /proc/diskstats |
head -1 | awk '{print $$8}'
UserParameter=custom.vfs.dev.write.ms[*],grep $1 /proc/diskstats |
head -1 | awk '{print $$11}'
UserParameter=custom.vfs.dev.io.active[*],grep $1 /proc/diskstats |
head -1 | awk '{print $$12}'
UserParameter=custom.vfs.dev.io.ms[*],grep $1 /proc/diskstats |   head
-1 | awk '{print $$13}'
UserParameter=custom.vfs.dev.read.sectors[*],grep $1 /proc/diskstats |
head -1 | awk '{print $$6}'
UserParameter=custom.vfs.dev.write.sectors[*],grep $1 /proc/diskstats
| head -1 | awk '{print $$10}'
```

Once done, we need to restart the agent. We can now test the metric on the agent side itself with:

```
[root@ localhost ~]# zabbix_get -s 127.0.0.1 -k custom.vfs.dev.
io.active[sda]
27
```

Now, let's define **Item prototype** using #SHORTDISKNAME, as shown in the next screenshot:

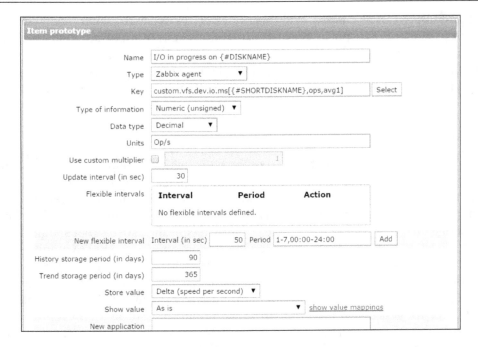

The {#SHORTDISKNAME} macro is used in the item's key, and, in the item's name, we're going to use {#DISKNAME}. Note that the $1 macro from the script references the first argument of the item's key. With the same process, we can create the prototype for all the other registered items. When you configure a template's discovery rules, there is no need to care about the actual values returned in their lists or about the list's length. The only thing that you have to know is the name of the macro that you can reference in your prototypes.

You can create them as regular template entities, such as **Item prototype**, **Trigger prototype**, **Graph prototype**, and **Host prototype**, making sure you use the discovery item macros where needed, and Zabbix will take care of the rest for you, by creating as many items as there are elements in the list returned by the discovery rule for each item prototype, as many triggers as there are elements in the list returned for each trigger prototype, and so on. The following screenshot shows this:

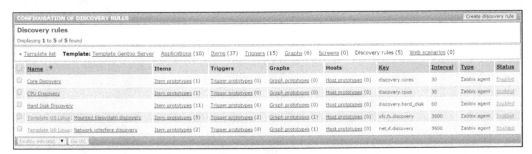

Host prototypes can be created with the low-level discovery rule, and then, when a server is discovered, the prototypes become real hosts. It is important to know that prototypes, before becoming discovered, cannot have their own items and triggers other than those from the linked templates. When a host is discovered, the hosts will belong to an existing host and will take the same IP of the existing host.

Summary

This chapter concludes the central part of the book, which is dedicated to developing a deeper understanding of the Zabbix monitoring system's core functions. The effective configuration and use of templates build on all the knowledge gained from using and analyzing items, graphs and screens, triggers, and actions. To this knowledge, this chapter has added a few template-specific aspects that should help to tie all of the previous chapters together. From choosing what to monitor and how to configure different item types, to putting together information-rich visualization items, at this point in the book, you can perform all the tasks associated with implementing and managing a monitoring system. You should also be able to select the triggers and actions that are most significant in order to maximize the expressiveness of your alerts, while avoiding false positives. Finally, you should not have any problems bringing it all together through the use of macros and nested and combined templates in order to apply a consistent and meaningful configuration to a wide range of hosts and to further automate these operations through host-level discovery actions and the low-level discovery facilities of Zabbix's templates.

The final part of the book will be about further customization options for Zabbix, how to extend its functionality, and how to really integrate it with the rest of your IT management systems in order to bring out its full power.

The next chapter will focus on writing extension scripts for Zabbix and its monitoring protocol.

8
Handling External Scripts

Until now, you have learned how most of a server's components work and how to leverage Zabbix to acquire data from various external sources. Considering that, set up your monitoring system in a large, heterogeneous, and complex infrastructure. Most probably, you will find a different custom device, server appliance, and proprietary hardware. Usually, all those devices have an interface to be enquired, but, unfortunately, it often happens that most of the metrics are not exposed via **Simple Network Management Protocol (SNMP)** or any other standard query method.

Let's consider a practical example. Nowadays, all the UPSes own a temperature sensor, and if you are in a complex infrastructure, it is possible that those UPS's are custom made and out of standard, and, most probably, this sensor can be enquired only with a tool provided from the UPS vendor. Now, the temperature of a UPS is a critical parameter, especially if the UPS is a big, custom-made UPS. It is really important to monitor these metrics.

Imagine that your cooling system is not working properly; receiving an alarm right when the temperature reaches over the warning level is fundamental. On the other hand, predicting the failure will save a lot of money. Also, even if the physical damage is not really expensive, the downtime can cost a lot of money and have a terrible impact on your business. A good example is the case of a trading company. In this scenario, everything should be in perfect working order. In this environment, there is terrible competition to achieve better performance against competitors— buying a stock option some milliseconds before the others is a big advantage. Here, it is easy to understand that, if servers are not performing well, it is already an issue; if they are down, it is a complete disaster for the company. This example explains how critical it is to predict a failure. Moreover, it is important to understand how critical it is to retrieve all functioning parameters of your infrastructure. This is where Zabbix comes to the rescue, providing interesting methods to retrieve data that interacts with the operating system, eventually enabling you to use a command-line tool. Zabbix's responses to this kind of requirement are as follows:

- External checks (server side)

- UserParameter (agent side)
- Zabbix_sender: This binary can be used on both the agent side and the server side
- A simple, efficient, and easy-to-implement communication protocol

This chapter will entirely explore those alternatives to interact with the operating system and receive data from external sources. In this chapter, you will learn that there isn't a general, optimal, valid solution for all the problems, but each of them has its pros and cons. This chapter will make you aware of all the things that need to be considered when you implement a custom check. The analysis proposed in this chapter will enable you to choose the best solution for your problems.

This chapter will cover the following points:

- Writing a script and making it available as external scripts
- The advantages and disadvantages of scripts on the server side and on the agent side
- Exploring alternative methods to send data to your Zabbix server
- Detailed documentation about the Zabbix protocol
- Commented educational implementation of the Zabbix sender protocol

External checks

Zabbix provides features to cover all the items that cannot be retrieved with the standard agent. In real life, it is possible that you are not able to install the standard agent on the device that you would like to monitor. A practical example is the UPS, all the servers that, for some reason, cannot be compromised when installing external software, or all the appliances that cannot have custom software installed.

Now, for all those reasons, you cannot have an agent on your device but you need to monitor the vital parameters of this device, the only feasible solution for which is to use an external check.

The script's placement

The script's location on Zabbix is defined in the zabbix_server.conf configuration file. Since Zabbix Version 2.0, the default location has changed to /usr/local/share/zabbix/externalscripts.

The default location depends on the compile time from the `datadir` variable. Actually, the default location is `${datadir}/zabbix/externalscripts`. This rule is valid for both proxy and server components.

Previously, it was defined as `/etc/zabbix/externalscripts`; anyway, you can change it by simply specifying a different location on `zabbix_server.conf` using the `ExternalScripts` parameter:

```
### Option: ExternalScripts
# Mandatory: no
# Default:
# ExternalScripts=${datadir}/zabbix/externalscripts
ExternalScripts=/usr/lib/zabbix/externalscripts
```

There are some important enhancements in external checks and scripts have been introduced since Zabbix versions 2.2 and 2.4:

- The key syntax now supports multiple comma-separated parameters
- There is support for user macros in script commands
- User parameters, global scripts, and external checks now return the standard error along with the standard output—this can be managed within your trigger
- There is support for multiline values

Now, let's see how external checks work in detail.

Going deep into external checks

Now, it is time for a practical example. This is an easy example to understand how an external script works. In the following example, we will count the number of open files for a specified user. The first thing to do is create the script and place it in the `ExternalScripts` location. The script will be called `lsof.sh` and will contain the following code:

```
#!/bin/bash
if grep -q  $1 /etc/passwd
        then  lsof -u $1 | tail -n +2 |wc -l
 else
        echo 0
 fi
```

This software requires the username as an input parameter; check whether the username exists on the system, and then return the number of open files for that account.

Now, you only need to create a new item of the External check type. In the **Key** field, enter `lsof.sh["postgres"]`, as shown in the following screenshot:

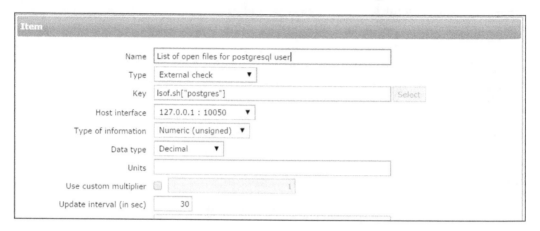

Now, on navigating to **Monitoring | Latest Data**, it is possible to see the data retrieved by our script:

The external script must be come back in a reasonable time; otherwise, the item will be marked as unsupported.

 Until now, we've considered the case of a Zabbix server that directly monitors a host using an external script. Bear in mind that if your host is monitored via a Zabbix proxy, the script needs to be placed on the proxy itself as the script must run from the proxy.

Now that you know how ExternalScripts works, it is time to see how we can implement something more complex thanks to this feature.

In the next example, we will monitor certain remote Oracle instances. There are some prerequisites to have this setup fully working: an Oracle client installed with a working `sqlplus`, a `tnsping`, and an account configured on your Oracle database target.

The latest version of this software is available for download at `http://www.smartmarmot.com/product/check_ora`.

Anyway, it is interesting to see how it evolved from Version 1.0. Version 1.0 is available for download directly on the Zabbix forum at `https://www.zabbix.com/forum/showthread.php?t=13666`.

This script is a good example of an external check. Basically, to have everything properly configured, you need to do the following:

1. Create a user account on all your monitored databases.
2. Configure your Oracle client.
3. Decompress the package on your external script location.
4. Configure your database account at `<EXTERNAL_SCRIP_LOCATION>/check_ora/credentials`.
5. Create a host with the same name as your database instance.

The last point is of particular importance and is a particular mode of using Zabbix. This method can be reused every time you need to aggregate metrics that are not tied to a real host but to a service. To do a practical example, if you have a DBMS that can failover against another server, you can simply create a Zabbix fake host that is called with the same name as that of your database. Now, if the services do failover, you don't have an interruption on your collected data because the failover process is transparent from the server that provides the service. This method is applied here because the Oracle client will handle a failover automatically once properly configured.

Now, you can go ahead and create a host with the same name as that of your SID, for example, you have an Oracle instance to monitor that is defined as ORCL on `tnsnames.ora`; thus, the Zabbix host will be ORCL.

> You can create hosts tied to the name of the service; this enables you to abstract the service from the host that is providing the service.

The detailed configuration of an Oracle client is out of the scope of this book. Once you complete the configuration, you can test the script by simply running the following command:

```
check_ora.sh[-i <instance> -q <query>]
```

In the preceding command line, `<instance>` represents your instance name and `<query>` is the query file that you would like to run. There is a large number of query files prebuilt in the `check_ora` directory; you can check all of them against your database.

> The usage of Oracle SID or an Oracle instance name as the hostname on Zabbix is really useful here. It can be expanded by the {HOSTNAME} macro, so you can simply create a key such as `check_ora.sh [-i {HOSTNAME} -q query]` on your template, and it will be expanded across all your databases.

Now, in the Zabbix host, you need to create the item to retrieve the external check, and the key will be as follows:

```
check_ora.sh[-i {HOSTNAME} -q <queryhere>]
```

For example:

```
key="check_ora.sh[-i {HOSTNAME} -q lio_block_changes]"
```

The template is available on the forum at the same location. Note that {HOSTNAME} is expanded with the hostname, which, in our case, is exactly the Oracle instance name. You can have a generalized template using the {HOSTNAME} macro, and their items are propagated across all your databases' hosts.

Now, the life cycle of this item will be the following:

1. Zabbix calls the script.

2. The script will perform the following:

   ○ Log in to the database

   ○ Execute the query and retrieve the value

   ○ Return the value on the standard output; Zabbix will receive the value, and, if it is valid, it will be stored

Going inside the script

The core function of `check_ora.sh` is `execquery()`. The function is the following:

```
execquery () {
start_time=$(date +%s)
#         echo "Time duration: $((finish_time - start_time)) secs."
echo "BEGIN check_ora.sh  $1 $2 `date`"  >> /tmp/checkora.log
   cd $SCRIPTDIR;
   sqlplus -S $1 <<EOF | sed  -e 's/^\ *//g'
```

```
set echo off;
set tab off;
set pagesize 0;
set feedback off;
set trimout on;
set heading off;
ALTER SESSION SET NLS_NUMERIC_CHARACTERS = '.,';
@$2
EOF
finish_time=$(date +%s)
echo "END check_ora.sh $1 $2 `date`" >> /tmp/checkora.log
echo "check_ora.sh $1 $2 Time duration: $((finish_time - start_time))
secs." >> /tmp/checkora.log
}
```

This function will begin producing log information on /tmp/checkora.log:

```
start_time=$(date +%s)
#        echo "Time duration: $((finish_time - start_time)) secs."
echo "BEGIN check_ora.sh $1 $2 `date`" >> /tmp/checkora.log
```

Those are useful to understand which external check is ongoing and against which database. Plus, in the log file, you will find the elapsed time for the whole operation:

```
finish_time=$(date +%s)
echo "END check_ora.sh $1 $2 `date`" >> /tmp/checkora.log
echo "check_ora.sh $1 $2 Time duration: $((finish_time - start_time))
secs." >> /tmp/checkora.log
}
```

Since this file is shared (between the check_ora.sh process) and the Zabbix calls are not serialized, it is important to report the script-calling line twice so that you can identify exactly which stating line corresponds to which finish line. Here, to avoid any doubt, the elapsed is calculated and reported on the finish message.

After the script, call sqlplus:

sqlplus -S $1 <<EOF | sed -e 's/^\ *//g'

Here, sed cleans up the white space at the beginning of the output. This is because the returned data is a number that cannot begin with blank spaces; if that happens, the item will become unsupported!

The following code snippet makes an Oracle client less verbose:

```
set echo off;
set tab off;
```

```
set pagesize 0;
set feedback off;
set trimout on;
set heading off;
```

The preceding lines are important to avoid noise in the output. The following code snippet explains the separator that should be used:

```
ALTER SESSION SET NLS_NUMERIC_CHARACTERS = '.,';
```

This section is important because you can have databases installed for different reasons with different character sets. Also, the client can use a different separator for decimals. You need to avoid all the uncontrolled charset conversions, and this is a general rule. Finally, the script executes the query file in the following way:

```
@$2
EOF
```

The output is returned in a standard output and is collected from Zabbix.

General rules for writing scripts

This script covers all the critical points that you need to pay attention to:

- Don't introduce unwanted characters into the output
- Be aware of the type; so, if a number is expected, remove all the unneeded characters (such as heading spaces)
- Avoid local conversions of numbers; the case of the dot and comma is a good example
- Have a log, keeping in mind that external scripts are not serialized, so you can have your log messages mixed in your log file
- Be aware of the time spent by the script from when the script is called until the script provides the output
- Those scripts, of course, run with the Zabbix server user, so perhaps you need to take care of file permissions and sudo privileges

> Starting with Zabbix 2.4, the standard output is tied together with the standard error; it is important to manage all the exceptions and errors within the script.

Remember that, if the requested script is not found or the Zabbix server has no permissions to execute it, the item will become unsupported. Also, in the case of a timeout, in both of the preceding cases an error message will be displayed and the forked process for the script will be killed.

Considerations about external checks

In this section, you have seen how external checks can be executed and how a complex task, such as database monitoring, is handled with them. If you have few external checks to implement, this can be a feasible solution to retrieve metrics. This kind of approach with externals checks, unfortunately, is not the solution to all the problems. On the other hand, you need to consider that they are really resource intensive and were once widely applied. Since external checks are on the server side, it is better not to overload the Zabbix server.

 Each ExternalScripts script requires the Zabbix server to start a fork process; running many scripts can decrease Zabbix's performance a lot.

The Zabbix server is the core component of your monitoring infrastructure, and you can't steal resources from this server.

The user parameter

The simple thing to do is to avoid extensive resource usage by your script by placing the script on the agent side. Zabbix provides an alternative method, and the script should instead be on the server side and load the Zabbix server; it can be offloaded to the agent side with UserParameter.

UserParameter is defined on the agent configuration file. Once it is configured, it is treated in the same way as all the other Zabbix agent items by simply using the key specified in the parameter option. To define a user parameter, you need to add something similar to the following to the agent configuration file:

```
UserParameter=<key>,<shell command>
```

Here, key must be unique and the shell command represents the command to execute. The command can be specified here inline and doesn't need to be a script, as shown in the following example:

```
UserParameter=process.number, ps -e |wc -l
```

In this example, the `process.number` key will retrieve the total number of processes on your server.

With the same kind of approach, you can check the number of users currently connected with the following code:

```
UserParameter=process.number, who |wc -l
```

The flexible user parameter

It is easy to understand that using this method you are going to define a large number of entries inside the agent configuration file. This is not the right approach because it is better to keep the configuration file simple.

Zabbix provides an interesting `UserParamenter` feature to avoid the proliferation of those items on the agent side — the flexible user parameter. This feature is enabled with an entry of this kind:

```
UserParameter=key[*],<shell command>
```

Here, `key` still needs to be unique, and the `[*]` term defines that this key accepts the parameters. The content between the square brackets is parsed and substituted with $1...$9; please note that $0 refers to the command itself. An example of `UserParameter` can be the following:

```
UserParameter=oraping[*],tnsping $1 | tail -n1
```

This command will execute `tnsping` to your SID, passing it as $1. You can apply the same method in the process to count specified users as follows:

```
UserParameter=process.number[*], ps -e |grep ^$1 | wc -l
```

Then, if we want to move to the agent side for the first script that returns the number of open files for a defined user, the configuration will be the following:

```
UserParameter=lsof.sh[*],/usr/local/bin/lsof.sh $1
```

Once this has been added, you only need to restart the agent. On the server side, you need to switch the item **Type** to **Zabbix agent** and save it. The following screenshot depicts this discussion:

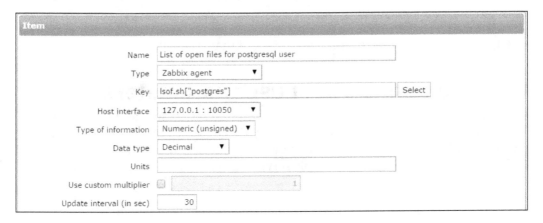

With the same method, you can configure the check_ora.sh script to check the database with the following code:

```
UserParameter=check_ora.sk[*],check_ora.sh -i $1 -q $2
```

On the Zabbix server side, you need to create an item of the Zabbix agent type or the Zabbix agent (active) type, and on the key you need to specify:

```
check_ora.sk[<databasename> <query_to_execute>]
```

You can test UserParameter using the command line, as previously described, or using the zabbix_get utility. With zabbix_get, you don't need to wait to see data between the latest data, and it is easier to debug what is happening on the agent side.

There are methods to test whether your UserParameter is working fine and the agent is able to recognize it. The first one is with zabbix_get; for example, in the case of losf.sh from the Zabbix server, we can use the following:

```
# zabbix_get -s 127.0.0.1 -p 10050 -k lsof.sh["postgres"]
2116
```

The response is the result of the operation. Alternatively, we can log on to the monitored host and run the following command:

```
#/usr/sbin/zabbix_agentd -t lsof.sh["postgres"]
lsof.sh[postgres] [/usr/local/bin/lsof.sh postgres]  [t|2201]
```

Again, this will display the output and the script that is called.

Considerations about user parameters

With `UserParameter`, you moved the script from the server side to the agent side. The workload introduced by the script is now on the agent side, and you avoided resource stealing on the server side. Another point to consider is that this approach divides the workload between multiple servers. Obviously, each agent will monitor the database present on its hosts.

The `UserParameter` parameters are really flexible. To enable them on the agent side, you need to change the configuration file and restart the agent. Also, here you need to be sure that the returned value is properly set; if it isn't properly set, it will be discarded.

Now, between the cons, you need to consider the observer effect (discussed in *Chapter 1, Deploying Zabbix*) introduced with this kind of monitoring. You need to keep things as lightweight as possible, especially because the agent runs on the same server that provides the service.

The usage of `UserParameter` implies that you need to distribute the scripts and the relative updates across all your servers. In this example, where you want to monitor Oracle, you need to consider how many different versions of operating systems and software you need to handle. It is possible that in time, you will need to handle a myriad of different flavors of your scripts and software. This myriad of scripts, versions, and so on will force you to have centralized deployment, that is, all the versions of the scripts are stored in a centralized repository. In addition, you need to take care of the workload added by your scripts and, if they don't handle all the possible exceptions well, this can be a really complex scenario to manage.

`UserParamenter` is really good, flexible, and sometimes indispensable to solve some monitoring requirements, but is not designed for massive monitoring against the same host. For all these reasons, it is time to explore another way to massively monitor the items that Zabbix doesn't support natively.

The following are certain very important points about external scripts and
UserParamenter:

- All pieces of input are passed as parameters to the script and should properly be properly sanitized within the script to prevent command injection.

- All values are returned via STDOUT and should be in the format of the expected return type. Returning nothing will cause the Zabbix server to flag this item as unsupported.

- Make sure that all scripts terminate in a short period of time.

- Make sure that scripts do not share or lock any resources, or have any other side effects, to prevent race conditions or incorrect interactions from incurring multiple executions.

Sending data using zabbix_sender

Until now, you have seen how to implement external checks on both the server side and the agent side, which involves moving the workload from the monitoring host to the monitored host. You can understand how both methods in the case of heavy and extensive monitoring are not the best approach since we are thinking of placing Zabbix in a large environment. Most probably, it is better have a server dedicated to all our checks and use those two functionalities for all the checks that are not widely run.

Zabbix provides utilities designed to send data to the server. This utility is zabbix_sender, and with it, you can send the item data to your server using the items of a Zabbix trapper type.

To test the zabbix_sender utility, simply add a Zabbix trapper item to an existing host and run the command:

```
zabbix_sender -z <zabbixserver> -s <yourhostname> -k <item_key> -o
<value>
```

You will get a response similar to the following:

```
Info from server: "Processed 1 Failed 0 Total 1 Seconds spent 0.0433214"
sent: 1; skipped: 0; total: 1
```

You just saw how easy the zabbix_sender utility is to use. That said, now we can dedicate a server to all our resource-intensive scripts.

The new script

Now, we can change the script that has been previously used as an external check and add `UserParameter` to a new version that sends traps to your Zabbix server.

The core part of the software will be as follows:

```
CONNECTION=$( grep $HOST\; $CONNFILE | cut -d\; -f2) || exit 3;
RESULT=$( execquery $CONNECTION $QUERY.sql);
if [ -z "$RESULT" ]; then
        send $HOST $KEY "none"
        exit 0;
fi
send $HOST $QUERY "$RESULT"
exit 0;
```

This code executes the following steps:

1. Retrieving the connection string from a file:

   ```
   CONNECTION=$( grep $HOST\; $CONNFILE | cut -d\; -f2) || exit 3;
   ```

2. Executing the query specified into the `$QUER.sql` file:

   ```
   RESULT=$( execquery $CONNECTION $QUERY.sql);
   ```

3. Checking the result of the query and if it is not empty, sending the value to Zabbix; otherwise, the value is replaced with `"none"`:

   ```
   if [ -z "$RESULT" ]; then
           send $HOST $KEY "none"
           exit 0;
   fi
   send $HOST $KEY "$RESULT"
   ```

In this code, there are two main functions in play: one is the `execquery()` function that basically is not changed, and the other is the `send()` function. The `send()` function plays a key role in delivering data to the Zabbix server:

```
send () {
   MYHOST="$1"
   MYKEY="$2"
   MYMSG="$3"
   zabbix_sender -z $ZBX_SERVER -p $ZBX_PORT -s $MYHOST -k $MYKEY -o
"$MYMSG";
}
```

This function sends the values passed by using a command line just as with the one already used to test the `zabbix_sender` utility. The value sent on the server side will have the corresponding item of the trapper kind, and Zabbix will receive and store your data.

Now, to automate the whole check process, you need a wrapper that polls between all your configured Oracle instances, retrieves the data, and sends it to Zabbix. The wrapper acquires the database list and the relative credential to log in from a configuration file, and you need to call your `check_ora_sendtrap.sh` script recursively.

Writing a wrapper script for check_ora_sendtrap

Since this script will run from `crontab`, as the first thing, it will properly set up the environment to source a configuration file:

```
source /etc/zabbix/externalscripts/check_ora/globalcfg
```

Then, go down to the script directory. Please note that the directory structure has not been changed for compatibility purposes:

```
cd /etc/zabbix/externalscripts
```

Then, it begins to execute all the queries against all the databases:

```
for host in $HOSTS; do
  for query in $QUERIES; do
          ./check_ora_sendtrap.sh -r -i $host -q ${query%.sql} &
          sleep 5
  done;
  ./check_ora_sendtrap.sh -r -i $host -t &
  sleep 5
  ./check_ora_sendtrap.sh -r -i $host -s &
done;
```

Note that this script executes all the queries and retrieves the `tnsping` time and the connection time for each database. There are two environment variables that are used to cycle between hosts and queries; they are populated with two functions:

```
HOSTS=$(gethosts)
QUERIES=$(getqueries)
```

The `gethost` functions retrieve the database name from the configuration file:

```
/etc/zabbix/externalscripts/check_ora/credentials
gethosts () {
    cd /etc/zabbix/externalscripts/check_ora
    cat credentials | grep -v '^#' | cut -d';' -f 1
}
```

The `getquery` function goes down into the directory tree, retrieving all the query files present:

```
getqueries () {
    cd /etc/zabbix/externalscripts/check_ora
    ls *.sql
}
```

Now, you only need to schedule the wrapper script on crontab by adding the following entry to your crontab:

```
*/5 * * * * /etc/zabbix/externalscripts/check_ora_cron.sh
```

Your Zabbix server will store and graph data.

> All the software discussed here is available on SourceForge at https://sourceforge.net/projects/checkora released on GPLv3 and at http://www.smartmarmot.com/.

The pros and cons of the dedicated script server

With this approach, we have a dedicated server that retrieves data. This means you do not overload the server that provides your service or the Zabbix server, and this is really a good point.

Unfortunately, this kind of approach lacks flexibility, and in this specific case, all the items are refreshed every 5 minutes. On the other hand, with the external checks or `UserParameter`, the refresh rate can vary and be customized per item.

In this particular case, where a database server is involved, there is an observer effect introduced by our script. The query can be as lightweight as you want, but to retrieve an item, `sqlplus` will ask Oracle for a connection. This connection will be used only for a few seconds (the time needed to retrieve the item), after which the connection is closed. All this workflow basically lacks connection pooling. Using connection pooling, you can perceptibly reduce the observer effect on your database.

Reducing the overhead with connection pooling is a general concept, and it is not tied with a vendor-specific database. Databases, in general, will suffer if they are hammered with frequent requests for a new connection and a close connection.

Pooling the connection is always a good thing to do in general. To better understand the benefit of this methodology, you can consider a complex network with a path that crosses different firewalls and rules before arriving at a destination; this is the clear advantage to have a persistent connection. To have a pool of persistent connections kept valid with keep-alive packed reduces the latency to retrieve the item from your database and, in general, the network workload. Creating a new connection involves the approval process of all the firewalls crossed. Also, you need to bear in mind that, if you are using Oracle, first a connection request is made against the listener that will require a callback once accepted and so on. Unfortunately, connection pooling can't be implemented with the shell components. There are different implementations of connection pooling, but before we go deep into the programming side, it is time to see how Zabbix protocols work.

Working with Zabbix protocols

Zabbix protocols are quite simple; this is a strong point because it is simple to implement your own custom agent or software that sends data to Zabbix.

Zabbix supports different versions of protocols. We can divide the protocols into three families:

- Zabbix get
- Zabbix sender
- Zabbix agent

The Zabbix get protocol

The Zabbix get protocol is really simple and easy to implement. Practically, you only need to send data to your Zabbix server at the port 10050.

This protocol is so simple that you can implement it with a shell script as well:

```
This is a textual protocol and is used to retrieve data from the agent
directly. [root@zabbixserver]# telnet 127.0.0.1 10050
Trying 127.0.0.1...
Connected to 127.0.0.1.
Escape character is '^]'.
```

```
agent.version
ZBXD2.0.6Connection closed by foreign host.
```

This example shows you how to retrieve the agent version simply with a telnet. Please note that the data is returned with a header that is ZBXD, followed by the data that represents the actual response 2.0.6.

This simple protocol is useful to retrieve data directly from the agent installed into our server and use it in a shell script.

This protocol is useful to identify the agent version without logging on to the server and to check all the instances of UserParameter defined against an agent.

The Zabbix sender protocol

The Zabbix sender protocol is a JSON-based protocol. The message composition is the following:

```
<HEADER><DATA_LENGTH><DATA>
```

The <HEADER> section is of 5 bytes, and it is in the form ZBXD\x01. Actually, only the first 4 bytes are the header; the next byte is used to specify the protocol version. Currently, only Version 1 is supported (0 x 01 HEX).

The <DATA_LENGTH> section is 8 bytes in length and in the hex format. So, for instance, 1 is formatted as 01/00/00/00/00/00/00/00, an 8-byte (or 64-bit) number in the hex format.

It is followed by <DATA>. This section is expressed in the JSON format.

From version 2.0.3, Zabbix can receive only 128 MB of data to prevent the server from running out of memory. This limit has been added to protect the server from crashes caused by a large amount of data input.

To send the value, the JSON message needs to be in the following form:

```
<HEADER><DATALEN>{
  "request":"sender data",
  "data":[
  {
    "host":"Host name 1",
    "key":"item_key",
    "value":"XXX",
    "clock":unix_time_format
```

```
    },

    {
      "host":"Host name 2",
      "key":"item_key",
      "value":"YYY"
    }
    ],
  "clock":unix_time_format
  }
```

In the previous example, as you can see, multiple items are queued on the same message if they come from different hosts or are referred to as different item keys.

 The "clock" term is optional in this protocol and can be omitted on the JSON object as well as at the end of the data section.

Once all the items are received, the server will send back the response. The response has the following structure:

```
<HEADER><DATALEN>{
  "response":"success",
  "info":"Processed 6 Failed 1 Total 7 Seconds spent 0.000283"
}
```

This example reports a response message; the following are some considerations:

- The response has a status that can be [success|failure] and refers to the whole transmission of your item list to the Zabbix server.
- It is possible, as shown in this example, that some of the items failed. You simply receive a notification and you can't do much more than notify and write this status in a log file.

 It is important to keep track of the time spent to send your item list because if this value becomes high or has a detectable variation, it means that our Zabbix server suffers on receiving items.

Unfortunately, this protocol does not give you feedback on which items failed and the reason for failure. At the time of writing this, there are two requested features that are still pending:

- To have a more readable output, visit `https://support.zabbix.com/browse/ZBXNEXT-935`

- To identify the failed items, visit `https://support.zabbix.com/browse/ZBXNEXT-246`

Now you know how the Zabbix sender protocol works on version 1.8 and higher.

Another issue is that the Zabbix sender protocol until now doesn't support any kind of encryption, which can cause an issue in the case of sensitive data that is sent in clear text. We also need to consider the case of a hacker who would like to hide his activity behind a large number of alarms or triggers on fire. With this protocol, the hacker can easily send a false alarm in order to set the trigger on fire and then proceed with his activity unnoticed.

Fortunately, this feature has now been taken into consideration, and the team is working on an SSL version or, better, a TLS version.

For more information, you can have a look at the ticket at `https://support.zabbix.com/browse/ZBXNEXT-1263`.

An interesting undocumented feature

There is an interesting sender's feature that is not widely known and not well documented. While going deep into protocol analysis, the first thing to do is read the official documentation, and the second is to check how Zabbix will implement it; it is possible that not all the minor changes are updated in the documentation.

Then, looking into the `zabbix_sender` code, you can find the section where the protocol is implemented:

```
zbx_json_addobject(&sentdval_args.json, NULL);
zbx_json_addstring(&sentdval_args.json, ZBX_PROTO_TAG_HOST, hostname,
ZBX_JSON_TYPE_STRING);
zbx_json_addstring(&sentdval_args.json, ZBX_PROTO_TAG_KEY, key, ZBX_
JSON_TYPE_STRING);
zbx_json_addstring(&sentdval_args.json, ZBX_PROTO_TAG_VALUE, key_
value, ZBX_JSON_TYPE_STRING);
```

The preceding code snippet implements the Zabbix JSON protocol and, in particular, this section:

```
"host":"Host name 1",
"key":"item_key",
"value":"XXX",
```

Until here, the protocol has been well documented. Right after these lines there are interesting sections that add one more property to our JSON item.

```
if (1 == WITH_TIMESTAMPS)
    zbx_json_adduint64(&sentdval_args.json, ZBX_PROTO_TAG_CLOCK,
atoi(clock));
```

Here, a timestamp is provided within the item and is added as a property of the JSON object, after which the item is closed as follows:

```
zbx_json_close(&sentdval_args.json);
```

 The clock is defined as an unsigned `int64` variable.

This is a really important property because, if you write your own `zabbix_sender`, you can specify the timestamp of when the item has been retrieved.

The important thing is that by testing this section, Zabbix stores the clock time of when the item has been retrieved at the specified clock time on the database.

Using the clock properties in JSON items

Now this property can be used to optimize your sender. Zabbix supports 128 MB of data for a single connection. Of course, it is better to be far from that limit because if we reach that limit, it is a sign that our implementation is not well done.

The clock feature can be used in two scenarios:

- If buffer items need to be sent and if they are sent inside a single connection in bursts
- If the server is not available, you can cache and send the item later

The first usage of this feature is clearly an optimization to keep the whole communication as lightweight as possible, and reducing the number of connections against our Zabbix server can prevent issues.

The second way to enable this is to implement a robust sender, which can handle a Zabbix server downtime and preserve your item in a cache, ready to be sent once the server is backed up and running. Please be aware not to flood the server if it is not reachable for a long period of time. Manage the communication by sending a reasonable number of items and not a long trail of items.

The Zabbix agent protocol

This protocol is a bit more complex because it involves more phases and the dialogue is more articulated. When an active agent starts, the first thing it does is connect to the server and ask for a task to perform, in particular, which item is to be retrieved and the relative timing.

Also, in the following code, the form of the protocol is the same as used previously:

```
<HEADER><DATA_LENGTH><DATA>
```

The `<HEADER>`, `<DATA_LENGTH>`, and `<DATA>` tags are as explained in the previous section.

The dialogue begins when the agent sends the following request to the server:

```
<HEADER><DATALEN>{
    "request":"active checks",
    "host":"<hostname>"
}
```

With this kind of request, the agent is going to ask for a specified hostname in the active checklist. The server response will, for instance, be as follows:

```
<HEADER><DATALEN>{
  "response":"success",
  "data":[{
    "key":"log[\/var\/log\/localmessages,@errors]",
    "delay":1,
    "lastlogsize":12189,
    "mtime":0
  },
  {
    "key":"agent.version",
    "delay":"900"
    }]
  "regexp":[
    {
    "name":"errors",
    "expression":"error",
```

```
    "expression_type":0,
    "exp_delimiter":",",
    "case_sensitive":1
}]
}
```

The Zabbix server must respond with success, followed by the list of items and the relative delay.

 In the case of log and logrt items, the server should respond with lastlogsize. The agent needs to know this parameter to continue the work. Also, mtime is needed for all the logrt items.

"regexp", which, in this example, is the response back to the agent, will exist only if you have defined global or regular expressions. Note that if a user macro is used, the parameter key is resolved and the original key is sent as key_orig. The original key is the user macro name.

Once the response is received, the agent will close the TCP connection and will parse it. Now, the agent will start to collect the items at their specified period. Once collected, the items will be sent back to the server:

```
<HEADER><DATALEN>{
    "request":"agent data",
    "data":[
        {
            "host":"HOSTNAME",
"key":"log[\/var\/log\/localmessages]",
"value":"Sep 16 18:26:44 linux-h5fr dhcpcd[3732]: eth0: adding default
route via 192.168.1.1 metric 0",
"lastlogsize":4315,
"clock":1360314499,
"ns":699351525
},
        {
            "host":"<hostname>",
            "key":"agent.version",
            "value":"2.0.1",
            "clock":1252926015
        }
    ],
    "clock":1252926016
}
```

While implementing this protocol, make sure to send back `lastlogsize` for all the log-type items and `mtime` for the `logrt` items.

The server will respond with:

```
{
  "response":"success",
  "info":"Processed 2 Failed 0 Total 2 Seconds spent 0.000110"
}
```

Also, there is a possibility that some items have not been accepted, but, currently, there isn't a way to know which ones they are.

Some more possible responses

To complete the protocol description, you need to know that there are some particular cases to handle:

- When a host is not monitored
- When a host does not exist
- When the host is actively monitored but there aren't active items

In the first case, when a host is not monitored, the agent will receive the following response from the server:

```
<HEADER><DATALEN>{
  "response":"failed",
  "info":"host [Host name] not monitored"
}
```

In the second case, when the host does not exist, the agent will receive the following response:

```
<HEADER><DATALEN>{
  "response":"failed",
  "info":"host [Host name] not found"
}
```

In the last case, when the host is monitored but does not have active items, the agent will receive an empty dataset:

```
<HEADER><DATALEN>{
  "response":"success",
  "data":[]
}
```

The low-level discovery protocol

The low-level discovery protocol provides an automated way to create items, triggers, and graphs for different entities on a computer. For instance, Zabbix can automatically start monitoring filesystems or network interfaces on your machine without the need to create items for each filesystem or network interface manually. Actually, the results found thanks to the discovery can trigger many different actions, such as even removing unneeded entities such as items and so on. This functionality gives a lot of flexibility to our monitoring system. Zabbix, indeed, lets you customize and create a brand-new low-level discovery rule to discovery any type of Zabbix entity.

Let's see which one is the output used by a low-level discovery item such as `vfs.fs.discovery`. To see the output, we can simply run the following command:

```
$ zabbix_get -s 127.0.0.1 -k vfs.fs.discovery
{"data":[
{"{#FSNAME}":"/","{#FSTYPE}":"rootfs"},
{"{#FSNAME}":"/proc","{#FSTYPE}":"proc"},
{"{#FSNAME}":"/sys","{#FSTYPE}":"sysfs"}
...
]}]
```

Here, we've reduced the output; anyway, as you can see, the output is easy to understand. First of all, this is a JSON-formatted output and is mostly in key-value format.

Then, as we saw in *Chapter 7, Managing Templates*, we can create all the scripts we need to properly automate the discovery of entities that need to be monitored.

Of course, every agent-side script must be registered as `UserParameter` of `zabbix_agent.conf`. Otherwise, if it is a server-side global script, it must be deployed in `ExternalScriptspath` that you've configured in `zabbix_server.conf`.

Let's see another example of a low-level discovery script that can be reused and will be useful to map all the open ports across your network. As we discussed in *Chapter 7, Managing Templates*, we need to have a JSON-formatted output with the port open and the relative protocol. To acquire this information, we can use `nmap`. To install `nmap` on Red Hat, you need to run the following command from root:

```
$ yum install nmap
```

This will install the only external component that we require. Now, to map all the open ports on a server, the best option is to run the script from the Zabbix server as it is possible that those ports are opened locally but hidden behind a firewall and are not accessible from our Zabbix server. Then, if we cannot reach them, we can't even monitor them. A command to run a quick port scan uses the `-T<0-5>` option, which sets the timing template (a higher number means a faster template). In this script, we are using the option `-T4`, followed by the `-F` (fast mode) option:

```
#!/bin/sh
#Start with JSON Header
echo '{'
echo ' "data":['
PORTS=( $(nmap -T4 -F ${1} | grep 'open' | cut -d" " -f1 ) )
COUNTER=${#PORTS[@]}
for PORT in "${PORTS[@]}"; do
        COUNTER=$(( COUNTER - 1))
        if [ $COUNTER -ne 0 ]; then
                echo '  { "{#PORT}":"'$(echo $PORT| cut -d/ -f1)}'",
"{#PROTO}":"'$(echo $PORT| cut -d/ -f2)'" },'
        else
#it's the last element.
#To have valid JSON We don't add a trailing comma
                echo '  { "{#PORT}":"'$(echo $PORT| cut -d/ -f1)}'",
"{#PROTO}":"'$(echo $PORT| cut -d/ -f2)'" }'
        fi
done
#End with JSON footer
echo ' ]'
echo '}'
```

The script running a port scan against the IP address specified will retrieve all the open ports that are not firewalled and the relative protocol. The output that the script produces is the following:

```
# ports_ldd.sh 192.168.1.1
{
 "data":[
  { "{#PORT}":"22}", "{#PROTO}":"tcp" },
  { "{#PORT}":"25}", "{#PROTO}":"tcp" },
  { "{#PORT}":"53}", "{#PROTO}":"tcp" },
  { "{#PORT}":"80}", "{#PROTO}":"tcp" },
  { "{#PORT}":"111}", "{#PROTO}":"tcp" },
  { "{#PORT}":"631}", "{#PROTO}":"tcp" },
```

```
{ "{#PORT}":"3306}", "{#PROTO}":"tcp" },
{ "{#PORT}":"5432}", "{#PROTO}":"tcp" }
]
}
```

This is the kind of output that we are expecting and, as you can see, is ready to be used. Of course, the script must be placed in your ExternalScripts location. Then, we can start creating the new **Discovery rule** tab, as shown in the following screenshot:

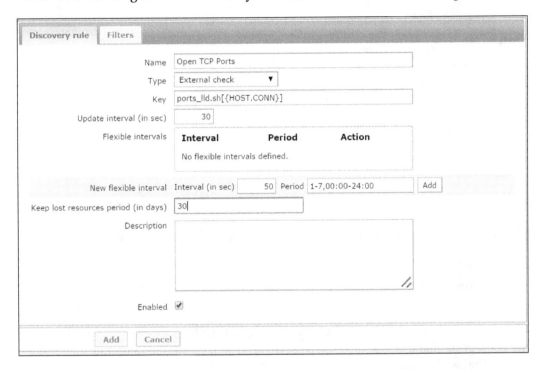

This will make the two variables {#PORT} and {#PROTO} ready to be used inside the prototypes. Let's create the Item prototype with the following properties:

- **Name:** Status of port {#PORT}/{#PROTO}
- **Type: Simple check**
- **Key:** net.tcp.service[{#PROTO},,{#PORT}]
- **Type of information: Numeric (unsigned)**
- **Data type: Boolean**

This is shown in the following screenshot:

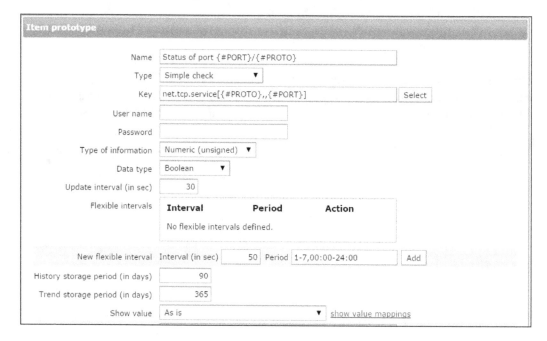

Then, we need to create the relative trigger prototype with the following information:

- **Name:** {#PROTO} port {#PORT}
- **Expression:** {Template_network:net.tcp.service[{#PROTO},,{#PORT}].last(0)}=0

With this kind of configuration, the discovery will do all the jobs for you, will find all the open ports that are reachable on a server, and will create the item and the relative trigger that will go on fire once the port is not accessible.

> Here, we are considering the case that you want to monitor all the services available on a server and then the trigger will send you an alarm if the port is not reachable. It is important to consider even the other case, where you're in a DMZ and you want to have a trigger if, for some reason, a service is reachable. One typical example is the database listener port, which should be accessible only within the DMZ and not from outside it.

This is just an example of automation, a simple one actually, but we can push the automation more. You can consider a network where you have a well-defined domain of services and you know the daemon in use or where at least the daemon banner is not changed to hide the service identity. In this case, a useful discovery customization would find all the open ports and, once the service behind them is identified, apply the relative template to the monitored server. For instance, we can think of port 80 as open, with an Apache service behind it, and then apply an Apache template ad hoc made to the host. This would definitely automate and reduce the initial startup cost and time.

Communicating with Zabbix

Now you know how the Zabbix protocol works, so it is time to see some code that implements this protocol. To keep things easy, we have described an example of the `zabbix_sender` protocol — the simplest way to send data to Zabbix.

Zabbix uses JSON to describe the object contained in the data. There are a lot of efficient JSON libraries that can be used, but to make things easier here, those libraries will not be used.

Implementing the Zabbix_sender protocol in Java

Here, you will see a really simple implementation of the `zabbix_sender` protocol that, as you know, is the easy way to send traps to Zabbix.

The piece of code that follows has been kept as simple as possible, and the scope is to provide an example from which you can start to develop your own Zabbix monitoring component:

```
private String buildJSonString(String host, String item,Long
timestamp, String value){
  return  "{"
    + "\"request\":\"sender data\",\n"
    + "\"data\":[\n"
    +          "{\n"
      +          "\"host\":\"" + host + "\",\n"
      +           "\"key\":\"" + item + "\",\n"
      +           "\"value\":\"" + value.replace("\\", "\\\\") +
"\",\n"
      +           "\"clock\":" + timestamp.toString()
    +          "}]}\n" ;
  }
```

This piece of code simply returns the JSON message to send it as a body. You only need to provide the host and item or, better, the item key, value, and timestamp to include into the message, and it will return a JSON-formatted string object.

Now, once you have retrieved all your item values, you simply need to generate the JSON message, open a connection, and send the message. To open a connection against your Zabbix server, we can use the following lines of code:

```
String data = buildJSonString( host,item,value);
    zabbix = new Socket(zabbixServer, zabbixPort);
    zabbix.setSoTimeout(TIMEOUT);
    out = new OutputStreamWriter(zabbix.getOutputStream());
    int length = data.length;
```

In this code, as you see the program open a socket, define the timeout, and retrieve the message length, it is now ready to send the message. Please remember that the message is composed with <HEADER><DATALEN><MESSAGE>. A simple way to send the header and the data length is the following:

```
out.write(new byte[] {
    'Z', 'B', 'X', 'D',
    '\1',
    (byte)(length & 0xFF),
    (byte)((length >> 8) & 0x00FF),
    (byte)((length >> 16) & 0x0000FF),
    (byte)((length >> 24) & 0x000000FF),
    '\0','\0','\0','\0'});
```

This portion of code writes the message on the socket that actually contains the host, item, and value:

```
out.write(data);
```

Remember to flush the data, close the socket, and complete the delivery as follows:

```
out.flush();
out.close();
```

Now, we need to see what the Zabbix server will say about our item:

```
in = zabbix.getInputStream();
final int read = in.read(response);
String respStatus = (String) getValue(response);
if (read !=2 || respStatus.equals(ZBX_SUCCESS)) {
in.close();
}
```

If the response is that of a success, you can close `InputStream`.

This example is fully working, but it is only for educational purposes. There are different things to improve before considering it ready for production. Anyway, this is a good starting point. This example can be extended by handling multiple JSON objects on the data section, thus increasing the number of objects passed per connection. You need to limit the connection numbers and avoid flooding your Zabbix server with connections just to send an item. Items can be buffered and sent together; for instance, if you have a group of items with the same schedule, all of them can be sent together.

When you retrieve your items, it is important to keep track of the timestamps. To do so, you can add the timestamp to your item and know when it has actually retrieved this metric.

In the previous example, the timestamp is not sent since it is optional, but it is a good practice to include it, especially if you're buffering an item; when you send it, the items will have the right timestamp.

Implementing the Zabbix sender protocol in Python

Nowadays, a lot of applications are written in Python, and it is a programing language that is widely diffused and known. For this reason, this is an example of a fundamental threat that can be the starting point for your custom `zabbix_sender` in Python. This piece of code can be extended and integrated directly into your software. Having a functionality integrated into the application can be really interesting because the application itself can send its health status to your Zabbix server. Now, it is time to take a look at the piece of code and how it works.

First, you need to define the structure and import `simplejson` used here to add the host, key, item value, and clock in the JSON format:

```
import simplejson as smplj
items_data = []
```

Now, retrieve the timestamp from the items; if it is null, we will get the current timestamp:

```
clock = zbxit.clock or time.time()
```

Now, you can begin to create the JSON object to include it in the Zabbix message:

```
items_data.append(('\t\t{\n'
                    '\t\t\t"host":%s,\n'
                    '\t\t\t"key":%s,\n'
                    '\t\t\t"value":%s,\n'
                    '\t\t\t"clock":%s}') % (smplj.dump(zbxit.
host), smplj.dump(zbxit.key), smplj.dump(zbxit.value), clock))
```

Now that your item has been transformed into a JSON object, it is time for the header:

```
json_items = ('{\n'
              '\t"request":"sender data",\n'
              '\t"data":[\n%s]\n'
              '}') % (',\n'.join(items_data))
```

The next step is to retrieve the length of our message to add it on the header:

```
data_len = struct.pack('<Q', len(json_items))
```

As previously discussed, here the message is put on the form
<HEADER><DATALEN>+<JSON ITEM> as follows:

```
packet = 'ZBXD\1' + data_len + json_items
```

Then, the socket is going to be open and the packet will be sent:

```
zabbix = socket.socket()
zabbix.connect((zabbix_host, zabbix_port))
zabbix.sendall(packet)
```

Once the packet has been sent, it is time to retrieve the Zabbix server response:

```
resp_hdr = _recv_all(zabbix, 13)
```

Next check whether it is valid:

```
if not resp_hdr.startswith('ZBXD\1') or len(resp_hdr) != 13:
    return False
resp_body_size = struct.unpack('<Q', resp_hdr[5:])[0]
resp_body = zabbix.recv(resp_body_size)
zabbix.close()
resp = smplj.loads(resp_body)
 if resp.get('response') != 'success':
    return False
return True
```

This piece of code is a good starting point to develop the Zabbix sender protocol in Python.

Some considerations about agent development

Now, you probably don't see when to begin the development of your software that sends a trap to Zabbix. But before beginning to write the code, it is fundamental to keep in mind the requirements and the problem.

Until now, you have two examples, and you can easily start to send a trap to the Zabbix server even if they are not completely engineered components.

As the first point, it is important to understand whether it is only needed to send the data to Zabbix at a specified time schedule that is not directed from the Zabbix server. Those two pieces of code implement the Zabbix sender protocol, but the frequency with which the items are retrieved and sent can't be defined from the Zabbix server. Here, it is important to keep in mind who will drive your software. Is it the Zabbix server or your software? To enable Zabbix to drive the sampling frequency, you need to implement the Zabbix agent protocol. The agent protocol is a bit more articulated and a bit more complex to implement. Anyway, the two examples proposed have all the components needed to properly handle the agent protocol.

There is another point to consider. Usually, developers have their own preference for a programming language. Here, it is important to use the right instrument to solve the problem. A practical example would be to monitor your Oracle database. So, your software will need to interact with commercial software; the easy and logical choice is to use Java. Now, all the Python fans will stick up their nose! Here, more than the preference, it is important keep in mind what is better supported from the monitored entity.

Oracle and databases in general produce standard industry-engineered drivers for Java to interact with them. Most of the database vendors provide and, more importantly, update, fix, and develop their JDBC drivers continuously. It is better to delegate a bit of work to vendors. Also, they know their products better, and you can get assistance on that.

Java has a lot of well-engineered components that will make your life easy in the difficult task of monitoring a database. For instance, the JDBC framework, together with the database driver, will provide efficient connection pooling that can be configured to:

- Handle a minimum number, and a maximum number, of connections
- Validate the connection before using it for your software
- Send a keep-alive packet (useful to avoid firewall issues)
- Handle a reap time, removing all the idle connections (reducing the total number of connections on the monitored server)

Those are only a few of the points covered by JDBC. All these points will help you to keep the monitoring lightweight and efficient.

 An example of software made to monitor databases in general is DBforBIX available at `http://sourceforge.net/projects/dbforbix/` or `http://www.smartmarmot.com/product/dbforbix/`.

Summary

In this chapter, we introduced you to the all the possible ways that will help you to interact with the server, thus enabling Zabbix to acquire items and metrics that are otherwise unsupported. In this chapter, we saw the steps required to move the Oracle monitoring script from the server side to the client side and then to its final destination—the dedicated server. Here, you learned how a simple script grows until it becomes a complex external software. In each step, you saw the progress and an analysis of the pros and cons of each location that the script passed. This does not mean that you need a dedicated server for all your checks, but if your monitoring of the script is widely and extensively used, then it is a good practice. For each location passed, you saw the positive side and the negative side of that particular placement. Now, you have a global vision of what can be done and which is the right place or point to act. Now, the Zabbix protocols have no more secrets, and you can extend Zabbix ideally without any limits.

In the next chapter, you will learn how to interact with Zabbix using the API. The next chapter will explain how you can take advantage of the Zabbix API for massive deployments of hosts and users, and massive and repetitive operations in general.

9
Extending Zabbix

Understanding the Zabbix monitoring protocol allows us to write scripts, agents, and custom probes. In other words, it allows us to freely extend Zabbix's monitoring capabilities by expanding its means to collect data.

When it comes to actually controlling and administrating its monitoring objects, though, the only point of access that we have mentioned until now is the web frontend. Whether you need to add a user, change the sampling frequency of an item, or look at historical data, you always need to use the frontend as a user interface.

This is certainly a convenient solution for day-to-day activities as all you need to have is access to a simple browser. The frontend itself is also quite powerful and flexible as you can conveniently perform mass operations on many objects of the same type and control different proxies from the same spot.

On the other hand, not every large and complex operation can be performed conveniently through a web application, and sometimes, you don't need to just visualize data, but you need to export it and feed it to other programs in order to further analyze it. This is where the Zabbix API comes in. As you will learn in this chapter, Zabbix's JSON-RPC API provides all the functions available to the frontend, including user management, monitoring configurations, and access to historical data.

In the following pages, we will cover the following topics:

- Writing code to connect to the API and make queries through it
- Creating custom operations to manage your installation
- Writing complex and conditional mass operations
- Exporting monitoring data in a number of different formats

Let's start with a look at the general API architecture and the way to set up your code in order to interact with it.

Exploring the Zabbix API

Zabbix provides an entry point to interact with, manipulate, configure, and create objects in Zabbix. This API is available through its PHP frontend at `http://<your-zabbix-server>/zabbix/api_jsonrpc.php`.

The communication protocol is JSON-based, and the medium used is obviously HTTP/HTTPS.

Zabbix's JSON-RPC API provides a nice interface and exposes a lot of functionalities. Once authenticated, it will allow you to perform any kind of operation on Zabbix objects. Now, if you need to configure Zabbix in a large or very large network, this Zabbix API can be really useful. As a practical example, you can consider that you may need to add a large number of devices that, most probably, are already defined in a separate document. The API provides the entry point to add all of them in Zabbix by simply using a dedicated script.

The Zabbix API was introduced with Zabbix Version 1.8 and went through changes up until the current Version 2.4. This version can be considered more stable and mature, but it is still officially in the draft state, so things may change a little in the future versions. This does not mean that it's not suitable for a production environment; on the contrary, the bigger the installation, the more beneficial can be the usage of the API to script for complex and time-consuming operations.

The following code is a simplified JSON request to the Zabbix API:

```
{
  "jsonrpc": "2.0",
  "method": "method.name",
  "params": {
    "param_1_name": "param_1_value",
    "param_2_name": "param_2_value"
  },
  "id": 1,
  "auth": "159121ba47d19a9b4b55124eab31f2b81"
}
```

The following points explain what the preceding lines of code represent:

- `"jsonrpc": "2.0"`: This is a standard JSON PRC parameter that is used to identify the protocol version; this will not change across your requests.

- `"method": "method.name"`: This parameter defines the operation that should be performed; for instance, it can be `host.create` or `item.update`.

- `"params"`: This specifies the parameter needed by the method in JSON. Here, if you want to create an item, the most common parameters will be `"name"` and `"key_"`.

- `"id": 1`: This field is useful to tie a JSON request to its response. Every response will have the same `"id"` provided in the request. This `"id"` is useful when you are going to send multiple requests at once if those requests don't need to be serialized or be sequential.

- `"auth": "159121ba47d19a9b4b55124eab31f2b81"`: This is the authentication token used to identify an authenticated user; for more details, refer to the next section.

 For a detailed description of all the possible parameters and methods, refer to the official Zabbix documentation available at https://www.zabbix.com/documentation/2.4/manual/appendix/api/api.

Now, it is important to remember that the whole communication usually is on HTTP. This is something to consider if we interact with Zabbix from our workstation or from a different network location. To interact with the Zabbix API, the first thing you need is authentication by the server, and here, it is clear how important it is to have the whole communication encrypted and to use a secured channel. There are two different exposures for you to consider:

- Use `https` instead of `http`; otherwise, the whole authentication will be in the clear format and readable

- Be aware of the sensitivity of the data being transmitted

Now, it is time to perform the first step here with the API. The step you can do is ask the version after the authentication.

First steps through the API

The first thing we can do is start interacting with the Zabbix API. Since the API requires POST to better understand the protocol, we will use `curl`.

With `curl`, you can quickly and easily transfer data from/to a service using different protocols, and here, we use HTTP in this first example; even if the channel is not secure, it is not a problem as we're simply asking the Zabbix version and as we are not yet logging in or receiving sensitive data.

```
$ curl --include --netrc --request POST --header "Content-Type:
application/json"  http://127.0.0.1/zabbix/api_jsonrpc.php -d @-
```

Between the options, we set the `Content-Type` header as JSON and enable `curl` to receive data from the standard input with `-d@-`. Once this is done, paste the following JSON envelope:

```
{
"jsonrpc":"2.0",
"method":"apiinfo.version",
"id":1,
"auth":null,
"params":{}
}
```

Take care to close the standard input with *Crtl + D*.

Now, let's see the response:

```
HTTP/1.1 200 OK
Date: Sat, 04 Jul 2015 06:32:36 GMT
Server: Apache/2.2.15 (CentOS)
X-Powered-By: PHP/5.3.3
Access-Control-Allow-Origin: *
Access-Control-Allow-Headers: Content-Type
Access-Control-Allow-Methods: POST
Access-Control-Max-Age: 1000
Content-Length: 41
Connection: close
Content-Type: application/json

{"jsonrpc":"2.0","result":"2.4.5","id":1}
```

After the standard HTTP header of the response, we can see the result of our query, that is, the Zabbix version `"result":"2.4.5"`.

> Please bear in mind that the `apiinfo.version` method has been introduced with Zabbix 2.0.4. If you're working with an old version of Zabbix, it might not be supported.

Authenticating through the API

Here, we discuss an example in a nutshell because this will show us how simple communication is; later, we will analyze an example with Python since it is widely used for rapid application development.

To test the authentication from our shell, we can use `curl` once again. Here, since we are going to authenticate our application to the Zabbix server, it is important to use a secured connection and then `https`. For this test, you can log on to your Zabbix server and write the following command:

```
$ curl --insecure --include --netrc --request POST --header "Content-
Type: application/json" https://127.0.0.1/zabbix/api_jsonrpc.php -d@-
```

Note that `--insecure` specifies to `curl` not to verify the server certificate. This option produces a less secure connection, but since we are the localhost, it is acceptable and will avoid a lot of certificate issues. Working on a practical example without `--insecure`, `curl` will respond with the following error:

```
curl: (60) Peer certificate cannot be authenticated with known CA
certificates
More details here: http://curl.haxx.se/docs/sslcerts.html
```

Once this command is run, you can paste the following JSON envelope:

```
{
"jsonrpc": "2.0",
"method": "user.login",
"params": {
"user": "Admin",
"password": "my secret password"
},
"auth": null,
"id": 0
}
```

Take care to replace the `"password"` properties with your own password, and then you can close the standard input using *Crtl + D*.

`curl` will take care to manage the whole HTTPS connection and will return the server's full HTTP response. In this case, we are interested in the authentication token that follows the standard web server response:

```
HTTP/1.1 200 OK
```

The remaining output is as follows:

```
Content-Type: application/json
{"jsonrpc":"2.0","result":"403bbcdc3c01d4d6e66f68f5f3057c3a","id":0}
```

This response contains the token that we need to use for all the following queries on the Zabbix server.

 The token will expire according to the `auto-logout` option set for the user who is authenticating.

Now, to see how all this work, we can use `curl` again:

```
# curl --insecure --include --netrc -request POST --header "Content-Type:
application/json" https://127.0.0.1/zabbix/api_jsonrpc.php -d @-
```

In this example, we are going to ask our server about the last history value for the Processor load (15 min average per core) item. In this particular case, on this server, the JSON envelope will be composed as follows:

```
{ "jsonrpc": "2.0",
    "method": "history.get",
    "params": {
        "output": "extend",
        "history": 0,
        "hostids": "10096",
         "itemid": "23966",
        "sortfield": "clock",
        "sortorder": "DESC",
        "limit": 1
    },
    "auth": "403bbcdc3c01d4d6e66f68f5f3057c3a",
    "id": 1
}
```

Remember that the request must contain the authentication token previously obtained using the `"user.authenticate"` method.

 Most of the APIs contain at least four methods: `get`, `create`, `update`, and `delete`, but please be aware that certain APIs may provide a totally different set of methods.

The server response in this case is the following:

```
HTTP/1.1 200 OK
```

```
{"jsonrpc":"2.0",
"result":[
{"hosts":
[{"hostid":"10096"}],
```

```
"itemid":"23840",
"clock":"1381263380",
"value":"0.1506",
"ns":"451462502"}
],"id":1}
```

In this example, you have seen a way to use the authentication token to query the historical data for a particular host/item. Of course, shell scripting is not the best method to interact with the Zabbix API because it requires a lot of coding to manage the "auth" token and it is better to use something more user friendly.

Using the PyZabbix library

Now that we have a clear understanding of the API's architecture and its JSON-RPC protocol, we can move beyond the manual construction of the JSON objects and rely on a dedicated library. This will allow us to focus on the actual features of the API and not on the specifics of the implementation.

There are quite a few Zabbix API libraries available for different languages, but the one we'll use for the rest of the chapter is PyZabbix, which is written by *Luke Cyca* (`https://github.com/lukecyca/pyzabbix/wiki`). It's a small, compact Python module that stays quite close to the API while still being easy to use. Moreover, Python's interactive console makes it quite convenient to try features and build a prototype before moving seamlessly to a complete script or application.

You can install PyZabbix very easily through Pip, the Python package installer:

$ pip install pyzabbix

Once the module has been installed, you'll be able to import it and use it in your scripts to manage a Zabbix installation.

The first thing to do is create an object for the API server and get an authentication token.

The following code fragments are shown as part of an interactive session, but they can also be part of any Python code:

```
>>> from pyzabbix import ZabbixAPI
>>> zh = ZabbixAPI("https://127.0.0.1/zabbix/")
>>> zh.login("Admin", "zabbix")
```

Needless to say, you have to use your actual Zabbix frontend URL and user credentials for this code to work in your environment. If all goes well, this is actually all there is to it. From now on, you can use the object handler to access any API method in the following way:

```
>>> zh.host.get(output="refer")
```

The "refer" options will give you only the primary key and the foreign key for any returned object:

```
[{'hostid': '9909900000010084'}, {'hostid': '9909900000010085'},
{'hostid': '9909900000010086'}, {'hostid': '9909900000010087'},
{'hostid': '9909900000010088'}]
```

Another advantage of using a Python library is that JSON data types map very cleanly onto Python ones, so much so that most of the time you won't even need to perform any additional type conversion. Here is a table that shows the specific types supported by the Zabbix API and a few examples of how they look both in JSON and within PyZabbix function calls:

Type	JSON	pyzabbix

bool	`{"jsonrpc" : "2.0"`
	`"method": "host.get",`
	`"params" : {`
	`"editable" : "true" }`
	`"auth" : <....>`
	`"id" : 1`
	`}}`
		`zh.host.`
		`get(editable="true")`

flag	`{"jsonrpc" : "2.0"`
	`"method": "host.get",`
	`"params" : {`
	`"countOutput" : "1" }`
	`"auth" : <....>`
	`"id" : 1`
	`}}`
		`zh.host.`
		`get(countOutput=1)`

integer	`{"jsonrpc" : "2.0"`
	`"method": "host.get",`
	`"params" : {`
	`"limit" : 10}`
	`"auth" : <....>`
	`"id" : 1`
	`}}`
		`zh.host.get(limit=10)`

Type	JSON	pyzabbix
string	```{"jsonrpc" : "2.0"` `"method": "host.get",` `"params" : {` `"sortfield": "name" }` `"auth" : <....>` `"id" : 1` `}}```	```zh.host.` `get(sortfield="name")```
timestamp	```{"jsonrpc": "2.0",` `"method":` `"event.get",` `"params": {` `"time_from":` `"1349797228",` `"time_till":` `"1350661228",},` `"auth": <...>,` `"id": 1` `}```	```zh.event.get(time_` `from="1349797228", time_` `till= "1350661228")```
array	```{"jsonrpc" : "2.0"` `"method": "host.get",` `"params" : {` `"hostids" : [1001, 1002,` `1003] }` `"auth" : <....>` `"id" : 1` `}}```	```zh.host.` `get(hostids=[1001, 1002,` `1003])```
object	```{"jsonrpc" : "2.0"` `"method": "host.get",` `"params" : {` `"filter": { "name":` `["Alpha", "Beta"] }` `"auth" : <....>` `"id" : 1` `} }```	```zh.host.` `get(filter={"name":` `["Alpha", "Beta"]})```
query	```{"jsonrpc" : "2.0"` `"method": "host.get",` `"params" : {` `"output": "extend" }` `"auth" : <....>` `"id" : 1` `}}```	```zh.host.` `get(output="extend")```

The library creates the method requests on the fly, so it's fairly futureproof, which means any new or updated methods in the API will be automatically supported.

We can now move on to explore a few concrete examples of API usage. In order to keep the code readable and to focus on the API, and not on general programming issues, all the examples will have a very simplistic and direct approach to data handling, without much data validation or error management. While you can certainly use the following fragments in interactive sessions or as part of more complex applications (or even to build a suite of dedicated command-line tools), you are strongly encouraged to make them more robust with the appropriate error-handling and data validation controls.

Exploring the Zabbix API with JQuery

Another interesting project that we can download and check is JQZabbix. For more information about this project, you can refer to https://github.com/kodai/jqzabbix.

JQZabbix is a demo application readymade to test the Zabbix API and, sometimes, it can be useful to have it installed somewhere as it allows a simple web browser to do a JSON-RPC query against our Zabbix server without the need to write scripts.

To install the package, we need to download the package; here, we can simply clone the GitHub repository with the following command:

```
$ mkdir jqzabbix && cd jqzabbix
$ git clone https://github.com/kodai/jqzabbix
```

The project will download a demo directory contained in the jqzabbix GitHub clone. We need to create a new location that we can call jqzabbix under DocumentRoot of httpd. Usually, the document root is located at /var/www/html, but it is better to check the DocumentRoot directive under /etc/httpd/conf/httpd. conf. Running the following command as root, we can now copy the required jqzabbix files:

```
$ mkdir /var/www/html/jqzabbix
$ cp <your-jqzabbix-location>/demo/* /var/www/html/jqzabbix/
$ cp <your-jqzabbix-location>/jqzabbix/* /var/www/html/jqzabbix/
Now all you have to do to see it in action is edit the file main.js
changing the following entry:
// Zabbix server API url
var url = 'http://localhost/zabbix/api_jsonrpc.php';
```

This `url` variable needs to contain the real IP address or DNS name of our Zabbix server.

Once this is done, you can simply check by opening a browser. The home page is available at `http://<your-zabbix-server>/jqzabbix/`.

Opening your browser, you'll see something similar to the following screenshot:

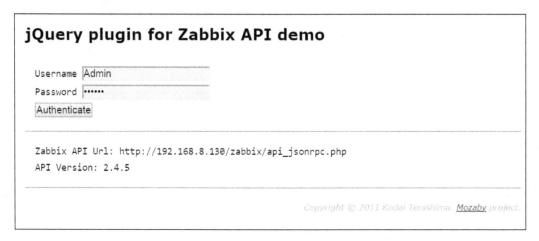

This application is interesting to see as it is an example of coding the Zabbix API using jQuery. This application enables you to use most of the methods supported by the Zabbix API:

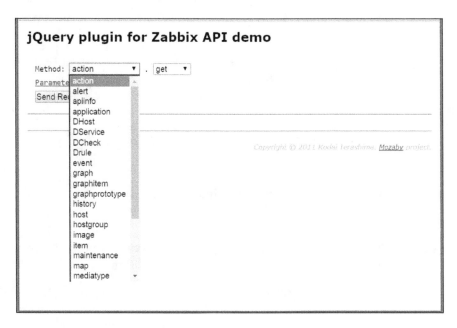

What follows, for instance, is the result of a `host.get` call:

jQuery plugin for Zabbix API demo

Method: host ▼ . get ▼
Parameters
Send Request

Result: 8

hostid	proxy_hostid	host	status	disable_until	error	available	errors_from	lastaccess	ipmi_authtype	ipmi_privilege	ipmi_username	ipmi_password	ipmi_disable_until
10112	10113	ZabbixProxy	0	0		1	0	0	-1	2			0
10107	0	OraSRVprd	0	0		0	0	0	-1	2			0
10084	0	Zabbix server	0	0		1	0	0	-1	2			0
10105	10111	Alpha	0	0		1	0	0	-1	2			0
10106	10111	Beta	0	0		1	0	0	-1	2			0
10109	10111	Gamma	0	0		1	0	0	-1	2			0
10110	10113	Lambda	0	0		1	0	0	-1	2			0
10114	0	Test Host 1	0	0		0	0	0	2	2	zabbix	you-password-here	0

Let's see with more details how this application works. You can take a look at the `main.js` file. The first thing that is done is the creation of the `jqzabbix` object with several options, which are mostly optional. The following are the default values:

```
server = new $.jqzabbix({
    url: 'http://localhost/zabbix/api_jsonrpc.php',   // URL of Zabbix
API
    username: 'Admin',    // Zabbix login user name
    password: 'zabbix',   // Zabbix login password
    basicauth: false,     // If you use basic authentication, set true
for this option
    busername: '',        // User name for basic authentication
    bpassword: '',        // Password for basic authentication
    timeout: 5000,        // Request timeout (milli second)
    limit: 1000,          // Max data number for one request
})
```

Then, check the Zabbix API version with the following calls:

```
server.getApiVersion();
```

If the request is completed successfully, it is time for authentication:

```
server.userLogin();
```

Once it is completed, the authentication ID is stored in server property. Now, you can execute the normal API method as per their own definition:

```
server.sendAjaxRequest(method, params, success, error)
```

Here, we have:

- `method`: The Zabbix API method listed on the Zabbix API document
- `params`: The Zabbix API method parameters
- `success`: The success callback function
- `error`: The error callback function

As you can see, this is a very simple package but it can be really useful to compare the values returned by the API with your own scripts and so on. Plus, it is a good starting point if you're thinking about coding a jQuery application. Here, thanks to the Zabbix API, the only limit we have is our imagination, but the API thanks the developer for allowing us to automate all the repetitive tasks and many maintenance tasks.

Mass operations

Now it is time to see the Python Zabbix API in action. Another common use of the API facility is to automate certain operations that you can perform from the web frontend, but they may be cumbersome or prone to errors. Things such as adding many users or updating the host IP addresses after merging two different networks fall under this category. The following fragments will assume that you already have a Zabbix API handle just as shown in the previous paragraphs. In other words, from now on, it will be assumed that your code will start with something similar to the following (remember that the Zabbix URL and user credentials here are just examples! Use your own URL and credentials):

```python
#!/usr/bin/python
from pyzabbix import ZabbixAPI
user='Admin'
pwd='password'
url = 'https://127.0.0.1/zabbix/'
zh = ZabbixAPI(url)
zh.login(user=user, password=pwd)
```

Redistributing hosts to proxies

We have seen in *Chapter 2, Distributed Monitoring*, that you can add hosts to a proxy through the proxy configuration form or by updating every single host's `monitored by` property. Both of these methods can be too slow and cumbersome if you have a great number of hosts and you need to update more than just a handful of them. If you just need to move an entire group of hosts from one proxy to another, you could also use the mass update functionality of the frontend, but if you need to distribute hosts to different proxies or work on just a few hosts from many different groups, this approach won't scale well.

Here is one way to redistribute all the hosts monitored by a proxy to all the other proxies in your Zabbix installation. A possible reason to do this is that you may be doing some proxy maintenance and you need to bring it down for a while, but you don't want to suspend monitoring for a whole bunch of hosts, so you redistribute them to other proxies.

First, let's get the proxy ID and the proxy name:

```
proxy_name = "ZBX Proxy 1"
proxy_id = zh.proxy.get(filter={"host": proxy_name}, output="refer")
[0]['proxyid']
```

Once you have the proxy's ID, get the list of monitored hosts:

```
hlist = zh.proxy.get(selectHosts=['hostid'], proxyids=proxy_id,
output="refer")[0]['hosts']
hosts = [x['hostid'] for x in hlist]
```

Next, for simplicity's sake, let's just get the list of all other proxies, excluding the one you are removing hosts from:

```
proxies =   [x['proxyid'] for x in zh.proxy.get() if x['proxyid'] !=
proxyid]
```

Now, we need to split the host list in as many roughly equal-sized chunks as the number of proxies available:

```
nparts = int(round(len(hosts)/len(proxies)))
hostchunks = [list(hosts[i:i+nparts]) for i in
range(0,len(hosts),nparts)]
```

The preceding code will divide your host list into as many sublists as the number of proxies you have. All that is left to do is actually assign the hosts to the proxies:

```
for c in len(hostchunks):
  zh.proxy.update(proxyid=proxies[c], hosts=hostchunks[c])
```

And that's it. The `proxy.update` method will automatically reassign hosts, so you don't even have to remove them first from the original one. You can, of course, make things more robust by only selecting proxies in the same network as the one you are doing maintenance on or by saving the host list so you can reassign it to the original proxy once it's available.

Adding or updating users

Even if you rely on some external authentication method for your Zabbix users, such as an LDAP server or Active Directory, no new user account will have any media information set, nor will it belong to any group. This means that you'll still need to manually configure every user unless you create new users or update existing ones through some kind of code. For simplicity's sake, let's assume that you already have a list of usernames, e-mail addresses, and the groups they should belong to, all gathered in a semicolon-separated `users.csv` file that looks like the following:

```
adallevacche,a.dallevacche@example.com,Admins
jdoe,jdoe@foo.bar,DB admins; App Servers
mbrown,mbrown@example.org,Net admins
```

The script that you are going to write will assume that the first field of every line will contain the username (called `alias` in the API). The second field will contain an e-mail address, while the last field will be a comma-separated list of user groups that the user should belong to. Updating your users' information is quite simple. First, you need to read into your script the contents of the `users.csv` file:

```
with open('users.csv', 'r') as f:
    users = f.readlines()
```

Assuming that your Zabbix API connection object is called `zh`, you can now define a couple of helper functions and variables. The `mediatypeid` will be needed to update your users' media information. Assuming that you have only one e-mail media type defined in your Zabbix installation, you can get its ID by calling the following:

```
mediatypeid = zh.mediatype.get(output="refer",
filter={"description": ['Email']})[0]['mediatypeid']
```

Unless you want to extend your `.csv` file with information about the severity and the time period for each one of your users' media, you can also define a common template for all e-mail contacts:

```
def mkusermedia(mediatype='', email='', mediaid=''):
return { "mediaid": mediaid
  "mediatypeid": mediatype,
  "sendto": email,
  "active": 0,
```

```
    "severity": 63,
    "period": "1-7,00:00-24:00"
}
```

Please note how 0 means *enabled*, while 1 means *disabled* for the active property. Also, while the period property is fairly self-explanatory, the severity property could look quite puzzling at first. It's actually a binary bitmap value and can be more easily understood if you take into consideration the trigger severity values and put them in order. Each severity level occupies a position of a 6-bit value:

Severity	Disaster	High	Average	Warning	Information	Not classified
Enabled?	1	1	1	1	1	1
Decimal value	111111 = 63					

Since 63 equals *111111* in binary form, this means that the user will receive notifications for every severity level. If you want to receive notifications only for the disaster severity, you will have a *100000* bitmap and so a severity value of *32*:

Severity	Disaster	High	Average	Warning	Information	Not classified
Enabled?	1	0	0	0	0	0
Decimal value	100000 = 32					

Similarly, to get notifications for disaster and higher levels, you'll need a *110000* bitmap and a severity value of *48*, and so on.

Severity	Disaster	High	Average	Warning	Information	Not classified
Enabled?	1	1	0	0	0	0
Decimal value	110000 = 48					

The following helper function will get a list of group names and return a list of user group IDs that actually exist, thus ignoring non-existing group names:

```
def getgroupids(grouplist):
    return zh.usergroup.get(output=['usergrpid'], filter={"name":
grouplist.split(",")})
```

We can now proceed to actually work the user list to either update existing users or create new ones:

```
for u in users:
    (alias, email, groups) = u.split(",")
    user = zh.user.get(output=['userid'], filter={"alias": [alias]})
    if not user:
        zh.user.create(alias=alias,
                        passwd="12345",
                        usrgrps=getgroupids(groups),
                user_medias=[mkusermedia(mediatype=mediatypeid,
                        email=email)])
```

The `if` statement checks whether the user exists. If not, the `user.create` method will take care of creating it, adding it to the appropriate groups and creating the media contact as well. You need to define a password even if your users will authenticate from an external source. Depending on your password management policies, your users should be strongly encouraged to change it as soon as possible, or, better yet, you could directly generate a random password instead of using a fixed string.

The second part of the `if` construct will get `userid` and update the user's information:

```
else:
    userid=user[0]['userid']
    zh.user.update(userid=userid,srgrps=getgroupids(groups))
    usermedia = zh.usermedia.get(filter={"userid" : userid},
                                output=['mediaid'])
    zh.user.updatemedia(users = [userid],
                    medias=[mkusermedia(
                    mediaid=usermedia[0]['mediaid'],
                    mediatype=mediatypeid,
                    email=email)])
```

 Please note the way you need to call two different methods here for user groups and media instead of just one. The first one will update group information; the second one will check for an already-defined e-mail address, and the third will update the said address or create a new one if it doesn't exist.

You can run the preceding code periodically to keep your user accounts updated. Obvious improvements would be adding each user's name and surname or getting user data directly from an LDAP server or any other source instead of from a .csv file.

Exporting data

Besides directly manipulating and monitoring internal objects, another compelling use of the Zabbix API is to extract data for further analysis outside of the Zabbix frontend. Maps, screens, graphs, triggers, and history tables can be excellent reporting tools, but they are all meant to be used inside the frontend. Sometimes, you may need the raw data in order to perform custom calculations on it—especially when it comes to capacity planning—or you may need to produce a document with a few custom graphs and other data. If you find yourself with such needs on a regular basis, it makes sense to write some code and extract your data through the API. An interesting feature of the get methods, which are the fundamental building blocks of any data extraction code, is that they come with quite a few filters and options out of the box. If you are willing to spend some time studying them, you'll find that you are able to keep your code small and clean as you won't usually have to get lots of data to filter through, but you'll be able to build queries that can be quite focused and precise.

Let's see a few short examples in the following paragraphs.

Extracting tabular data

Zabbix provides a way to group similar items in a host in order to navigate them more easily when looking at the latest monitoring data. These item containers, called applications, come in very handy when the number of items in a host is quite consistent. If you group all CPU-monitoring items together under a label, say CPU, all filesystem-related items under filesystems, and so on, you could find the data you are looking for more easily. Applications are just labels tied to a specific template or host and are just used to categorize items. This makes them simple and lightweight. But it also means that they are not really used elsewhere in the Zabbix system.

Still, it's sometimes useful to look at the trigger status or event history, not just by the host but by the application too. A report of all network-related problems regardless of the host, host group, or specific trigger, could be very useful for some groups in your IT department. The same goes for a report on filesystem events, database problems, and so on.

Let's see how you can build a script that will export all events related to a specific application into a .csv file. The setup is basically the same as the previous examples:

```python
#!/usr/bin/python
from pyzabbix import ZabbixAPI
import sys
import csv
from datetime import datetime
appname = sys.argv[1]
```

```
timeformat="%d/%m/%y %H:%M"
zh = ZabbixAPI("http://locahost/zabbix")
zh.login(user="Admin", password="zabbix")
```

As you can see, the application name is taken from the command line, while the API's URL and credentials are just examples. When you use your own, you can also consider using an external configuration file for more flexibility. Since events are recorded using a Unix timestamp, you'll need to convert it to a readable string later on. The `timeformat` variable will let you define your preferred format. Speaking of formats, the `.csv` module will let you define the output format of your report with more flexibility than a series of manual prints.

Now, you can proceed to extract all applications that share the name you passed on the command line:

```
applications = zh.application.get(output="shorten", filter={"name":
[appname]})
```

Once we have the list of applications, you can get the list of items that belong to the said application:

```
items = zh.item.get(output="count", applicationids=[x['applicationid']
for x in applications])
```

From there, you still need to extract all the triggers that contain the given items before moving on to the actual events:

```
triggers = zh.trigger.get(output="refer", itemids=[x['itemid'] for x
in items])
```

Now, you can finally get the list of events that are related to the application you are interested in:

```
events = zh.event.get(triggerids=[j['triggerid'] for j in triggers])
```

Here, only the event IDs are extracted. You didn't ask for a specific time period, so it's possible that a great number of events will be extracted. For every event, we'll also need to extract all related hosts, triggers, and items. To do that, let's first define a couple of helper functions to get the host, item, and trigger names:

```
def gethostname(hostid=''):
    return zh.host.get(hostids=hostid, output=['host'])[0]['host']

def getitemname(itemid=''):
    return zh.item.get(itemids=itemid, output=['name'])[0]['name']

def gettriggername(triggerid=''):
    return zh.trigger.get(triggerids=triggerid,
expandDescription="1", output=['description'])[0]['description']
```

Finally, you can define an empty `eventstable` table and fill it with event information based on what you have extracted until now:

```
eventstable = []
triggervalues = ['OK', 'problem', 'unknown']
for e in events:
        eventid = e['eventid']
        event = zh.event.get(eventids=eventid,
                        selectHosts="refer",
                        selectItems="refer",
                        selectTriggers="refer",
                        output="extend")
        host = gethostname(event[0]['hosts'][0]['hostid'])
        item = getitemname(event[0]['items'][0]['itemid'])
        trigger = gettriggername(event[0]['triggers'][0]['triggerid'])
        clock = datetime.fromtimestamp(int(event[0]['clock'])).
strftime(timeformat)
        value = triggervalues[int(event[0]['value'])]
        eventstable.append({"Host": host,
                        "Item": item,
                        "Trigger": trigger,
                        "Status": value,
                        "Time" : clock
                })
```

Now that you have all the events' details, you can create the output `.csv` file:

```
filename = "events_" + appname + "_" + datetime.now().
strftime("%Y%m%d%H%M")
fieldnames = ['Host', 'Item', 'Trigger', 'Status', 'Time']
outfile = open(filename, 'w')
csvwriter = csv.DictWriter(outfile, delimiter=';',
fieldnames=fieldnames)
csvwriter.writerow(dict((h,h) for h in fieldnames))
for row in eventstable:
        csvwriter.writerow(row)
outfile.close()
```

The report's filename will be automatically generated based on the application you want to focus on and the time of execution. Since every event in the `eventstable` array is `dict`, a `fieldnames` array is needed to tell the `csv.DictWriter` module in what order the fields should be written. Next, a column header is written before finally looping over the `eventstable` array and writing out the information we want.

There are a number of ways that you can expand on this script in order to get even more useful data. Here are a few suggestions, but the list is limited only by your imagination:

- Ask for an optional time period to limit the number of events extracted
- Order events by host and trigger
- Perform calculations to add the event duration based on the change in the trigger state
- Add acknowledged data if present

Creating graphs from data

At this point in the book, you should be familiar with Zabbix's powerful data visualization possibilities. On the frontend, you can create and visualize many kinds of graphs, maps, and charts that can help you to analyze and understand item history data, changes in the trigger status over time, IT services availability, and so on. Just as any other Zabbix capabilities, all of the visualization functions are also exposed through the API. You can certainly write programs to create, modify, or visualize screens, graphs, and maps, but unless you are building a custom frontend, it's quite unlikely that you'll ever need to do so.

On the other hand, it may be interesting to extract and visualize data that is otherwise too dispersed and hard to analyze through the frontend. A good example of such data is trigger dependency. You may recall from *Chapter 6, Managing Alerts*, that a trigger can depend on one or more other triggers such that it won't change to a **PROBLEM** state if the trigger it depends on is already in a **PROBLEM** state.

As useful as this feature is, there's no easy way to see at a glance the triggers that depend on other triggers, if those triggers, in turn, depend on other triggers, and so on. The good news is that with the help of the Graphviz package and a couple of lines of Python code, you can create a handy visualization of all trigger dependencies.

The Graphviz suite of programs

Graphviz (http://www.graphviz.org) is a suite of graph visualization software utilities that enables you to create arbitrary complex graphs from specially formatted text data. The suite provides you with many features for data visualization and can become quite complex to use, but it is quite simple to create a basic, functional setup that you can later build on.

If you do not have it installed on your system, Graphviz is just a `yum install` command away if you are on a Red Hat Enterprise Linux system:

```
# yum install 'graphviz*'
```

The program you will use to create your graphs is called dot. Dot takes a graph text description and generates the corresponding image in a number of formats. A graph description looks similar to this:

```
digraph G {
        main → node1 → node2;
        main → node3;
        main → end;
        node2 → node4;
        node2 → node5;
        node3 → node4;
        node4 → end;
}
```

Put the preceding graph in a `graph.gv` file and run the following command:

```
$ dot -Tpng graph.gv -o graph.png
```

You will obtain a PNG image file that will look somewhat similar to the following diagram:

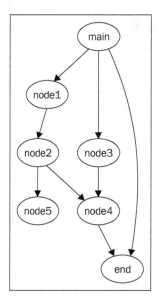

As you can see, it should be fairly simple to create a trigger-dependency graph once we have extracted the right information through the API. Let's see how we can do it.

Creating a trigger dependency graph

The following is a Python script that will extract data about trigger dependencies and output a dot language graph description that you can later feed into the dot program itself:

```
#!/usr/bin/python
from pyzabbix import ZabbixAPI
zh = ZabbixAPI("https://127.0.0.1/zabbix")
zh.login(user="Admin", password="zabbix")

def gettriggername(triggerid=''):
    return zh.trigger.get(triggerids=triggerid,
output=['description'])[0]['description']
```

In the first part, there are no surprises. A Zabbix API session is initiated and a simple helper function, identical to the one shown before, is defined:

```
tr = zh.trigger.get(selectDependencies="refer", expandData="1",
output="refer")
dependencies = [(t['dependencies'], t['host'], t['triggerid']) for t
in tr if t['dependencies'] != [] ]
```

The next two lines extract all triggers and their dependencies and then create a list, filtering out triggers that don't have any dependencies:

```
outfile = open('trigdeps.gv', 'w')
outfile.write('digraph TrigDeps {\n')
outfile.write('graph[rankdir=LR]\n')
outfile.write('node[fontsize=10]\n')
```

Here, the first few lines of the graph are written out to the output file, thus setting up the graph direction from left to right and the font size for the nodes' labels:

```
for (deps, triggerhost, triggerid) in dependencies:
    triggername = gettriggername(triggerid)

    for d in deps:
        depname = gettriggername(d['triggerid'])
        dephost = d['host']
        edge = '"{}:\\n{}" -> "{}:\\n{}";'.format(dephost, depname,
triggerhost, triggername)
        outfile.write(edge + '\n')
```

This is the core of the script. The double `for` loop is necessary because a single trigger may have more than one dependency and you want to map out all of them. For every dependency-trigger relationship found, an edge is defined in the graph file:

```
outfile.write('}\n')
outfile.close()
```

Once the script reaches the end of the list, there is nothing more to do except close the graph description and close the output file.

Execute the script:

```
$ chmod +x triggerdeps.py
```

```
$ ./triggerdeps.py
```

You will get a `trigdeps.gv` file that will look somewhat similar to this:

```
digraph TrigDeps {
graph[rankdir=LR]
node[fontsize=10]
"Template IPMI Intel SR1630:\nPower" -> "Template IPMI Intel SR1630:\
nBaseboard Temp Critical [{ITEM.VALUE}]";
"Template IPMI Intel SR1630:\nBaseboard Temp Critical [{ITEM.VALUE}]"
-> "Template IPMI Intel SR1630:\nBaseboard Temp Non-Critical [{ITEM.
VALUE}]";
"Template IPMI Intel SR1630:\nPower" -> "Template IPMI Intel SR1630:\
nBaseboard Temp Non-Critical [{ITEM.VALUE}]";
"Template IPMI Intel SR1630:\nPower" -> "Template IPMI Intel SR1630:\
nBB +1.05V PCH Critical [{ITEM.VALUE}]";
"Template IPMI Intel SR1630:\nBB +1.05V PCH Critical [{ITEM.VALUE}]"
-> "Template IPMI Intel SR1630:\nBB +1.05V PCH Non-Critical [{ITEM.
VALUE}]";
"Template IPMI Intel SR1630:\nPower" -> "Template IPMI Intel SR1630:\
nBB +1.05V PCH Non-Critical [{ITEM.VALUE}]";
"Template IPMI Intel SR1630:\nPower" -> "Template IPMI Intel SR1630:\
nBB +1.1V P1 Vccp Critical [{ITEM.VALUE}]";
}
```

Just run it through the dot program in order to obtain your dependencies graphs:

```
$ dot -Tpng trigdeps.gv -o trigdeps.png
```

The resulting diagram will probably be quite big; the following is a close up of a sample resulting image:

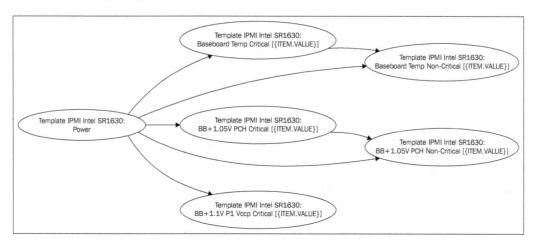

From improving the layout and the node shapes, to integrating the graph generating part into Python with its `graphviz` bindings, once again, there are many ways to improve the script. Moreover, you could feed the image back to a Zabbix map using the API, or you could invert the process and define trigger dependencies based on an external definition.

Generating Zabbix maps from dot files

Now, it is interesting to see how starting with a `Graphviz` dot file, we can generate a Zabbix map in an automated way. Here, the automation is quite interesting as Zabbix is affected by certain boring issues, such as:

- You can't move multiple elements at the same time: `https://support.zabbix.com/browse/ZBXNEXT-161`

- You can't add hosts in bulk: `https://support.zabbix.com/browse/ZBXNEXT-163`

- You can't clone any existing map element: `https://support.zabbix.com/browse/ZBXNEXT-51`

- When you are using icons, you can't select them automatically, so you need to check their size and check whether they fit on your map: `https://support.zabbix.com/browse/ZBXNEXT-1608`

Those are already a good set of points to think about an automated way to speed up a long and slow process. Graphviz provides us with a good tool to be used in this case to generate an image and transform it into Zabbix's API calls. What we need to do is:

1. Read out the dot file.
2. Generate the topology using `graphviz`.
3. Acquire all the coordinates from our topology that has been generated.
4. Use PyZabbix to connect to our Zabbix server.
5. Generate our topology in a fully automated way.

We can now, finally, start coding lines in Python; the following example is similar to the one presented by Volker Fröhlich. Anyway, the code here has been changed and fixed (it did not work well with Zabbix 2.4).

As the first thing, we need to import the `ZabbixApi` and `networkx` libraries:

```
import networkx as nx
from pyzabbix import ZabbixAPI
```

Then, we can define the Graphviz DOT file to use as a source; here, we can generate our DOT file by exporting data from Zabbix itself, which involves taking care to populate all the relations between the nodes. In this example, we are using a simple line of code:

```
dot_file="/tmp/example.dot"
```

In the next lines, we will define our username, password, map dimension, and the relative map name:

```
username="Admin"
password="zabbix"
width = 800
height = 600
mapname = "my_network"
```

What follows here is a static map to define the element type:

```
ELEMENT_TYPE_HOST = 0
ELEMENT_TYPE_MAP = 1
ELEMENT_TYPE_TRIGGER = 2
ELEMENT_TYPE_HOSTGROUP = 3
ELEMENT_TYPE_IMAGE = 4
ADVANCED_LABELS = 1
LABEL_TYPE_LABEL = 0
```

Then, we can define the icons to use and the relative color code:

```
icons = {
    "router": 23,
    "cloud": 26,
    "desktop": 27,
    "laptop": 28,
    "server": 29,
    "sat": 30,
    "tux": 31,
    "default": 40,
}
colors = {
    "purple": "FF00FF",
    "green": "00FF00",
    "default": "00FF00",
}
```

Now, we will define certain functions: the first one is to manage the login and the second one is to define a host lookup:

```
def api_connect():
    zapi = ZabbixAPI("http://127.0.0.1/zabbix/")
    zapi.login(username, password)
    return zapi

def host_lookup(hostname):
    hostid = zapi.host.get({"filter": {"host": hostname}})
    if hostid:
        return str(hostid[0]['hostid'])
```

The next thing to do is read our dot file and start converting it into a graph:

```
G=nx.read_dot(dot_file)
```

Then, we can finally open our graph:

```
pos = nx.graphviz_layout(G)
```

> Here, you can select your preferred algorithm. Graphviz supports many different kind of layouts. You can change the look and feel of your map as desired. For more information about Graphviz, please check the official documentation available at http://www.graphviz.org/.

Then, the next thing to do, as the graph is already generated, is find the maximum coordinates of the layout. This will enable us to scale our predefined map output size better:

```
positionlist=list(pos.values())
maxpos=map(max, zip(*positionlist))
for host, coordinates in pos.iteritems():
    pos[host] = [int(coordinates[0]*width/maxpos[0]*0.95-
coordinates[0]*0.1), int((height-coordinates[1]*height/maxpos[1])*0.95
+coordinates[1]*0.1)]
nx.set_node_attributes(G,'coordinates',pos)
```

 Graphviz and Zabbix use two different data origins—Graphviz starts from the bottom left corner and Zabbix works starting from the top left corner.

Then, we need to retrieve `selementids` as they are required for links and even for the node data coordinates:

```
selementids = dict(enumerate(G.nodes_iter(), start=1))
selementids = dict((v,k) for k,v in selementids.iteritems())
nx.set_node_attributes(G,'selementid',selementids)
nx.set_node_attributes(G,'selementid',selementids)
```

Now, we will define the map on Zabbix, the name, and the relative map size:

```
map_params = {
    "name": mapname,
    "label_type": 0,
    "width": width,
    "height": height
}
element_params=[]
link_params=[]
```

Finally, we can connect to our Zabbix server:

```
zapi = api_connect()
```

Then, prepare all the node information and the coordinates, and then set the icon to use:

```
for node, data in G.nodes_iter(data=True):
    # Generic part
    map_element = {}
    map_element.update({
```

```
            "selementid": data['selementid'],
            "x": data['coordinates'][0],
            "y": data['coordinates'][1],
            "use_iconmap": 0,
            })
```

Check, whether we have the hostname:

```
if "hostname" in data:
    map_element.update({
            "elementtype": ELEMENT_TYPE_HOST,
            "elementid": host_lookup(data['hostname'].strip('"')),
            "iconid_off": icons['server'],
            })
else:
    map_element.update({
        "elementtype": ELEMENT_TYPE_IMAGE,
        "elementid": 0,
        })
```

We will now set labels for the images:

```
if "label" in data:
    map_element.update({
        "label": data['label'].strip('"')
        })
if "zbximage" in data:
    map_element.update({
        "iconid_off": icons[data['zbximage'].strip('"')],
        })
elif "hostname" not in data and "zbximage" not in data:
    map_element.update({
        "iconid_off": icons['default'],
        })


    element_params.append(map_element)
```

Now, we need to scan all the edges to create the element links based on the element. We've identified `selementids`:

```
nodenum = nx.get_node_attributes(G,'selementid')
for nodea, nodeb, data in G.edges_iter(data=True):
    link = {}
    link.update({
        "selementid1": nodenum[nodea],
        "selementid2": nerodenum[nodeb],
```

```
            })

    if "color" in data:
        color =  colors[data['color'].strip('"')]
        link.update({
            "color": color
        })
    else:
        link.update({
            "color": colors['default']
        })

    if "label" in data:
        label =  data['label'].strip('"')
        link.update({
            "label": label,
        })

    link_params.append(link)

# Join the prepared information
map_params["selements"] = element_params
map_params["links"] = link_params
```

Now, we have populated all `map_params`. We need to call Zabbix's API with that data:

```
map=zapi.map.create(map_params)
```

The program is now complete, and we can let it run! In a real-case scenario, the time spent to design a topology of more than 2,500 hosts is only 2-3 seconds!

We can test the software here that has been proposed against a dot file that contains 24 hosts:

```
[root@localhost]# time ./Generate_MyMap.py
real    0m0.005s
user    0m0.002s
sys     0m0.003s
```

As you can see, our software is really quick… but let's check what has been generated. In the next picture, you can see the map generated automatically in 0.005 seconds:

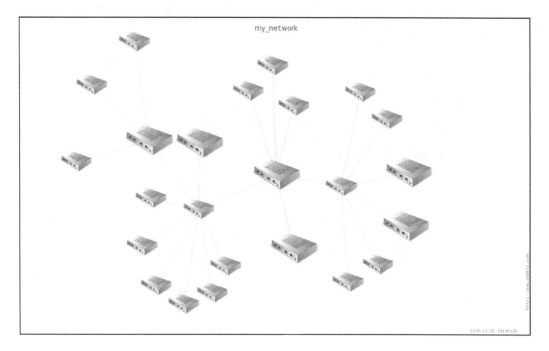

The goal of this example was to see how we can easily automate complex and long tasks using the Zabbix API. The same method proposed here is really useful when you have to create or do the initial startup. Also, nowadays, there are quite a few tools that can provide you with the data of the host already monitored, for example, Cisco Prime or other vendor-specific management tools from where you can extract a considerable amount of data, convert it into .dot, and populate the Zabbix hosts, maps, and so on.

Summary

In this chapter, we barely scratched the surface of what is possible once you begin playing with the powerful Zabbix API. If you worked through the examples, we can assume that you are comfortable with the JSON-RPC protocol, which is the foundation of the API. You should know how to explore the various methods and have some ideas on how to use them to make your Zabbix management tasks easier or to further expand the system's data manipulation possibilities.

With the discussion of the API, we conclude our exploration of Zabbix's features. The next and final chapter will build upon the knowledge you have gained until now and use it to make Zabbix a more integral part of your IT infrastructure by opening communication channels with other management systems.

10
Integrating Zabbix

A monitoring system is, by definition, all about connecting and communicating with other systems. On the one hand, it needs to connect to its monitored objects in order to take measurements and evaluate the service status. On the other hand, it needs to be able to communicate the collected information outside of itself so that system administrators can act on the data and an alarm is raised. In the previous chapters of the book, we focused mainly on the first part of the equation, namely collecting data, and always assumed that the second part, exposing data and warnings, would involve sending a series of messages to human operators. While this is certainly the most common setup, the one that will be at the core of every Zabbix deployment, it's also true that it can prove to be quite limited in a large, complex IT environment.

Every managing system has a specific, detailed view of its environment that is directly dependent on the function it must perform. Identity management systems know all about users, passwords, and permissions, while inventory systems keep track of hardware and software configurations and deployment. Trouble ticketing systems keep track of current issues with users, while monitoring systems keep track of the availability status and performance metrics of anything they can connect to. As many of these systems actually share some common data among them, whether it is user information, connection configuration, or anything else, it is vital that as much of this data as possible is allowed to pass from one system to the next without constant manual intervention on the part of the administrators.

It will be impossible for Zabbix or any monitoring system to come with an out-of-the-box integration with any other arbitrary system in the world. Its open source nature, clear protocol, and powerful APIs make it relatively easy to integrate your monitoring system with any other IT management tools you have deployed in your environment. This can be the subject of a book in itself, but we will try to get you started on the path of Zabbix integration by looking at one such integration possibility.

In this chapter, you will see a concrete example of integration between Zabbix and WhatsApp™ and an example of integration between Zabbix and **Request Tracker** (**RT**). I don't think there is any need to explain what WhatsApp is as it is a widely known messaging system that now supports encryption and even phone calls using VoIP.

Request Tracker is the open source trouble ticket management system from Best Practical (http://bestpractical.com/rt/). By the end of the chapter, you will be able to do the following:

- Route an alert directly to your Unix system administrator and support via WhatsApp
- Integrate custom media with Zabbix
- Relay an alert to a trouble ticketing system
- Keep track of which tickets relate to which events
- Update event acknowledgments based on the status of a ticket
- Automatically close specific tickets when a trigger returns to an OK state

There won't be any new concepts or Zabbix functionality explained here as we'll explore some of the real-world applications made possible by the features we have already learned about in the rest of the book.

Stepping into WhatsApp

WhatsApp is so widely used that it does not require any kind of presentation. More interesting is that, on the other hand, the libraries that have been developed using the WhatsApp communication protocol. In this example, we are going to use a Python library, **Yowsup**, that will enable us to interact with WhatsApp. Anyway, during the year, we had quite a few libraries that were developed around this service. Yowsup has been used to create an unofficial WhatsApp client for Nokia N9 through the Wazapp project, which was in use by more than 200K users. Another fully featured unofficial client for Blackberry 10 has been created using Yowsup, which is a robust component that we can use for our integration.

Let's have a look at the requirements:

- Python 2.6+, or Python 3.0 +
- Python packages: `python-dateutil`
- Python packages for end-to-end encryption: `protobuf`, `pycrypto`, and `python-axolotl-curve25519`
- Python packages for `yowsup-cli`: `argparse`, `readline`, and `pillow` (to send images)

Then, we can start installing the required packages as root with `yum`:

```
$ yum install python python-dateutil python-argparse
```

`Yum`, as usual, will resolve all the dependencies for us; now we can finally start downloading Yowsup. You need to decide whether you prefer to clone the Git repository or download directly archive packages of `master`. In this example, we will download the package:

```
# wget https://github.com/tgalal/yowsup/archive/master.zip
```

Once the zip archive has been saved, we can extract it using:

```
# unzip master.zip
```

This will expand the zip archive by reproducing the Git directory structure. Now, we can step into the main directory:

```
# cd ./yowsup-master
```

And from there, we can build the project. To build the software, you need to have installed even `python-devel`. You can install it with:

```
# yum install -y python-devel
```

Now, you can finally build the project using:

```
# python setup.py install
```

`setup.py` will resolve all the dependencies for us, avoiding the use of `pip`, which installs all the dependencies and the required packages manually.

Getting ready to send messages

Now that we are finally ready to configure our package, the first thing to do is create the configuration file. The configuration needs to be in the following form:

```
# cat ./yowsup.config
cc=
phone=
id=
password=
```

The field `cc` must be filled with the country code.

The `phone` field is composed of *country code + area code + phone number*. Please remember that the country code must be provided without + or 00 leading.

The ID field is used in registration calls and for logging in. WhatsApp has recently deprecated using IMEI/MAC to generate the account's password in updated versions of their clients. Use the --v1 switch to try it anyway. Typically, this field should contain the phone's IMEI if your account is set up on a Nokia or Android device or the MAC address of the phone's WLAN for iOS devices. If you are not trying to use existing credentials, you can leave this field blank or remove it.

Finally, password has the login password. You will get this password when you register the phone number using yowsup-cli. If you are registering a number, you need to leave this field blank and populate it once you have your password.

> It is recommended that you set a permission 600 to the configuration file, and since the command line will be used by our Zabbix server account, you can enforce the security with a sudo role provided only to your Zabbix account. Only then the Zabbix server will be able to send out messages.

Registering the yowsup client

Now it's time to register our client, thus enabling it to send messages.

First of all, we need a phone number to sacrifice; this phone number will then be used for this application. Here, it is important to have a real mobile number where we can receive SMS.

To register our client, we need to properly fill in the configuration file as previously explained. We need then to populate id and phone number in our yowsup.config configuration file. We can let the other fields remain empty for now.

Once this is done, we can run the following command:

```
# ./yowsup-cli registration -c ./yowsup.config -r sms
INFO:yowsup.common.http.warequest:{"status":"sent","length":6,"method":"s
ms","retry_after":1805}
status: sent
retry_after: 1805
length: 6
method: sms
#
```

Once this is done, we should receive an SMS in our phone in the *NNN-NNN* form. We need to use this command as follows:

```
# ./yowsup-cli registration -c ./yowsup.config -R 117-741
INFO:yowsup.common.http.warequest:{"status":"ok","login":"41076XXXXXX","p
w":"w3cp6Vb7UAU1KG6/xhx/1K4hA=","type":"existing","expiration":146511959
9,"kind":"free","price":"\u20ac 0,89","cost":"0.89","currency":"EUR","pri
ce_expiration":1439763526}


status: ok
kind: free
pw: w3cp6Vb7UAU1KG6/xhx/1K4hA=
price: € 0,89
price_expiration: 1439763526
currency: EUR
cost: 0.89
expiration: 1465119599
login: 41076XXXXXX
type: existing
#
```

Now, we have received the password encoded in **BASE64**. The password is specified in the field as `pw: w3cp6Vb7UAU1KG6/xhx/1K4hA=`. We need to include this password in our `yowsup.config` configuration file.

Sending the first WhatsApp message

Finally, we have everything ready to be used. The first thing that we can try to do is send a message. Now, for all the time required for those tests, we can use the new yousup account. From there, we can run the following:

```
# $HOME/yowsup-master/yowsup-cli demos -c ./yowsup.config -s 4176XXXXX
"Test message form cli"
WARNING:yowsup.stacks.yowstack:Implicit declaration of parallel layers in
a tuple is deprecated, pass a YowParallelLayer instead
INFO:yowsup.demos.sendclient.layer:Message sent


Yowsdown
```

We can now send another message and test whether the messages are getting delivered. Then, we can run the following from `yowsup`:

```
# $HOME/yowsup-master/yowsup-cli demos -c ./yowsup.config -s 4176XXXXX
"Test message form cli. 2nd test"
WARNING:yowsup.stacks.yowstack:Implicit declaration of parallel layers in
a tuple is deprecated, pass a YowParallelLayer instead
INFO:yowsup.demos.sendclient.layer:Message sent
```

Now, we can see the result on our phone or directly online using WhatsApp web. The result is the following:

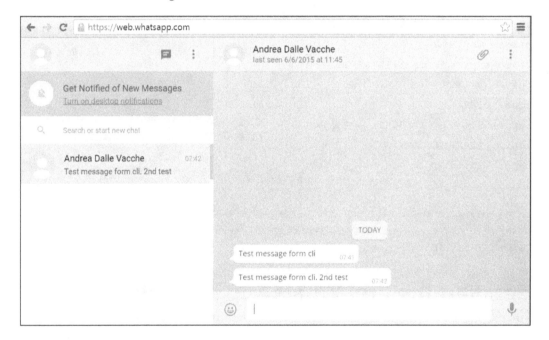

Now, let's see what the options used are. First of all, we've used the demo client.

Securing the yowsup setup

Before proceeding any further, it makes sense to restrict access to `yowsup` to Zabbix and the relative Zabbix server account.

To do that, we need to create a user ad hoc, for example, `yowsup`. Then from root, we can run the following command:

```
# useradd yowsup
```

Create the relative password that executes the following command from root:

```
# passwd yowsup
Changing password for user yowsup.
New password:
Retype new password:
passwd: all authentication tokens updated successfully.
```

Now it is time to edit the sudoers and allow the account using your Zabbix server to execute the required command. Then, we need to run the following from root:

```
#visudo -f /etc/sudoers.d/Zabbix
```

We need to add the following content:

```
    zabbix ALL=(ALL) NOPASSWD: /usr/bin/sudo -l
    zabbix ALL=(ALL) NOPASSWD: /home/yowsup/yowsup-master/yowsup-cli *
```

Now, we can test whether the account with which Zabbix will be able to run all the required commands can become our Zabbix account. Then, type the following command:

```
$ sudo -l
```

The output must contain the following section:

```
User zabbix may run the following commands on this host:
    (ALL) NOPASSWD: /usr/bin/sudo -l
    (ALL) NOPASSWD: /home/yowsup/yowsup-master/yowsup-cli *
```

Now, the last thing to do is transfer all the files and data to our new yowsup account by running the following command as root:

```
# cp -r -a yowsup-master /home/yowsup/
# chown -R yowsup:yowsup /home/yowsup/*
```

 Yowsup stores all the history at $HOME/.yowsup/ just in case you are relocating a preexistent setup. This is something you need to consider.

Test whether everything works as expected by running the following command from the Zabbix account:

```
$ sudo -u yowsup  /home/yowsup/yowsup-master/yowsup-cli
Available commands:
```

```
====================
```

```
demos, version, registration
```

Now, if you don't get the same output, it is better to check your configuration. Now, as a final test, we can send a message from the Zabbix account, and then, from Zabbix, you can run:

```
$ sudo -u yowsup /home/yowsup/yowsup-master/yowsup-cli demos -c /home/
yowsup/yowsup-master/yowsup.config -s 4176XXXXXX "Test message form
zabbix 1st test"
```

```
WARNING:yowsup.stacks.yowstack:Implicit declaration of parallel layers in
a tuple is deprecated, pass a YowParallelLayer instead
```

```
INFO:yowsup.demos.sendclient.layer:Message sent
```

Yowsdown

To confirm that everything works as expected, you should see the message arrive at your terminal or WhatsApp web, as shown in the following screenshot:

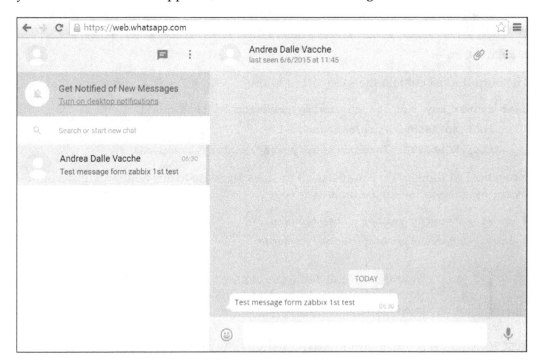

Here, you see that the message has been sent by me as I have saved the number that I use to send messages from Zabbix under my name.

Creating our first Zabbix alert group

Now that we've secured and locked down our setup by taking care to grant Zabbix the required privilege to send messages, but to avoid reading the configuration password file, it is time to think about a real scenario of usage. Now, you've tasted the basic functionality of this software, but in a real scenario, we need to consider that the messages need to be delivered to a team or a group of people that might change from time to time following the nightshift plan, the weekly support shift plan, and so on. To solve this problem, we can simply create a WhatsApp group. Luckily, the software provides us with the functionality to create a group and add/ remove people from a group, among many other functions.

Here, we will see how we can create a group called `zabbix_alert` in this example. From the `yowsup` account, we can then run the following command:

```
# cd yowsup-master && ./yowsup-cli demos -c yowsup.config  --yowsup
```

This command starts the Yowsup command-line client. It is actually an interactive shell that allows us to send extended commands to WhatsApp. The following is the welcome message:

```
Yowsup Cli client

==================

Type /help for available commands
```

Now, if we type `/help`, we can have an idea of the power of this shell; let's do it:

```
[offline]:/help

------------------------------------------------

/profile   setPicture    [path]                   Set profile picture

/profile   setStatus     [text]                   Set status text

/account   delete                                 Delete your account

/group     info          [group_jid]              Get group info

/group     picture       [group_jid] [path]       Set group picture

/group     invite        [group_jid] [jids]       Invite to group. Jids are a
comma separated list

/group     leave         [group_jid]              Leave a group you belong to

/group     setSubject    [group_jid] [subject]    Change group subject

/group     demote        [group_jid] [jids]       Remove admin of a group. Jids
are a comma separated list

/group     promote       [group_jid] [jids]       Promote admin of a group.
Jids are a comma separated list
```

```
/group      kick         [group_jid] [jids]    Kick from group. Jids are a
comma separated list

/help                                          Print this message

/seq                                           Send init seq

/contacts   sync         [contacts]            Sync contacts, contacts
should be comma separated phone numbers, with no spaces

/keys       set                                Send prekeys

/keys       get          [jids]                Get shared keys

/image      send         [number] [path]       Send and image

/presence   available                          Set presence as available

/presence   subscribe    [contact]             Subscribe to contact's
presence updates

/presence   unsubscribe  [contact]             Unsubscribe from contact's
presence updates

/presence   name         [name]                Set presence name

/presence   unavailable                        Set presence as unavailable

/ping                                          Ping server

/L                                             Quick login

/state      paused  [jid]                      Send paused state

/state      typing  [jid]                      Send typing state

/contact    picture [jid]                      Get profile picture for
contact

/contact         picturePreview [jid]          Get profile picture preview
for contact

/contact         lastseen       [jid]          Get lastseen for contact

/groups          create [subject] [jids]       Create a new group with the
specified subject and participants. Jids are a comma separated list. Use
'-' to keep group without participants but you.

/groups          list                          List all groups you belong
to

/disconnect                                    Disconnect

/login           [username] [b64password]      Login to WhatsApp

/ib              clean          [dirtyType]    Send clean dirty

/message         broadcast [numbers] [content] Broadcast message. numbers
should comma separated phone numbers

/message         send [number] [content]       Send message to a friend

------------------------------------------------

[offline]:
```

As you can quickly spot, this is a very complete client as it allows us to operate against all the possible options that the messaging service provides us.

Now, before being able to create a group, we need to log in. Note that the shell provides you your status. In this case, we are still [offline]. We can use the quick login as we've specified in our configuration file after the -c option. Then, we can simply run this command:

```
[offline]:/L
Auth: Logged in!
[connected]:
```

Now, the status is changed to [connected], and we can finally send commands. Now we will create the group with group create, followed by group name and a comma separated list of phone numbers we would like to add; in this example, it is only one number, but you can add all the numbers you wish to add here in a comma-separated list:

```
[connected]:/groups create zabbix_alert 4176XXXXXX
```

The following is the output:

```
[connected]:INFO:yowsup.layers.protocol_groups.layer:Group create success
Iq:
ID: 1
Type: result
from: g.us


Notification: Notification
From: 39340XXXXXXX-1436940409@g.us
Type: w:gp2
Participant: 39340XXXXXXX@s.whatsapp.net
Creator: 39340XXXXXXX @s.whatsapp.net
Create type: new
Creation timestamp: 1436940409
Subject: zabbix_alert
Subject owner: 39340XXXXXXX@s.whatsapp.net
Subject timestamp: 1436940409
Participants: {39340XXXXXXX@s.whatsapp.net': 'admin', '4176XXXXXXX@s.
whatsapp.net': None}


[connected]:
```

The result of this command is shown in the following screenshot:

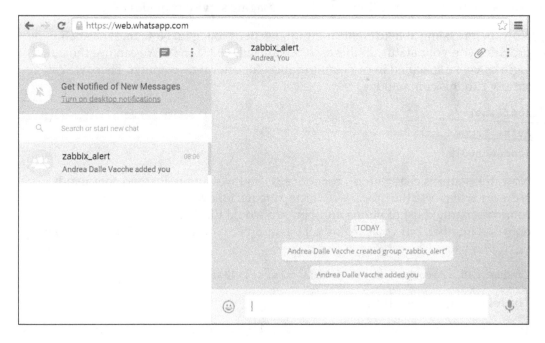

Here, the group JID and the group identifier are:

```
From: 39340XXXXXXX-1436940409@g.us
```

The JID is composed of the phone number that creates the group, followed by a unique identifier. Now we are ready to send the first message to this group using a command line. We can run the following command:

```
# ./yowsup-cli demos -c ./yowsup.config -s 39340XXXXXXX-1436940409@g.us
"Test message to zabbix_alert group"
```

The result is shown in the following screenshot:

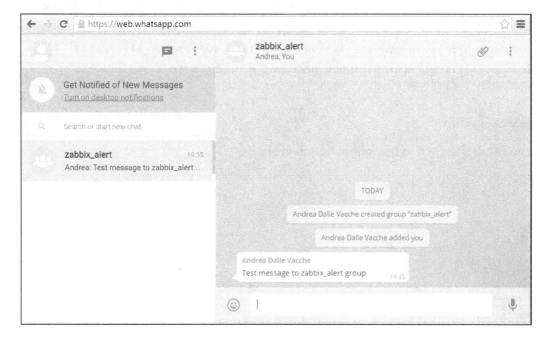

Now, as the final step, it make sense to have more than one group administrator as it is safer to have someone human that can manage the emergency by adding a newcomer who is not included in the automated process, and so on.

To add one more group administrator, we need to log in and access the interactive shell with:

```
# ./yowsup-cli demos -c ./yowsup.config --yowsup
Yowsup Cli client
==================
Type /help for available commands

[offline]:/L
Auth: Logged in!
[connected]:
```

Now, we can run our command, which will be a group command. Then promote the group JID and the list of numbers that we want promote to admin. Here is just one number:

```
[connected]:/group promote 39340XXXXXXX-1436940409@g.us 4176XXXXXX
[connected]:INFO:yowsup.layers.protocol_groups.layer:Group promote
participants success


[connected]:
```

The result is shown in the following screenshot:

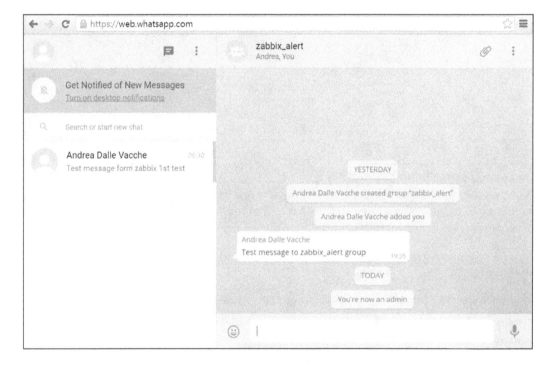

Now, I can personally add and remove contacts from this group.

Integrating yowsup with Zabbix

Now we are finally ready to integrate Zabbix with our WhatsApp gateway. First of all, we need to create the appropriate script to use the command line by using the proper sudo command. The script needs to be placed at the AlertScript location that we can retrieve from here:

```
grep AlertScript /etc/zabbix/zabbix_server.conf
### Option: AlertScriptsPath
# AlertScriptsPath=${datadir}/zabbix/alertscripts
AlertScriptsPath=/usr/lib/zabbix/alertscripts
```

Then, we can create our script in the /usr/lib/zabbix/alertscripts directory.

We can create a script called whatsapp.sh with the following content:

```
$ cat /usr/lib/zabbix/alertscripts/whatsapp.sh
#!/bin/bash
BASEDIR=/home/yowsup/yowsup-master
sudo -u yowsup $BASEDIR/yowsup-cli demos -c $BASEDIR/yowsup.config -s $1
"$2 $3"
```

Now it's time to create a new notification method that will use our brand-new script. To create a new media type, you need to navigate to **Administration | Media type | Create media type** and fill in the form, as shown in the following screenshot:

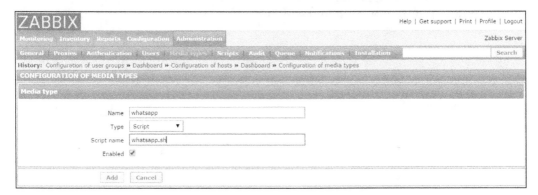

Now, we need to create the action that will use our new media type. Let's then go on to **Configuration | Actions**, select **Trigger** in the drop-down menu, and click on **Create action**, as shown in the following screenshot:

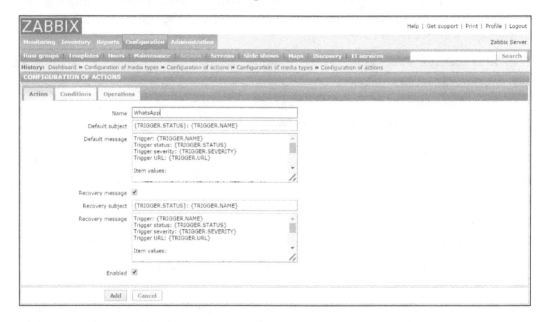

Then, we need to define in the **Operations** tab to whom we would like to send this message. Here, we've decided to send the message to the entire **Zabbix administrators** group, as shown in the following screenshot:

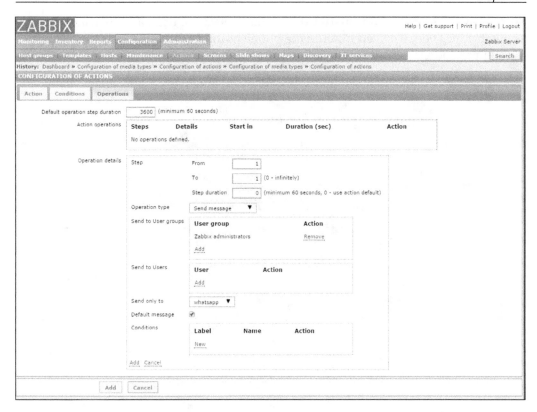

Now, we need to populate all the media fields of all the accounts that would like to receive alerts and that are part of this example of the Zabbix administrators group.

Then, we need to go to **Administration | Users**, select the user, and then add media as **whatsapp**. Then, we need to write the phone number without + or 00 in front of the country code, as shown in the following screenshot:

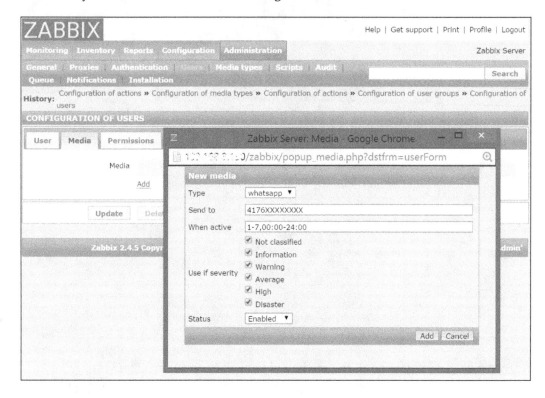

Here, of course, we can select which severity can be sent out using this media.

Now, we can act in two different ways — either send the messages to all the accounts listed in a group in the media section, or use the WhatsApp group. Then, in our case, we can define just a group with one account or even only an account that uses the group 39340XXXXXXX-1436940409@g.us (that we created a few pages ago) as media.

We can debug and see the flow of messages sent to our media by looking at the actions and monitoring them after navigating to **Administration | Audit** and selecting **Action log**. There, we can see all the actions that are triggered. In the following screenshot, you see an event, which I've caused, to test whether everything works as expected. In the next screenshot, you can see the event caused by a temporary iptables rule that has been properly tracked:

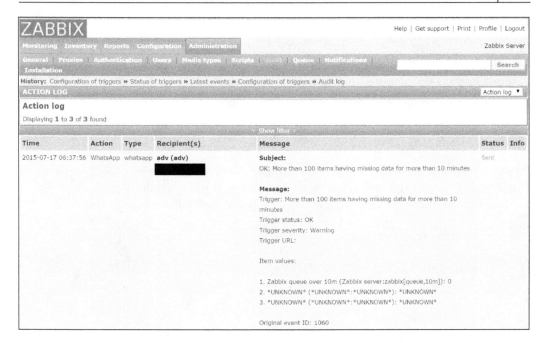

I've also slightly changed our `whatsapp.sh` script in order to properly track how it is called:

```
$ cat /usr/lib/zabbix/alertscripts/whatsapp.sh
#!/bin/bash
BASEDIR=/home/yowsup/yowsup-master
echo "sudo -u yowsup $BASEDIR/yowsup-cli demos -c $BASEDIR/yowsup.
config -s $1 \"$2 $3\"" >> /var/log/whatsapp.log
sudo -u yowsup $BASEDIR/yowsup-cli demos -c $BASEDIR/yowsup.config -s
$1 "$2 $3"
```

As you can see in the highlighted line, I've added a sort of log. Now, let's see how our script has been called:

```
$ tail -n 12 /var/log/whatsapp.log
```

```
sudo -u yowsup /home/yowsup/yowsup-master/yowsup-cli demos -c /home/
yowsup/yowsup-master/yowsup.config -s 4176XXXXXXX "OK: More than 100
items having missing data for more than 10 minutes Trigger: More than 100
items having missing data for more than 10 minutes
```

```
Trigger status: OK
```

```
Trigger severity: Warning
```

```
Trigger URL:
```

```
Item values:

1. Zabbix queue over 10m (Zabbix server:zabbix[queue,10m]): 0
2. *UNKNOWN* (*UNKNOWN*:*UNKNOWN*): *UNKNOWN*
3. *UNKNOWN* (*UNKNOWN*:*UNKNOWN*): *UNKNOWN*


Original event ID: 1060"
```

As you can see in the following screenshot, the command has been called properly, and even if the message is written in multiple lines, it has been delivered properly. Now, for our end-to-end test, we can close our check with the message received:

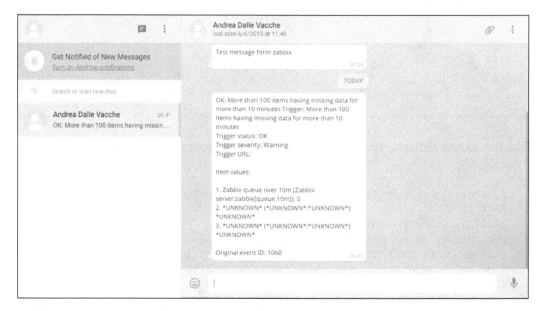

This integration can be really useful, especially nowadays that people have smartphones always connected to the network. Here, there are some things to take into account. First of all, we need to decide whether we want to send an alarm to a specific group, or people individually. If we want to alarm the group, we need to use the group JID and then 39340XXXXXXX-1436940409.

The same message has also been delivered to the Zabbix_alert group as, within the Zabbix administrator group we previously configured, the WhatsApp group JID is the default WhatsApp media for Admin (Zabbix administrator).

The following screenshot displays the result:

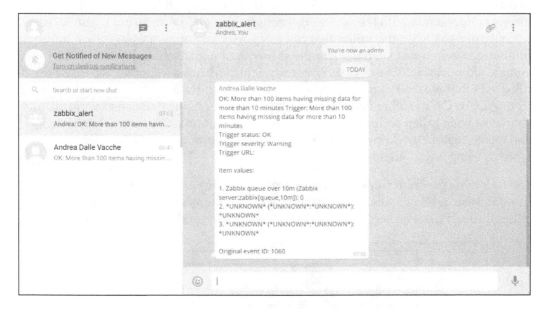

Now, we can move on and see how to integrate Zabbix with RT.

An overview of Request Tracker

Quoting from the Best Practical website:

> "RT is a battle-tested issue tracking system which thousands of organizations use for bug tracking, help desk ticketing, customer service, workflow processes, change management, network operations, youth counseling and even more. Organizations around the world have been running smoothly thanks to RT for over 10 years."

In other words, it's a powerful, yet simple, open source package to display the Zabbix integration. This is not to say that it is the only issue tracking system that you can use with Zabbix; once the principles behind the following sample implementation are clear, you will be able to integrate any product with your monitoring system.

Request Tracker (**RT**) is a web application written in Perl that relies on a web server to expose its frontend and on a relational database to keep all its data on. The main means of interaction with the system is through the web interface, but it also features a powerful e-mail-parsing utility that can categorize an e-mail message, turn it into a full-fledged ticket, and keep track of the subsequent mail exchange between the user and the support staff. Closer to our interests, it also features a simple, yet effective, REST API that we'll rely on in order to create and keep track of the existing tickets from Zabbix. On the other hand, a powerful scripting engine that can execute custom chunks of code called **scripts** not only allows RT to automate its internal workings and create custom workflows, but also allows it to communicate with external systems using any available protocol.

The following diagram shows the basic application architecture. All the data is kept in a database, while the main application logic can interact with the outside world either through the web server or via e-mail and custom scripts.

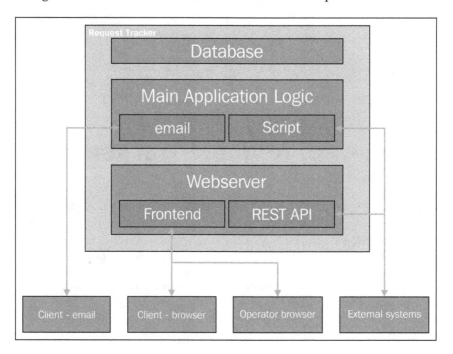

This is not the place to cover an in-depth installation and configuration of RT, so we will assume that you already have a working RT server with at least a few users and groups already set up. If you need to install RT from scratch, the procedure is quite simple and well documented; just follow the instructions detailed at `http://www.bestpractical.com/docs/rt/4.2/README.html`. Refer to the Request Tracker website link provided earlier for further information.

Setting up RT to better integrate with Zabbix

The two basic elements of RT are tickets and queues. The function of a ticket is to keep track of the evolution of an issue. The basic workflow of the tracks' said evolution can be summarized in the following points:

- A ticket is created with the first description of the problem
- An operator takes ownership of the ticket and starts working on it
- The evolution of the problem is recorded in the ticket's history
- After the problem's resolution, the ticket is closed and archived

All of the ticket's metadata, from its creation date to the amount of time it took to close it, from the user who created it to the operator that worked on it, and so on, is recorded and grouped with all the other tickets' metadata in order to build statistics and calculate service-level agreements.

A queue, on the other hand, is a specific collection of tickets and a way to file new tickets under different categories. You can define different queues based on the different organization departments, different products you are providing support for, or any other criteria that can make it easier to organize tickets.

Let's see what we can do to configure RT queues and tickets so that we can transfer all the information we need to and from Zabbix, while keeping any existing functionality as a generic issue tracker as is.

Creating a custom queue for Zabbix

A nice feature of queues is that from the fields that need to be filled out to the details of the workflow, you can customize every aspect of a ticket that belongs to a specific queue. The first step is, therefore, to create a specific queue for all tickets created from a Zabbix event action. This will allow us to define specific characteristics for the corresponding Zabbix tickets.

Creating a queue is quite simple. Just go to **Admin | Queues | Create** and fill in the form. For our purposes, you don't need to specify more than a name for the queue and an optional description, as shown in the following screenshot:

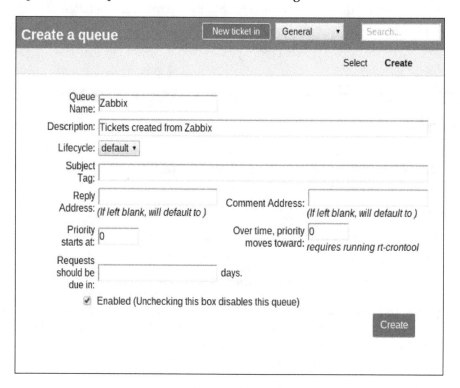

After the queue is created, you will be able to configure it further by going to **Admin | Queues | Select** and choosing the Zabbix queue. You should grant the user and staff rights to a user group or, at the very least, to some specific users so that your IT staff can work on the tickets created by Zabbix. You will also want to create custom fields, as we will see in a couple of paragraphs.

First, let's move on to look at what parts of a ticket are most interesting from an integrator's point of view.

Customizing tickets – the links section

Keeping in mind our goal to integrate Zabbix actions and events with RT, the **Links** section of a ticket is of particular interest to us. As the name suggests, you can define links to other tickets as dependencies or to other systems as further referrals. You can insert useful links during ticket creation or while editing it. The following screenshot shows this:

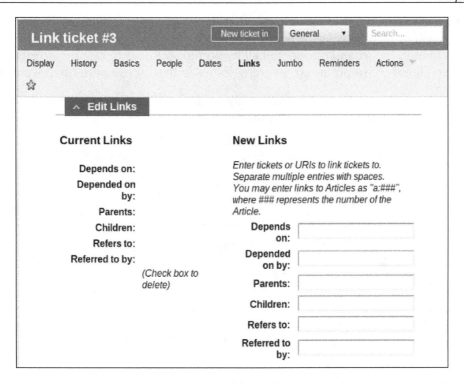

As you probably already imagined, we'll rely on the **Refers to:** link field to link back to the Zabbix event that created the ticket. As we will see in the following pages, the event's acknowledge field will, in turn, show a link to the corresponding ticket so that you can move easily from one platform to the other in order to keep track of what's happening.

Customizing tickets – ticket priority

Another interesting field in the **Basics** section of a ticket is the ticket's priority. It's an integer value that can be from 0 to 100, and it's quite useful to sort tickets depending on their severity level. There is no official mapping of RT priority and a few other descriptive severity levels, such as those used by the Zabbix triggers. This means that if you want to preserve information about trigger severity in the ticket, you have two choices:

- Ignore the ticket's priority and create a custom field that shows the trigger severity as a label
- Map the trigger severity values to the ticket's priority values as a convention, and refer to the mapping while creating tickets

The only advantage of the first option is that the single ticket will be easily readable, and you will immediately know about the severity of the corresponding trigger. On the other hand, the second option will allow you to sort your tickets by priority and act first on the more important or pressing issues with a more streamlined workflow.

While creating a ticket from Zabbix, our suggestion is, therefore, to set ticket priorities based on the following mapping:

Trigger severity label	Trigger severity value	Ticket priority value
Not classified	0	0
Information	1	20
Warning	2	40
Average	3	60
High	4	80
Disaster	5	100

There is nothing to configure either on Zabbix's or on RT's side. This mapping will use the full range of priority values so that your Zabbix tickets will be correctly sorted not only in their specific queue, but also anywhere in RT.

Customizing tickets – the custom fields

As we have seen in *Chapter 6, Managing Alerts*, a Zabbix action can access a great number of macros and, thus, expose a lot of information about the event that generated it. While it makes perfect sense to just format this information in a readable manner while sending e-mails, with the availability of custom fields for RT tickets, it makes less sense to limit all of the event details just to the ticket description.

In fact, one great advantage of custom fields is that they are searchable and filterable just as any other native ticket field. This means that if you put the host related to a ticket event in a custom field, you'll be able to search all tickets belonging to the said host for reporting purposes, assign a host's specific tickets to a particular user, and so on. So, let's go ahead and create a couple of custom fields for the tickets in the Zabbix queue that will contain information, which we'll find useful later on. Go to **Admin | Custom Fields | Create** and create a **Hosts** custom field, as shown in the following screenshot:

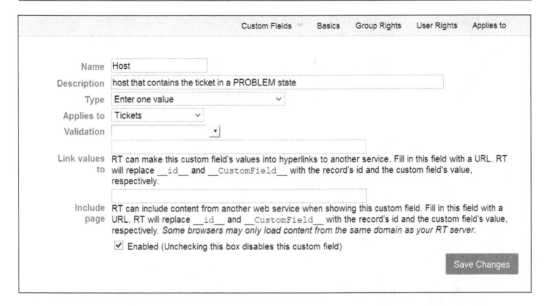

Make sure that you select **Enter multiple values** as the field type. This will allow us to specify more than a single host for those complex triggers that reference items from different hosts.

Speaking of triggers and items, you can follow the same procedure to create other custom fields for the trigger name, item names, or keys. After you are done with this, you will need to assign these fields to the tickets in the Zabbix queue. Select the Zabbix queue by navigating to **Admin | Queues | Select**, and for the **Tickets** form, go to **Custom fields | Tickets**. Select the fields that you wish to assign to your tickets:

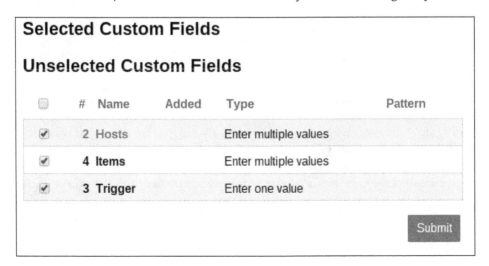

After you are done, you will see the following fields in every ticket of the Zabbix queue:

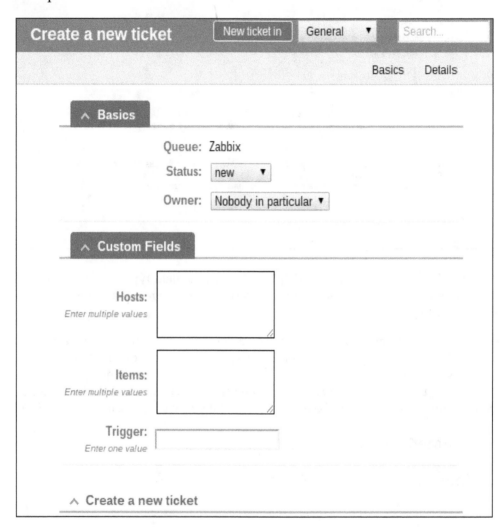

Depending on your needs, you can create as many custom fields as you want for the trigger and event acknowledge history, host's IP interfaces, custom macros, and so on. You will be able to search for any of them, and for the three shown earlier, you can do so by selecting the Zabbix queue in the search page of the RT frontend. At the bottom of the search form, you can see the newly created fields just as expected:

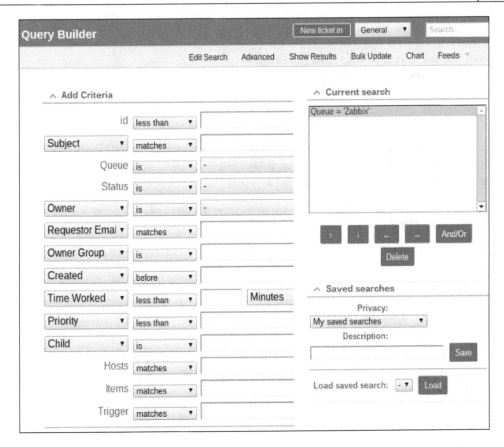

Connecting to the Request Tracker API

RT exposes a REST-type API that relies directly on the HTTP protocol to handle requests and responses. This means that the API is easily tested and explored using tools such as wget and netcat. Let's do that to get a feel of how it works before introducing the Python library that we'll use for the rest of the chapter.

The base URL for the RT API is located at ../REST/1.0/ after the base URL of Request Tracker itself. This means that if your base URL is http://your.domain.com/rt, the API will be accessible at http://your.domain.com/rt/REST/1.0/. If you try to connect to it, you should get a message asking for credentials (some response headers are removed to improve readability):

```
$ ncat example.com 80
GET /rt/REST/1.0/ HTTP/1.1
Host: example.com
```

```
HTTP/1.1 200 OK
[...]
Content-Type: text/plain; charset=utf-8


22
RT/4.2.0 401 Credentials required
```

The API doesn't have a special authentication mechanism separated from the rest of the application, so the best way to authenticate is to get a session cookie from the main login form and use it for each API request. To get the cookie, let's use wget:

```
$ wget --keep-session-cookies --save-cookies cookies.txt --post-data
'user=root&pass=password' http://example.com/rt/
```

The command that will save the session cookie in the cookies.txt file is as follows:

```
$ cat cookies.txt
# HTTP cookie file.
# Generated by Wget on 2015-07-10 10:16:58.
# Edit at your own risk.


localhost  FALSE  /rt  FALSE  0  RT_SID_example.com.80
2bb04e679236e58b406b1e554a47af43
```

Now that we have a valid session cookie, we can issue requests through the API. Here is the GET request for the general queue:

```
$ ncat localhost 80
GET /rt/REST/1.0/queue/1 HTTP/1.1
Host: localhost
Cookie: RT_SID_example.com.80=2bb04e679236e58b406b1e554a47af43


HTTP/1.1 200 OK
[...]
Content-Type: text/plain; charset=utf-8


RT/4.2.0 200 Ok


id: queue/1
Name: General
Description: The default queue
```

```
CorrespondAddress:
CommentAddress:
InitialPriority: 0
FinalPriority: 0
DefaultDueIn: 0
```

As you can see, the API is quite easy to interact with without any special encoding or decoding. For our purposes, however, it is even easier to use a library that will spare us the burden of parsing each HTTP request. `Rtkit` is a Python 2.x library that makes it even easier to connect to the API from within a Python program, for which it allows us to send requests and get responses using native Python data structures. The installation is very simple using `pip`:

```
$ pip install python-rtkit
```

Here, we're supposing that you have already installed pip. If not, please install it with this command here:

```
$ yum install -y python-pip
```

Once installed, the library will be available upon importing various `Rtkit` modules. Let's see the same preceding interaction (authenticating and requesting the general queue) from within a Python 2.x session:

```
 $ python2
Python 2.7.5 (default, Sep  6 2013, 09:55:21)
[GCC 4.8.1 20130725 (prerelease)] on linux2
Type "help", "copyright", "credits" or "license" for more information.
>>> from rtkit.resource import RTResource
>>> from rtkit.authenticators import CookieAuthenticator
>>> from rtkit.errors import RTResourceError
>>>
>>> res = RTResource('http://localhost/rt/REST/1.0/', 'root', 'password',
CookieAuthenticator)
>>>
>>> response = res.get(path='queue/1')
>>> type(response)
<class 'rtkit.resource.RTResponse'>
>>> type(response.parsed)
<type 'list'>
>>> response.parsed
```

```
[[('id', 'queue/1'), ('Name', 'General'), ('Description', 'The
default queue'), ('CorrespondAddress', ''), ('CommentAddress', ''),
('InitialPriority', '0'), ('FinalPriority', '0'), ('DefaultDueIn', '0')]]
```

As you can see, a response is parsed into a list of tuples with all the attributes of an RT object.

Now that we have a custom queue and custom fields for Zabbix tickets, we are able to interact with the API through the Python code, and the setting up process on RT's side is complete. We are ready to actually integrate the Zabbix actions and the RT tickets.

Setting up Zabbix to integrate with Request Tracker

Our goal is to define a Zabbix action step that, when executed, will:

- Create a ticket with all the relevant event information
- Link the ticket back to the Zabbix event that generated it
- Acknowledge the event with a link to the ticket just created

While the first point can be covered with a simple e-mail action to RT, we need custom code to take care of the other two. The best way to do this is to define a new media type in Zabbix as a custom alert script. The script will do the following:

- Take the action message
- Parse it to extract relevant information
- Create a ticket with all custom fields and link the referrals filled out
- Get back the ticket ID
- Write a link to the created ticket in the event's acknowledgment field

Before actually writing the script, let's create the media type and link it to a user (you can assign the media type to any user you want; the custom `rt_tickets` user has been used here, as shown in the following screenshot):

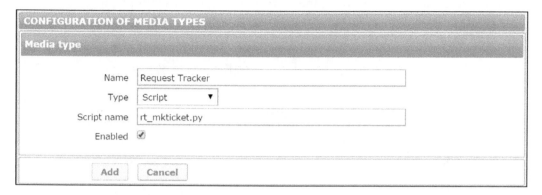

While linking the media type to the user, use the RT base URL in the **Send to** field, so you won't need to define it statically in the script. This is shown in the following screenshot:

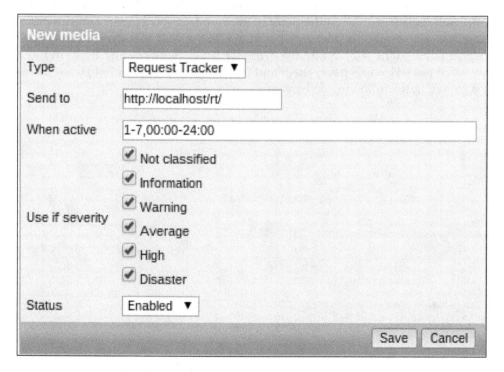

Once saved, you'll see all relevant information at a glance in the Media tab, as shown in the following screenshot. Just after the URL address, you'll find the notification periods for the media and, after that, a six-letter code that shows the active severity levels. If you disabled any of them, the corresponding letter would be in gray:

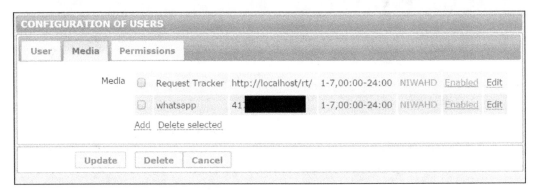

Now, let's create an action step that will send a message to our rt_tickets user through the custom media type. Needless to say, the rt_tickets user won't receive any actual message as the alert script will actually create an RT ticket, but all of this is completely transparent from the point of view of a Zabbix action. You can put any information you want in the message body, but, at the very least, you should specify the trigger name in the subject and the event ID, severity, hosts, and items in the body so that the script will parse them and fill them in the appropriate ticket fields. This is shown in the following screenshot:

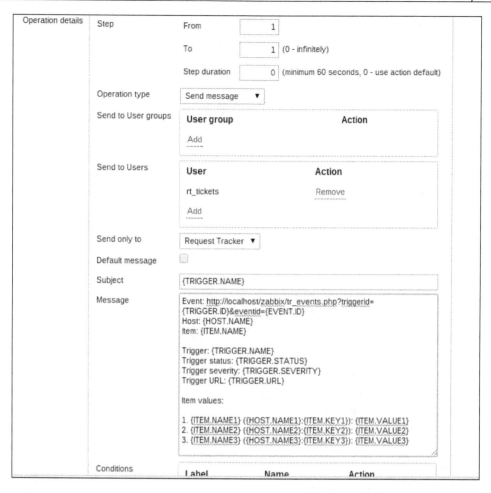

We are now ready to actually write the script and use it to create tickets from Zabbix.

Creating RT tickets from the Zabbix events

Zabbix will search for custom alert scripts in the directory specified by AlertScriptsPath in the zabbix_server.conf file. In the case of a default install, this would be ${datadir}/zabbix/alertscripts, and in Red Hat, it is set to /usr/lib/zabbix/alertscripts /.

This is where we will put our script called `rt_mkticket.py`. The Zabbix action that we configured earlier will call this script with the following three arguments in this order:

- Recipient
- Subject
- Message

As we have seen, the content of the subject and the message is defined in the action operation and depends on the specifics of the event triggering action. The recipient is defined in the media type configuration of the user receiving the message, and it is usually an e-mail address. In our case, it will be the base URL of our Request Tracker installation.

So, let's start the script by importing the relevant libraries and parsing the arguments:

```python
#!/usr/bin/python2
from pyzabbix import ZabbixAPI
from rtkit.resource import RTResource
from rtkit.authenticators import CookieAuthenticator
from rtkit.errors import RTResourceError
import sys
import re
lines = re.findall(r'^(?!(Host:|Event:|Item:|Trigger severity:))
(.*)$', message, re.MULTILINE)
desc = '\n'.join([y for (x, y) in lines])

rt_url = sys.argv[1]
rt_api = rt_url + 'REST/1.0/'
trigger_name = sys.argv[2]
message= sys.argv[3]
```

Now, we need to extract at least the event URL, trigger severity, list of host names, and list of item names from the message. To do this, we will use the powerful regular expression functions of Python:

```python
event_id = re.findall(r'^Event: (.+)$', message, re.MULTILINE)[0]
severity = re.findall(r'^Trigger severity: (.+)$', message,
re.MULTILINE)[0]
hosts = re.findall(r'^Host: (.+)$', message, re.MULTILINE)

items = re.findall(r'^Item: (.+)$', message, re.MULTILINE)
lines = re.findall(r'^(?!(Host:|Event:|Item:|Trigger severity:))
(.*)$', message, re.MULTILINE)

desc = '\n'.join([y for (x, y) in lines])
```

While the event ID has to be unique, a trigger can reference more than one item and, thus, more than one host. The preceding code will match any line beginning with `Host:` to build a list of hosts. In the preceding action message, we just put one `Host:` {HOST.NAME} line for readability purposes, but your actual template can contain more than one (just remember to use {HOST.NAME1}, {HOST.NAME2}, {HOST.NAME3}, and so on, or you'll end up with the same host value repeatedly). Of course, the same goes for item names. The rest of the message is then extracted with the opposite of the regexps used before and joined back in a single multiline string.

Now, the macro we used for trigger severity is {TRIGGER.SEVERITY}. This means that it will be substituted by a string description and not a numerical value. So, let's define a simple dictionary with severity labels and RT ticket priority values mapped, as explained earlier in the chapter:

```
priorities = {
        'Not classified': 0,
        'Information': 20,
        'Warning': 40,
        'Average': 60,
        'High': 80,
        'Disaster': 100 }
```

We also need to know in advance the name of the queue we are creating the ticket in or, better yet, its ID number:

```
queue_id = 3
```

Now that we have everything we need, we can proceed to build the request to create a new ticket and then send it over to Request Tracker:

```
ticket_content = {
        'content': {
        'Queue': queue_id,
        'Subject': trigger_name,
        'Text': desc,
        'Priority': priorities[severity],
        'CF.{Hosts}': ','.join(hosts),
        'CF.{Items}': ','.join(items),
        'CF.{Trigger}': trigger_name
    }
}

links = {
        'content': {
        'RefersTo': event_url
    }
}
```

First, we create two dictionaries, one for the main ticket content and the second for the links section, which must be edited separately.

Then, we get to the main part of the script: first, we log in to the RT API (make sure to use your actual username and password credentials!), create a new ticket, get the ticket ID, and input the link to the Zabbix event page:

```
rt = RTResource(rt_api, 'root', 'password', CookieAuthenticator)
ticket = rt.post(path='ticket/new', payload=ticket_content,)
(label,ticket_id) = ticket.parsed[0][0]
refers = rt.post(path=ticket_id + '/links', payload=links,)
```

We are almost done. All that is left to do is acknowledge the Zabbix event with a link back to the ticket we just created:

```
event_id = re.findall(r'eventid=(\d+)', event_url)[0]
ticket_url = rt_url + 'Ticket/Display.html?id=' + ticket_id.split('/')
[1]
print(ticket_url)
zh = ZabbixAPI('http://localhost/zabbix')
zh.login(user='Admin', password='zabbix')
ack_message = 'Ticket created.\n' + ticket_url
zh.event.acknowledge(eventids=event_id, message=ack_message)
```

This preceding code is fairly straightforward. After extracting the eventid value and creating the URL for the ticket, we connect to the Zabbix API and edit the acknowledge field of the event, effectively closing the circle.

Now that the script is complete, remember to give ownership to the zabbix user and set the executable bit on it:

```
$ chown zabbix rt_mkticket.py
```

```
$ chmod +x rt_mkticket.py
```

The next time the action condition that you defined in your system returns true and the action operation is carried out, the script will be executed with the parameters we've seen before. A ticket will be created with a link back to the event, and the event itself will be acknowledged with a link to the ticket.

Here is an example event. The link in the acknowledgement field corresponds to the URL of the ticket:

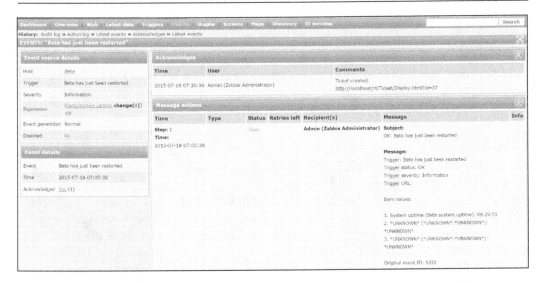

Here is the corresponding ticket. The **Refers to:** field contains a clickable link to the event shown earlier, while the **Custom Fields** section reports the host, item, and trigger information, just as expected:

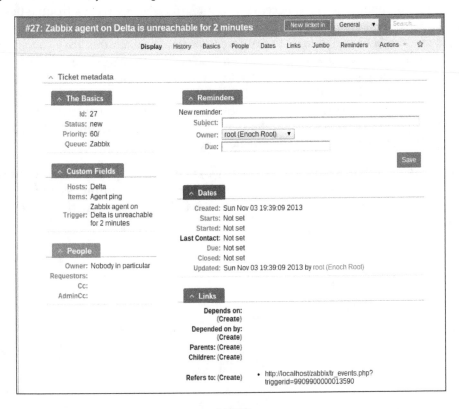

The script, in much the same way as those explained in *Chapter 9, Extending Zabbix*, is little more than a proof of concept, with as much focus on the readability and ease of explanation as on pure functionality. Make sure that you add as many condition checks and error-reporting functions as possible if you want to use it in a production environment.

Summary

We have finally reached the end of our journey to mastering the Zabbix monitoring system. In the course of the book, you learned how to plan and implement the general monitoring architecture; how to create flexible and effective items, triggers, and actions; and how to best visualize your data. You also learned how to implement custom agents by understanding the Zabbix protocol and how to write the code to manipulate every aspect of Zabbix through its API. In this chapter, we barely scratched the surface of what's possible once you start taking advantage of what you now know about Zabbix to integrate it better with your IT infrastructure. Many more integration possibilities exist, including getting and updating users and groups through an identity management system, getting inventory information through an asset management system, feeding inventory information to a CMDB database, and much more. Following the steps necessary to integrate Zabbix with a trouble ticket management system and integrate the Zabbix monitoring solution with external and different media, you learned how to prepare two systems such that they can share and exchange data and knowledge of how to use each system's API in a coordinated manner in order to get the systems to talk to each other. During our walkthrough, we also covered and analyzed all the critical security aspects in order to make you aware of the risk that a monitoring system can introduce and how you can mitigate them with a proper setup. At this point in the book, you're now able to implement and set up a segregated and secured monitoring system.

Our hope is that with the skills you just learned, you will be able to bring out the full potential of the Zabbix monitoring system and make it a central asset of your IT infrastructure. In doing so, your time and effort will be repaid many times over.

Index

A

C

Thank you for buying
Mastering Zabbix
Second Edition

About Packt Publishing

Packt, pronounced 'packed', published its first book, *Mastering phpMyAdmin for Effective MySQL Management*, in April 2004, and subsequently continued to specialize in publishing highly focused books on specific technologies and solutions.

Our books and publications share the experiences of your fellow IT professionals in adapting and customizing today's systems, applications, and frameworks. Our solution-based books give you the knowledge and power to customize the software and technologies you're using to get the job done. Packt books are more specific and less general than the IT books you have seen in the past. Our unique business model allows us to bring you more focused information, giving you more of what you need to know, and less of what you don't.

Packt is a modern yet unique publishing company that focuses on producing quality, cutting-edge books for communities of developers, administrators, and newbies alike. For more information, please visit our website at www.packtpub.com.

About Packt Open Source

In 2010, Packt launched two new brands, Packt Open Source and Packt Enterprise, in order to continue its focus on specialization. This book is part of the Packt Open Source brand, home to books published on software built around open source licenses, and offering information to anybody from advanced developers to budding web designers. The Open Source brand also runs Packt's Open Source Royalty Scheme, by which Packt gives a royalty to each open source project about whose software a book is sold.

Writing for Packt

We welcome all inquiries from people who are interested in authoring. Book proposals should be sent to author@packtpub.com. If your book idea is still at an early stage and you would like to discuss it first before writing a formal book proposal, then please contact us; one of our commissioning editors will get in touch with you.

We're not just looking for published authors; if you have strong technical skills but no writing experience, our experienced editors can help you develop a writing career, or simply get some additional reward for your expertise.

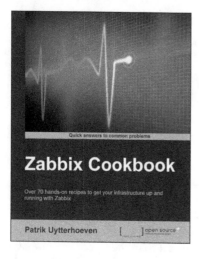

Zabbix Cookbook

ISBN: 978-1-78439-758-6   Paperback: 260 pages

Over 70 hands-on recipes to get your infrastructure up and running with Zabbix

1. Set up and configure your own Zabbix server by using packages or from source.

2. Automate your Zabbix infrastructure in order to maintain your Zabbix setup.

3. Create your own items and use them to monitor your Zabbix infrastructure with the help of this practical, step-by-step guide.

Zabbix Network Monitoring Essentials

ISBN: 978-1-78439-976-4   Paperback: 178 pages

Your one-stop solution to efficient network monitoring with Zabbix

1. Effectively monitor a number of network devices based on network security and segments.

2. Adapt your monitoring solution to an array of evolving network scenarios using Zabbix discovery features.

3. A fast-paced guide to Zabbix network monitoring with a strategic focus on the collection and organization of data.

Please check **www.PacktPub.com** for information on our titles

Zabbix Performance Tuning

ISBN: 978-1-78398-764-1   Paperback: 152 pages

Tune and optimize Zabbix to maximize performance

1. Get up to speed with the ins and outs of Zabbix's performance issues and their causes.

2. Identify the root cause of underperformance affecting implementation, and turn it around to your benefit.

3. A comprehensive guide, taking an engaging and conversational approach to making administrator and end user work easy by eliminating all Zabbix-related performance problems.

Mastering Zabbix

ISBN: 978-1-78328-349-1   Paperback: 358 pages

Monitor your large IT environment efficiently with Zabbix

1. Create the perfect monitoring configuration based on your specific needs.

2. Extract reports and visualizations from your data.

3. Integrate monitoring data with other systems in your environment.

4. Learn the advanced techniques of Zabbix to monitor networks and performances in large environments.

Please check **www.PacktPub.com** for information on our titles

Printed in the USA
CPSIA information can be obtained
at www.ICGtesting.com
LVHW071051090124
768489LV00043B/1627